S0-BYA-403

CHRISTIANITY

AN INQUIRY INTO ITS NATURE AND TRUTH

Awarded the Fiftieth Anniversary Bross Prize

Christianity

AN INQUIRY INTO ITS NATURE AND TRUTH

BY

HARRIS FRANKLIN RALL

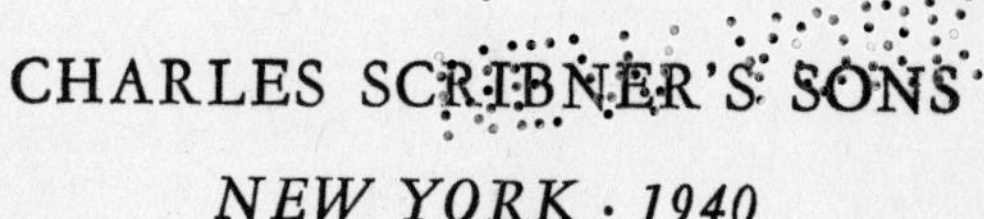

CHARLES SCRIBNER'S SONS

NEW YORK · 1940

Printed in the United States of America

A

To those with whom I have worked and from whom I have learned in twenty-five years of teaching at Garrett Biblical Institute: my colleagues, past and present, and my students, now serving in many lands.

FOREWORD

RELIGION is the supreme concern of the individual because here the ultimate questions of his mind and the ultimate needs of his life seek for answer. Religion is the supreme need of society in a world that is disintegrating before our very eyes for lack of an authority that shall be something more than force, for lack of a spirit that shall be stronger than its fears and hates and selfishness, and for lack of a faith that will give meaning to life and courage to live. Yet alike the validity of religion and its significance are disputed today. For one group it is impossible because its foundations have been destroyed, for another it is irrelevant to humanity's real problems. At the same time, great areas of human habitation are coming under the sway of movements which, beginning as revolutions in national governments, have become, in effect, religions, claiming the rule over all life, demanding absolute obedience, offering themselves as the saviors of their people, and avowedly or implicitly denying this place to Christianity.

Within the Christian tradition, in the meantime, we note two opposed tendencies. To the left are some who, giving up the traditional faith, seek to salvage the moral idealism of Christianity and join it to social devotion; in so doing, however, they not only lose the distinctive element of the religious life but the dynamic which this life supplies, and so become impotent even in the field of their special interest, that of social change. To the right are others who realize that the crucial matter in religion is faith in God, but in their defence of that faith tend to fall back upon traditional supernaturalism and authoritarianism.

The task that is set for us in such a situation is plain. We must start at the beginning. What is religion and what is its place in human life? More particularly, what is the Christian religion, and can it maintain its claim to be supreme and final? And these questions we must ask with a constant reference, first, to the world in which Christianity finds itself today, and, second, to the central Christian concern, the belief in a God whom man can know, with whom man can have fellowship, and who makes a difference in this world.

This volume is an attempt to deal with these questions. It is divided into four parts. I. The Christian Religion (What is religion and its function? What is the Christian religion and what of its claim to finality?) II. The Present-Day Setting of Religion (In what kind of world does Christianity find itself today? What of threat and what of help and what of need does this world show?) III. The Knowledge of God (Can we believe in God? How can we know God?) IV. Some Problems for Faith (What can we say and what may we learn as we face the questions raised for faith by science, history, psychology, and ethics, and even more by the fact of evil?).

One important distinction must constantly be kept in mind in such a study. The term Christianity has a double reference and so a double character. On the one side, it brings to man something transcendent and absolute, the living and unchanging God. On the other, it is something empirical, a movement that belongs to time and takes place in history, whose life and thought, whose practices and institutions are marked by the imperfection and change that belong to all things human. And that brings a double danger: first, that within the Church men shall claim for Scripture or creed or the empirical Church herself that finality and absolute authority which belong only to God himself; second, that the critic, looking on this empirical imperfection, shall miss the God to whom Church and Scripture point and whose living power is working in them. Emil Brunner has the first danger in mind when he says in his *Religionsphilosophie:* "For no one is it harder to believe than for the theologian. For no temptation is so great as this, to put a theological system in the place of faith." And both dangers are aptly suggested by William C. Dampier in his *History of Science,* when he suggests that "religion always mistakes what it says for what it means. And rationalism, so to speak, runs after it pointing out that what it says is untrue." For myself, I am more concerned about Christianity as a living faith than as a doctrinal system, and more about what the doctrine is trying to say than about the exact form of its expression.

A word in justification of the method followed in these studies seems to be called for at this point. Our discussion begins with the Christian religion and then inquires as to its validity and its adequacy for our day. As against this, some would say: Today we must be scientific and strictly empirical, and that means beginning at scratch, without any assumption whatever. To this I would reply: The discussion of religion has never yet served to make a man religious or supply him with a vital faith. It is significant only for those to whom life has already brought some conviction of the higher world and some real relation to it, that is, some kind of religion. These pages are addressed to the men of the Western world, and of the East, who have found the highest and most convincing expression of religion in Christianity. They find their convictions contradicted by the life of the modern world and challenged by much of its thought. Two things such men may rightly ask of any treatise like this: first, that it make clear what the Christian faith really means; second, that the questions raised be honestly faced, with a mind open to truth from every source, and with the most thorough critical consideration. These are the elements, then, to which I have tried to give place in the following pages: (1) the historical, an effort to understand and present the great tradition, the Christian faith and way; (2) the empirical, the data furnished by every field of experience and knowledge, not omitting, however, that which comes in the highest reach of human experience, the religious; (3) the rational and critical, the bringing to bear of every resource of mind upon the historical and empirical data thus presented.

In writing these pages I have had in mind three groups to whom I hope this work may be of value: the religious leader, whether minister or layman, who feels the need of aid alike in interpreting the Christian religion and in meeting the questions that confront it in the modern world; the college student who wishes to study religion, not primarily as a philosophical or historical or psychological discipline, but as offering a philosophy of life; the general reader brought up in the Christian Church but more or less aware of the changes affecting religion, and seeking to make his faith both honest and intelligent. I trust, however, that in addition to the larger circle which a Bross Foundation volume is designed to reach, this work may serve the intention with which it was originally prepared before its submission in the Bross competition, that is as an introduction to theology for those who conceive that discipline as rooting, indeed, in the past, but as oriented to the problems and needs of the present.

I have sought to make my style as clear and non-technical as possible. It is time that the discussion of religion was taken out of the closets of philosophers and theologians into the open roads of life. The primary vocation of the theologian is not to write books for other theologians to read. In the problems that it considers and the terms that it uses theology should keep close to that life of humanity in which religion roots and to which it ministers; and because religion is every man's concern, it should be possible, as A. E. Taylor argues, to state its problems in terms clear to every man.

Much of the material found in Part I was used by me in the Nathaniel W. Taylor Lectures on *Some Studies in Religion* which I gave in 1931 at Yale University. Though it has undergone much change in form and substance, I make this reference that I may voice a double appreciation: to the present faculty of the Yale Divinity School for the honor of this invitation, and to the faculty of my student days for the introduction to these fields of interest in my years of resident study and for the opportunity of continuing that work as a travelling fellow of Yale University.

The biblical quotations here used have been taken from the Standard Edition of the Revised Bible, copyright 1929 by the International Council of Religious Education. Permission to make use of this edition has been generously granted by the Council. I wish here to make acknowledgment of the assistance given me by my wife in the preparation of this manuscript for the press, an acknowledgment that falls far short of my larger indebtedness to her.

HARRIS FRANKLIN RALL.

Garrett Biblical Institute,
Northwestern University Campus,
Evanston, Illinois,
October, 1940.

Part One

THE CHRISTIAN RELIGION

Chapter One

THE NATURE OF RELIGION

THE persistence of religion is one of the most striking facts in human history. Religion belongs to every race and age. With advancing knowledge it has had to alter its ideas. Its institutions and practices have been modified with social change. Particular religions have passed away. Yet religion persists. Bread and love and religion have been the three great impelling interests of man. When, however, we seek a definition of religion, we find that scarcely any two students will agree. There are reasons for this, and to state them will help us to understand what religion is.

Religion is hard to define just because it is at once elemental, inclusive, and individual. It is elemental, one of those ultimates that cannot be defined in terms of something else. It is like life and beauty and truth and the right; you can say this thing and the other about it and point out where its interests lie and how it functions, but you cannot tell what it is in terms of something else because it is different from everything else. It is like a fourth dimension entering into life, adding a new quality and depth and meaning, indeed making all things new. Yet it is at the same time inclusive; it takes in all of life. In the words of Terence it can say: "I am human, and nothing that concerns man is alien to me." Finally, it is individual. There is no such thing as religion in general; it is always something specific, the way in which this individual or that group reacts to the world as seen under this special viewpoint. And so we have the multifarious variety of religion.

But though definition is difficult, understanding is possible; and what we need most is a sympathetic and intelligent understanding of what religion is about. We can best gain that by asking four questions. (1) What are the roots of religion, the sources from which it renews its life through the ages? (2) What are its main aspects, the features which constantly appear? (3) What is its spirit and attitude? What makes the religious man? (4) What is the function of religion? What does it do for man? Instead, then, of beginning with a definition of religion, we will attempt to describe the essential elements of religion, seeking in this way an answer to these questions.

I. THE ESSENTIAL ELEMENTS OF RELIGION

1. Religion arises from man's sense of need and his search for life. It did not begin with man's curiosity seeking an explanation of things, but with that impulse to self-assertion and self-achievement which is inseparable from all life but which takes new and distinctive forms with man. The urge to live is naturally expressed at first on the lower levels; life means physical self-preservation, food and safety and victory over one's enemy, and religion is seen as help to these ends. But it is a mistake to think that higher religion eliminates this element. Rather, it rebukes apathy and indifference and easy self-satisfaction. Its blessing is for those that hunger and thirst, that seek some pearl of great price, some supreme treasure. If it asks men to sell all that they have, it is only that they may be truly rich. Goethe's *Entbehren sollst du, sollst entbehren,* is not a Christian word, and even the Nirvana of Buddhism offers itself as a good. Religion calls men to live and offers men help.

This aspect of religion has received steadily increasing emphasis from students. Thus Harald Höffding insisted that the supreme interest of religion was in the values of life, that the supreme value was personal life, and the basic faith of religion was the conviction of a "fundamental relation between value and reality."[1] Still earlier Albrecht Ritschl had declared that the circle of religion was not described by two points, God and man, but by three, God, man, and the world. Religion is concerned with man's achievement of values in this world, or over against it, through the help of God. A pragmatist before James, Ritschl's anti-intellectual, anti-mystical, and social-ethical emphasis is still a strong influence in modern theology.[2] The historical-psychological study of religion, especially as developed in America, has made the same approach.[3] It sees religion as a phase of the struggle to live, and asks what religion contributes to this struggle.

2. The second source of religion is man's awareness of a world of a higher order, an unseen world in which are found the meaning of his life, the higher goods for his attainment, and the ultimate forces upon which his life depends. We may call the needs of man the "push" of religion, that which impels man from behind. But there is a "pull" of religion also. Religion is not merely desire, it is response. As the physical universe by its stimulus has created our organs of sense perception, and has called forth such varied responses in man as the scientific knowledge of its order and the creative control of its forces, so the impact of this spiritual world has brought forth religion. It has itself created the needs for which it affords satisfaction. The functional, or "biological," approach has helped to correct the mistaken idea that religion is primarily a matter of beliefs; but it is just as much a mistake to explain religion in terms of need and satisfaction alone. The quest for satisfaction belongs to all life, to the flower turning to the sun, to the animal after its prey. Of it-

[1]H. Höffding, *Philosophy of Religion,* pp. 102–130.

[2]A. Ritschl, *Die Christliche Lehre von der Rechtfertigung und Versöhnung,* III, 28, 29.

[3]*Cf.* Geo. A. Coe, *Psychology of Religion,* p. 57.

self it does not constitute religion. Nor is it enough to call this search religious when man shares it with others,[4] or when he discerns that some values are higher than others and proceeds to organize his life about some highest good.[5] Religion involves the belief in a higher world which has the answer to our needs.

Men of the most varied points of view have united in recognizing some such belief as an essential element in religion. Thus Gilbert Murray defines religion as "all that region of human emotion and activity which arises from man's sense that he is in the presence and at the mercy of mysterious and overwhelming forces with whom he can yet enter into some personal relation."[6] McTaggart speaks of religion as "an emotion resting on a conviction of a harmony between ourselves and the universe at large."[7] For William James "The life of religion . . . consists of the belief that there is an unseen order, and that our supreme good lies in harmoniously adjusting ourselves thereto."[8] From the standpoint of his study of primitive religion, J. G. Frazer declares: "By religion I understand a propitiation or conciliation of powers superior to man which are believed to direct and control the course of nature and of human life."[9]

Man's apprehension of this higher world comes slowly and its beginnings are crude. At first it may be simply a sense of power and mystery in the forces which he can neither con-

[4]So E. S. Ames, *The Psychology of Religious Experience,* p. viii, speaks of religion as "the consciousness of the highest social values," and A. E. Haydon, *The Quest of the Ages,* p. ix, sees it as "a shared quest of the good life."

[5]*Cf.* Geo. A. Coe, *op. cit.,* p. 70: "Any reaction may then be considered as religious to the extent that it seeks 'life' in the sense of completion, unification, and conservation of values—any values whatever."

[6]See Peake's *Commentary on the Bible,* p. 627.

[7]*Some Dogmas of Religion,* p. 3.

[8]*The Varieties of Religious Experience,* p. 53. *Cf.* 515.

[9]*The Golden Bough,* one vol. ed., p. 50.

trol nor understand, in the fury of the tempest, the incalculable lightning, and the awesome phenomena of life and death. But what he senses is not mere bigness and power; it is something that transcends not only man but nature itself. Rudolf Otto well describes this early stage in his *Idea of the Holy,* where he uses the term holy, or numinous, to indicate the more than natural that is thus perceived. Awe, wonder, fear, fascination, and a sense of dependence are all mingled here, and are called forth by man's feeling that he is in the presence of something more than himself or his fellows or the world of things, a Power that has supreme meaning for his life.[10] At the lower level, fear is apt to predominate, for the unseen is at once mighty and incalculable. Gilbert Murray has illustrated this by a quotation from an early Greek writer: "For we are surrounded above and below by Keres, or spirits, winged influences, shapeless or of unknown shape, sometimes the spirits of death, sometimes of disease, madness, calamity; thousands and thousands of them, as Sarpedo says, from whom man can never escape or hide; 'all the air so crowded with them,' says an ancient poet, 'that there is not one empty chink into which you could push the spike of a blade of corn.' "[11] Similarly Albert Schweitzer, in his *On the Edge of the Primeval Forest,* pictures the pall of fear that rests on the African native from which a higher religion delivers him.

Does this lowest stage represent religion? If we distinguish religion from magic and superstitious fear, then we may say that religion first appears when man senses in this higher world not merely power and mystery, but meaning and goodness as well, something to which he can aspire, in which he can trust, before which his soul must bow. It is on this higher level that the second element of religion comes clearly to expression; here first we see plainly its distinctive quality as

[10]See also N. Söderblom, *Das Werden des Gottesglaubens,* and his article "Holiness" in the *E. R. E.,* and R. R. Marett, *The Threshold of Religion.*

[11]*Four Stages of Greek Religion,* p. 58.

more than the mere sense of need and search for satisfaction. The test of religion, says Söderblom, is the awareness of the holy, of that which may be contrasted with the profane. The religious man is he who has found something that is holy and bows before it. The essential attitude of religion is reverence.[12] It involves more than awe and fear; it is marked by worship, whose derivation from worth-ship implies this sense of worth.

In recent years, under the influence of that naturalism which sees no reality beyond the space-time world revealed by the senses, there has been an effort to minimize or exclude from religion this aspect of faith in a higher world, or in God, making the one essential feature the search for satisfaction. "In his higher philosophical moments," says J. H. Leuba, "man wants to know; in his religious moments he wants to be."[13] "The heart of religion, the quest of the ages, is the outreach of man, the social animal, for the values of the satisfying life."[14] It is, of course, permissible for any one to put into the term religion what he wishes and frame his definition accordingly, but the great tradition of religion and the opinion of its most notable representatives are certainly not on this side. Religion is not merely a quest; it is a quest inspired by a conviction, the conviction that in some deep and significant way the world of the ideal and the world of the real are one. Religion means faith in God and in life. Such faith, for high religions, is not incidental or negligible; it is the heart of the matter. Confidence, courage, devotion, inner peace, outer activity, all hinge on this. Here, in W. P. Montague's words, is "a momentous possibility—the possibility namely that what is highest in spirit is also deepest in nature, that the ideal and the real are at least to some extent identified, not merely evanescently in our own lives, but enduringly in the universe itself. If this possibility were an actuality . . .

[12]*Das Werden des Gottesglaubens,* pp. 193–214.
[13]*A Psychological Study of Religion,* p. 206.
[14]A. E. Haydon, *The Quest of the Ages,* p. 68.

life would suddenly become radiant. For no longer would we be alien accidents in an indifferent world, uncharacteristic by-products of the blindly whirling atoms; and no longer would the things that matter most be at the mercy of the things that matter least."[15]

The instance of Buddhism is often cited as that of a religion without belief in God. It would be just as accurate to say that it contradicts the functional conception of religion which emphasizes needs and satisfaction, for its keynote is not search and satisfaction but insight and renunciation. As a matter of fact, however inadequate it may seem to us, Buddhism qualifies as a religion in both respects, and in the third aspect soon to be discussed; there is for it something holy before which it bows, not gods or spirits but an inviolable order; it indicates a way of satisfaction, though it be in the peace of Nirvana and not in the fulfillment of desire; and it calls for a definite relation to this order, a way by which man may find not only escape but attainment.

It is hardly necessary to say that for the religious man this higher world is not a fiction shaped to satisfy his needs, an imagined Companion when he finds himself lonely, or a cosmic Helper when he feels his impotence. He would describe his experience rather as awareness and response. There is the persistent sense of something higher upon which he depends, and which responds to him in turn. It is not only real for him, but the most real, the center to which all else is related, by which all else is understood.[16] The source of religion thus is to be found where everything else originates that is fundamental and enduring in human life: in man and his world, and in the interaction between the two. On one side is a deep and abiding need, on the other that which both evokes faith and responds to it. We may call these the push and the pull of religion. Nothing less can explain the fact

[15]*Belief Unbound,* pp. 6, 7.

[16]*Cf.* C. C. J. Webb, *Problems in the Relation of God and Man,* p. 10, and his quotation from Pringle-Pattison.

that with all the changes that man and his environment and his ideas undergo, religion persists.

3. But religion itself is not present until a third aspect appears: the active and reciprocal relation between man and this higher world. It is man's life as thus lived that constitutes religion, not his search for satisfaction nor his belief in God, but what happens to him when his life is brought under this all-transforming relation. In Hocking's phrase, it is "a revolution of the will, as determined by a radical insight." It is a two-way relation. From man's side it means insight, reverence, aspiration, worship, and surrender; from the other side it means for man salvation, the transformation and completion of life by help from above.

II. RELIGION AS INNER SPIRIT AND ATTITUDE

More important than any definition of religion is the sympathetic understanding of its inner spirit and attitude. With all its endless variations there is a spirit which the truly religious man will recognize as such wherever it is found. What is this spirit? Who is the religious man?

1. Religion is spiritual awareness and insight. We live in a dual world, the world of the seen and the unseen. The religious spirit knows the deeper meanings, the higher values, the hidden forces of our world. It sees the things that are unseen and lives in their presence.

2. Awe and reverence mark the religious spirit. There is a sense of majesty and power; man sees his God "high and lifted up." There is an element of mystery; man stands before that which is other than himself as well as like himself. "How unsearchable are his judgments," he cries, "and his ways past tracing out! For who hath known the mind of the Lord? or who hath been his counsellor?"[1]

But beyond this awe and fear in the presence of the *mysterium tremendum et fascinosum,* which Rudolf Otto so well describes, there is something higher, a reverence which has an

[1]See Rom. 11:33–36, with its echo of Isa. 40 and 55.

ethical quality and comes with deeper insight. It is the error of Otto to have overemphasized the aspect of the "wholly other," an overemphasis which has become almost an exclusive emphasis with Karl Barth. When the Highest is seen to be not only power but goodness, when the Holy is known as the righteous, then appears that reverence which is awe in its highest meaning. Reverence is the response of the soul in the presence of that which has not only power but worth. It is the soul's attitude toward that God in whom goodness and power are one. It is stirred in man whenever he finds those values which he counts as holy, to whose acknowledged claim all else must yield.

3. The religious spirit is one of trust. Religion is the conviction that this world "means intensely and means good." The inner attitude that corresponds to this we call faith. The Holy is good and calls for man's trust. We see this in the quiet calm that rests upon the Lord's Prayer. It breathes through the simple and beautiful confession of the twenty-third psalm. It gives the genuine note of religion to the words of a modern like John Burroughs:

> "I stay my haste, I make delays,
> For what avails this eager pace?
> I stand amid the eternal ways,
> And what is mine shall know my face."

It is not an idealism that "makes its reason blind," or shuts its eyes to unwelcome facts; neither does it rest upon reasoned philosophy or elaborate theodicy. Even in primitive religion, often so heavily weighted with fears, there is a confidence as to help secured and evil averted which makes possible religion instead of despair. "Religious faith is the conviction of a steadfastness, a certainty, an uninterrupted interconnexion in the fundamental relation between value and reality. . . . Faith is akin to faithfulness and presupposes faithfulness in its object."[2]

[2]Harald Höffding, *Philosophy of Religion,* p. 113.

4. The religious spirit is marked by loyalty. Even the crudest religion makes some demand on action and carries some sense of obligation. But in high religion, where the Holy has become wholly good, the Highest is no longer merely a resource for help and a power upon which we depend; it has the right to absolute loyalty and obedience. "Religion at its best," says G. W. Knox, in one of the finest brief definitions of religion, "is the deepest response of the self to the highest we know."[3] God is the home of all values and religion is supreme devotion. Find out that in which a man trusts for help and to which he gives his final obedience, and you will have learned his religion, whether it be in the creed that he professes or not.

5. Closely allied to this is the spirit of aspiration and adventure, the creative spirit in religion. Here religion links itself with the urge to live and shapes this into its highest form. "I tell you," says one of Bernard Shaw's characters, "that as long as I can conceive something better than myself I cannot be easy unless I am striving to bring it into existence or clearing the way for it."[4] Such aspiration religion clarifies and deepens. It gives man confidence that his world is shaped for such achievement; it gives the vision of a God who is working to such ends, and this obedience becomes no passive submission but loyalty in a common creative task. "Religion," says A. N. Whitehead, "is the vision of something which stands beyond, behind, and within the passing flux of immediate things; something which is real and yet waiting to be realized, something whose possession is the final good, and yet is beyond all reach; something which is the ultimate ideal, and the hopeless quest. The vision claims nothing but worship; and worship is surrender to the claim for assimilation, urged with the motive of mutual love. The worship of God is not a rule of safety—it is an adventure of the spirit, a flight

[3]In *The Harvard Theological Review,* 1908, p. 205. *Cf.* H. N. Wieman, *The Issues of Life,* pp. 138–141.

[4]*Man and Superman,* Act III.

after the unattainable. The death of religion comes with the repression of the high hope of adventure."[5] The beatitude of religion is not for the contented but for those that hunger and thirst; religion is supreme desire. But it is more; it is courage and adventure, because it is faith in God.

6. Finally, one may understand the spirit of religion by looking at its opposite. Over against the vision which apprehends the highest and the aspiration which desires it, there is the secularism which sees only the world of things and has no desire but to possess this world and enjoy it. Less common than secularism is the profane spirit, which knows the holy only to trample it under foot. Contrasted with the confidence of religion is the hopeless spirit that has turned from faith to despair, saying, with Joseph Wood Krutch in *The Modern Temper,* that since life has lost all high meaning, nothing is left us but to die like men since we will not live like beasts. Opposed to the humility and dependence of religion is the self-sufficient spirit, a little defiant, as in Henley's "Invictus," or simply self-confident and self-contented as with the mid-Victorians who found in natural science a new messiah.[6] Contrasted with religion's devotion are the selfishness and disloyalty, whether of men or nations, which refuse the high way of justice and good will and the common good, and cling to isolation and the rule of selfishness.

It is in this basic attitude of religion that we see how it differs from magic, which is so often viewed as a first stage of religion. Magic might be called a back-door neighbor of both religion and science. It is like science in assuming that the forces of nature can be controlled by knowledge; it is like religion in its belief in unseen powers, or a world of the spirit. It differs from science in that its knowledge is not grounded in fact; it differs from religion in its spirit and attitude. Re-

[5]*Science and the Modern World,* taken from pp. 267–269.

[6]Classically illustrated in Wynwood Reade, *The Martyrdom of Man,* a work still being issued after two generations by a belated rationalism.

ligion means reverence and dependence and humility; magic assumes superiority and mastery through knowledge. Religion means devotion to what is higher; magic seeks to exploit for individual advantage. Religion is social; magic is individualistic and anti-social. This does not exclude recognition of the fact that in practice magic has constantly been intermingled with religion.

III. AS TO DEFINITIONS OF RELIGION

We are now in better position to understand the widely varying definitions of religion and to attempt one of our own. We may note first some of the more common errors in attempting a determination of the nature of religion. Very common is the dogmatic error, the tendency to define religion in terms of our own particular interest or viewpoint. In other words, we fail to distinguish between our ideal of religion (a normative definition) and a characterization of that common interest and attitude in life which we call religious (a descriptive definition). It is important to evaluate the various forms of religious belief and practice and to determine an ideal for ourselves, but that is not to define religion.

The error of reduction lies in the opposite direction. In the effort to be objective, some have tried to find the nature of religion in a bare minimum which all religions have in common, while others, studying religion in its development, have identified it with its crude beginnings. The result is a caricature of religion. No one would think of applying this procedure to other cultural interests, art, let us say, or science, or the family. There we turn naturally to the highest forms of development to find what is most significant, realizing, as Aristotle saw long ago, that the true nature of any living reality is to be found not in its root but in its fruit.

Most common is the danger of a fragmentary conception, or a one-sided emphasis. For one, religion is individual, inner, and mystical, for another a matter of the customs and sanctions of the group, for a third beliefs, while a fourth sees only the cultus. Often individual interest is determinative; sometimes the philosophical world-view enters in. Thus one can understand the interest in social values evinced by A. E. Haydon, his stress upon religion as a social affair and an evaluating process. But when religion as such is limited to this, and it is suggested that the real nature of religion was not recognized until Professor E. S. Ames and "the Chicago School of pragmatists" discovered its essential meaning, then one has reason to suspect the influence of a particular philosophy which excludes belief in any possible transcendent reality as an object of religious faith. To hold that this is the only valid religion is one thing, to insist that nothing else is to be called religion is another matter. Indeed, viewing historical usage, one may well ask whether it would not be better to use some other term, such as a philosophy of life, for this humanistic-pragmatic position.

We may say then that religion is man's life as conceived and lived in relation to a world of a higher order, upon which he feels himself dependent, to which he knows himself under obligation, and in relation with which he finds life's meaning and seeks its completion.

Chapter Two

THE FUNCTION OF RELIGION

THE function of religion can be nothing less than to secure for man the highest and fullest life. No aspect of man's experience can be foreign to it. So simple an expression of religion as the Lord's Prayer shows this wide range; the God over all, the bread which stands for material needs, the inner life with its concern for peace and security and wholeness, the relations to our fellow men as seen in the words "our" and "we" and in the requirement of the forgiving spirit, all the great aspects of life are here. There is real danger that we shall conceive the function of religion too narrowly. One man tends to make it mystical, to lead men into fellowship with God. For another its task is to furnish a creed, a doctrine of God and the world. For a third its goal is ethical, the achievement of the highest values in individual life and social organization. Clearly, it should take in all of these, not in succession but in unity, since no one can come without the others.

But if religion be thus all-inclusive, is there left for it any distinctive field or function of its own? Except for the mystical, are there not a score of other agencies to supply these wants: science and philosophy to furnish knowledge and a world-view, with invention, engineering, medicine, sanitation, psychology, politics, and economics to meet our practical problems? And do not these have the advantage of being specific and practical and certain in method and result? Even in personal problems, are there not great numbers who turn to psychiatrist or physician rather than priest or pastor, and have we not in Russia a great people that has definitely declared that religion is an obstacle and not an aid in human affairs?

Now the striking fact is that religion shows no sign of perishing from the earth. It is receiving constant criticism and undergoing constant change, but it persists. It does not always function as it should, but it evidently has a necessary function. It suffers, as it always has, from man's ignorance and evil, and from that deadening secularism which knows only material forces, seeks only material goods, and is destructive of all ideal interests. But the new messiahs that threaten its place or primacy—science, the machine, communism, fascism, and the rest—one after another either pass away or take their subordinate position. What men are seeking today is not to abolish religion but to find one that is adequate.

1. THE WAY TO INSIGHT AND LIFE

Most simply stated, it is the function of religion to help man to see the highest in his world and to achieve the highest in his life. We may distinguish three aspects of this function: the rational, the mystical, and the ethical. (1) Religion as rational gives man an insight into final meanings and ultimate reality; it furnishes a world view and a philosophy of life. (2) Religion as mystical leads man into fellowship with the Eternal, into the supreme life-giving relation. (3) On the ethical side religion means both ideal and power. It reveals life's meaning and its highest goods. By its faith it gives men confidence and courage for the adventure of living. While science furnishes knowledge and techniques, it creates the needed inner spirit which makes possible our living and working together in mutual good will and common devotion. Where ethics presents goals, religion furnishes dynamic.

Where psychology analyzes, religion unifies and creates. It thus supplies the conditions necessary for man's higher life: vision, confidence, aspiration, loyalty, and love.

This does not mean that religion enters into competition with these other agencies or merely supplements them in a restricted field of its own. It has need of them all and makes use of them all; but it alone can bring them into unity and give them a meaning and a dynamic which of themselves they do not possess. And it does this by bringing men God. It transforms man's world by showing him the God who is creator and ruler and goal. It transforms his life by giving him an object of faith and worship and fellowship. It transforms his relations with his fellows by creating in him a spirit of reverence and good will. The function of religion then is to show man the meaning of his world in the light of God and to give man fullness of life through right relations with God and his world. Put in modern terms, it is to secure integration through insight and right relations; only, integration must mean, not simply overcoming inner disunity and social maladjustment, but achieving wholeness and richness of life. What this means must now be indicated in its major aspects.

II. THE WAY TO INTEGRATION THROUGH RIGHT RELATIONS

1. The first task of religion is to help a man to unify his world, to see things whole and to see their meaning, in other words, to give man a faith, or a philosophy of life. This is integration by insight. All human culture is witness to man's impelling need to relate, to unify, to bring into order, so that he may know the meaning and end of the world in which he lives. Such a world-view is precedent to intelligent and purposeful living. Religion is the conviction that our world is neither fragmentary nor meaningless. As John Oman declares, "It was religion and not science which first inspired men to try to unify all their experiences, and it is religion

still which alone seems to unify all experience—the corporeal and the mental, the inward and the outward, the ideas of value and the facts of existence, the events of time and their significance for eternity."[1] John Dewey, too, sees this meaning of religion: "Within the flickering inconsequential acts of separate selves dwells a sense of the whole which claims and dignifies them. In its presence we put off mortality and live in the universal."[2] Not only in nature, but in history, religion finds one Power that directs and one Purpose that rules. Wildon Carr has suggested that Paul was the father of the philosophy of history, but it was the still earlier prophetic writings of the Old Testament that furnished Paul with the idea of human history as the outworking of a divine purpose.[3] The crucial question is that of the relation of the two worlds in which man lives, the one the visible world, the world of things joined in causal relations, the other the world of ideals and values and ends. Can he integrate these two? Do they form a unity and a whole? Are truth and beauty and righteousness one with what is mightiest and most enduring in the universe? Or are all these, and he himself, but unmeaning incidents in an equally unmeaning world? The answer of religion is God, God who is on the one hand the sustaining energy of the universe and its all-embracing order, and on the other hand the home of all values and the answer to man's deepest needs and hopes.

Our own day gives abundant illustration of what the failure of such a faith means, as has, indeed, every age of history. Usually it means one of three things. It may be a fundamental dualism, as with the modern non-theistic humanism, where men still seek to cherish the world of human ideals and values while accepting a cosmos that has no knowledge of such a world and no concern for it, and that must ulti-

[1]In *Science, Religion, and Reality,* Joseph Needham, ed., p. 299. Similarly E. A. Burtt, *Religion in an Age of Science,* pp. 43, 44.

[2]*Human Nature and Conduct,* pp. 331, 332.

[3]See W. R. Matthews, *God In Christian Experience,* pp. 83, 84.

mately overwhelm what is after all only a momentary and inexplicable interlude. It may be a frank pessimism to which this unstable and somewhat forced humanistic optimism tends to give way, the mood illustrated by Thomas Hardy, "the secret of whose pessimism I take to be that he strove to combine the Christian valuation of man with the negation of the Christian view of the cosmic order."[4] Or it may be a final relapse, under that pressure for unity of thought which the mind always feels, into a naturalism that is sceptical as to ideals, cynical as to humanity, and hopeless as to life.

2. Religion integrates man's life through establishing right relations. It not only sees things whole but makes things whole; only so can man have life. What life actually is the biologist is not ready to declare, but it is clear that life on the lowest level and on the highest is a matter of relations. That is true of the parts of an organism, and of the unity which they form with each other and in which they work to a common end. That is true of the larger relations formed by the organism and its environment in mutual adjustment.[5] Of recent years this principle of integration through right relations has received increasing recognition in connection with our interpretation of the world whole and our idea of evolution. The theory of emergent evolution sees a process in which higher levels of existence appear through the association of elements of a lower order in new and more significant wholes. Taken by themselves, the constituent elements of a living cell have their appropriate laws of behavior, physical and chemical. But let these elements be united in the living cell and, though nothing has been added that you can discern by weighing or analyzing, one might well say: "Behold; all things are new." There is a new quality of being—life; there are new ways of behavior, new laws. No one can explain the why. We must simply accept the fact, "with natural piety," that the individual or particular can enter into relations to

[4]See D. S. Cairns, *The Faith That Rebels,* p. 216.

[5]See L. J. Henderson, *The Fitness of the Environment.*

form a new and larger whole, and that these new wholes bring a higher form of life. Here is the "organicistic" interpretation of the universe. The making of these wholes is the way of advance, and the study of things as "wholes" is the way of understanding our world. Physics and biology, psychology and the social sciences, all are concerned here.

The richest illustrations of this principle are to be found upon the human plane. Here, as elsewhere, pure individualism and isolation mean death; the way of life is the forming of larger wholes by entering into right relations. The unique position of man and the almost limitless possibilities of human life are connected with the extraordinary extent, variety, and significance of the relations upon which man can enter. Physically, chemically, biologically he belongs to the visible world of things, and his very existence depends upon right relations with this. Socially he is bound up with his fellow men in a myriad possible ties that spell either disaster or a wealth of life which humanity as yet has hardly envisaged. Ethically and religiously, through insight and imagination, he belongs to a world of spiritual forces and values which lifts him above all other beings. In addition to all else, man himself is a cosmos, a microcosm with a wealth of inner life and relations standing over against the macrocosm of the physical, the social, and the supernatural.

Religion is not the only agency concerned with establishing right relations. That is the task of industry and the state, of farmer and engineer, of physician and teacher and homemaker. But religion probes more deeply and reaches farther. It brings to life the highest ideals under which these relations are to be formed and releases the most potent forces. In overcoming division and discord, in uniting in right relations, religion is the greatest "togethering" power in human life. It is not independent of knowledge and skill gained in other fashion, it must use all such; yet at every point its task is unique and final.

This function of religion can be made clear by reference

to the four basic relations which are constructive for human life: man's relation to the physical order, the social order, the relations within himself, and his relation to God.

(1) Supreme is man's relation with God. But we must note at once, while supreme it is not separate. For God is not just one more added to the other relations of life; he is the final meaning in all relations. Tolstoi said that to find God was to live. When man has found God he has found the meaning of history, the purpose of his life, the power that rules, the good that summons him, the goodness that he may trust. Religion bids him relate himself to this God in trust and loyalty, and in that relation to find strength and peace. It sets itself to overcome the disunion caused by ignorance and fear and selfishness, to lead man to God in faith and devotion, and so to establish a fellowship which is the source of life.[6]

(2) Upon the basis of this first relation religion establishes the second, man's right relation to the physical universe. Science gives him knowledge, invention puts tools into his hands; but more than this is needed for the right relation to the world of things. Religion gives him perspective in values so that the world of things shall serve his need and pleasure and yet not seduce or enslave. Religion gives meaning to his daily task, links the common life with the larger welfare, and with the final purpose of God himself. Religion delivers from fear. Many fears have been banished by science, but science may simply make more acute the great fear as man stands in the presence of the illimitables of time and space which dwarf him to nothingness. For religion the immensities of nature suggest only a greater glory of God, whose greatest glory is the goodness that calls forth man's trust. So man through God feels himself at home in the cosmos; its beauty, its sublimity,

[6]"A friend once wrote to Turgenev: 'It seems to me that to put one's self in the second place is the whole significance of life.' To which Turgenev replied: 'It seems to me that to discover what to put before one's self, in the first place, is the whole problem of life.'" John C. Schroeder in *The Christian Century,* July 26, 1939.

its goods, and its very burdens and pains become ministers to the larger life.

(3) Religion helps man to secure life by right relations to his fellows, that is, by social integration. Recent years have made us more acutely aware of the problems that belong to our social life, whose dangers have become ever more threatening as that life has become increasingly complex. There is the age-old conflict between the individual and the group: how shall the self-assertion of the individual be reconciled with the needs of the group calling for subordination and service and sacrifice? There is the effect of the group life upon the individual: man's organized life, becoming ever more complex, shows a frequent tendency, not to elevate the individual life and enrich it, but to depress its level and make it a mere instrument. A world war motivated by selfish nationalism and economic imperialism takes a toll of twenty million lives. The old order gave the workman a task which had variety and interest and engaged his whole personality; modern industry tends to make him a robot, a number on a pay roll, an instrument like the machine before him. Society in a thousand ways seeks to further a submissive conformity in which intelligence and individuality are suppressed. Big business commonly, and the state in such emergencies as war, determine by press and movie and radio what men shall think. And the new nationalism, autocratic, militaristic, totalitarian, accomplishes the final reduction of the individual. Must social advance come at the cost of individual degeneration?[7] A final danger lies in the imperfect relations between groups, in the divisions and hatreds and destructive conflicts between races and nations and within economic groupings.

The absolute need of religion at this point grows increasingly apparent. Its fourfold task will be: to assert the sacred-

[7]See the discussion by W. M. Wheeler in *Emergent Evolution and the Development of Societies,* with the authorities there cited, pp. 43–52; and compare the picture of the masses in Aldous Huxley's *Brave New World* and its keen satire on a hundred per cent technological civilization.

ness of human personality; to set free the spirit of man from the divisive forces of selfishness, hatred, and fear; to reshape the institutions of our social life so that they will minister to humanity and not be the exploitative instruments of the few; to show how the life of the individual is fulfilled in the life of the group, and the life of the group in that of the larger whole.

(4) Religion must secure inner wholeness, personal integration. Personality is not an endowment but an achievement. It does not come by mere "self-expression" any more than by suppression. It means the harmonizing of warring impulses through some higher goal and master motive that will insure alike unity and energy and satisfaction. It is a way of freedom through mastery of one's world. It offers a faith which brings the quietness of confidence and the courage for adventure. And as an inner creative power, coming through the right relations with God and one's world, it works to secure the final harmony between ideal and attainment. Thus religion, in the individual and in the group, brings integration not by reduction but by fulfillment, a fulfillment through rich and right relations which rest finally upon the vision of God and fellowship with God.

Chapter Three

THE POLARITY OF RELIGION

I. THE PRINCIPLE OF POLARITY

THE complexity of religion, on the one hand, and its function of bringing unity into life, on the other, can both be better understood if considered in the light of the principle of polarity. At the same time this principle will aid us in the consideration of certain questions affecting the nature of religion and its relations which we have still to take up before we discuss the nature of the Christian religion. These are the problems of religion as individual and social, religion as activity and rest, religion and ethics, permanence and change in religion, and duality in the experience of God.

The term polarity originated with physics. It is defined by the *New International Dictionary* as "that quality or condition in virtue of which a body exhibits opposite, or contrasted, properties or powers, in opposite, or contrasted, parts or directions." The *Encyclopedia Britannica* speaks of "two poles or parts at which certain properties are the opposite to one another, as in a magnet." But the principle is one which obtains on every level of existence. Everywhere we find in the same field or object the pull of opposing forces, and the contrast, if not opposition, of different qualities. Our universe reveals a common and inclusive order which makes it a cosmos; we are not dealing here, therefore, with the concept of dualism. But within that order there is a tension, not a dualism of principles but a duality of process. Thus we have order and freedom, the calculable and the unpredictable, dependence and self-assertion, the tension between organism and environment, and that underlying duality which is expressed in the problem of the One and the Many.

The principle of duality, or bipolarity, becomes even more evident as we move higher. It culminates on the highest level in such dualities as fact and value, matter and spirit, evil and good, man and God. Here the naturalisms and idealisms of philosophy face each other, and too often each attempts to secure a premature unity by denying the element of truth that underlies the other. The principle of polarity suggests that there is a unity which not only admits such opposition but gives it an important place. "I cannot quite see," writes W. M. Urban, after setting forth his philosophy of values, "just how fact and value, value and existence, are related, although I do see perfectly that to separate them means ultimately unintelligibility."[1]

Such polarity involves two significant elements. (1) It means, not an opposition which leads to deadlock and stagnation, but a tension which is the spring of action and progress. Such tension is apparently a condition of life and development. In the happy phrase of Professor Sheldon, we have "productive duality." "The principle of duality suggests . . . another side, wherein freedom and law, static and dynamic, individual and universal, have a positive relationship. They do not merely fail to conflict, they are not only mutually indifferent; they are also mutually contributory."[2] The tension of polarity is like the spring of the bow for the flight of the arrow. Fact and value, goodness and power, may be one in some ultimate and enduring sense, but in our finite world goodness is in process of achievement and the product comes out of a duality of process with its inherent tension or

[1]*Contemporary American Philosophy,* II, 380.

[2]W. H. Sheldon, *Strife of Systems and Productive Duality,* p. 493.

strain. That was the insight of Browning's Rabbi Ben Ezra.

"Then, welcome each rebuff
That turns earth's smoothness rough,
Each sting that bids nor sit nor stand but go!
Be our joy three-parts pain!
Strive, and hold cheap the strain;
Learn, nor account the pang; dare, never grudge the throe!"

To the principle of tension we must add (2) that of interpenetration, or, better, of mutual completion.[3] The problem of the pull of opposing forces or interests is not solved by the familiar formula of "both-and," nor yet by the principle of alternation which Hocking has developed finely in relation to the demands of action and rest in religion.[4] Something more than addition or alternation is involved here. The opposing aspects or tendencies of this duality are not only both needed for individual life and progress, but each demands the other for its own completion; and if each be pursued far enough and explored in its fullest meaning, it will lead, like the straight line in Einstein's curved universe, not simply away but back again. Rest brings the call to action and is the spring of action. Thus there is a constant pull between the individual and social in religion, as in all life, but neither comes to real expression without the other. So obedience, as Paul insisted, is the way to freedom. It is as if you stood at either pole of our earth and found the other by digging deep enough.

Polarity is thus something more than paradox. Paradox moves in the realm of thought. It is a matter of statements which seem to contradict each other while yet each is true in its own right. It rests upon the fact that life has to do with many different relations and levels.[5] On one level I am

[3]The term interpenetration in this sense is used by Sheldon, *op. cit.*, p. 476, and is fully discussed by E. W. Lyman, *The Meaning and Truth of Religion*, pp. 94–99.

[4]See his *Meaning of God in Human Experience* and consult his Index under this term.

[5]See the interesting discussion of Daniel Lamont, *Christ and the World of Thought*, pp. 62–67.

bound (in the physical order), on another I am free (as rational and self-determining spirit). I have a relation to myself as individual moral personality, and here I am an end in myself; I have a relation to society, and here I am obligated to service. So, with Paul, I am free and yet the servant of all. These paradoxes with which the mind deals point to the tensions of polarity which lie deep in life itself. These tensions, relatively simple on the physical level, increasing with the biological, become complex beyond description in human life. But it is this that has made man's life at once so full of conflict and so rich in possibilities. It need hardly be stated that the polarity here considered is not the Hegelian dialectic, the immanent and unceasing process in which the opposition of thesis and antithesis is constantly being resolved in the unity of the higher synthesis, a process of which man is the spectator. This is rather the pull of forces remaining in tension, going to constitute that life of man at whose heart is the need of constant decision and action.

It is in religion that the principle of polarity comes to its most significant expression. That is to be expected since it is religion as the highest level of lfe that takes up into itself all other relations, and since it is the task of religion to bring the tensions of life and the paradoxes of thought into rich and productive unity. We turn now to the specific problems indicated above in which this principle at once receives illustration and gives us guidance.

II. RELIGION AS INDIVIDUAL AND SOCIAL

The polarity of religion appears first in the opposition of individual and social. Some have stressed the individual side. So we recall Augustine's insistence: "I wish to know God and the soul." "Nothing more?" he is asked. "Nothing at all."[1] Quite as vigorous is A. N. Whitehead: "Religion is the art and theory of the internal life of man," and this inner

[1]See Fr. Loofs, *Dogmengeschichte,* 4th ed., p. 352, for citation and comment.

life "is the self-realization of existence. This doctrine is the direct negation of the theory that religion is primarily a social fact. Religion is what the individual does with his own solitariness. If you are never solitary, you are never religious."[2] On the other side Wundt, in his *Völkerpsychologie,* and Durkheim, in *The Elementary Forms of the Religious Life,* find the source of religion in the interests and ideas and practices of the group. For E. S. Ames "religion consists in this social consciousness." It is "a phase of all socialized human experience." "Non-religious persons are accordingly those who fail to enter vitally into a world of social activities and feelings."[3]

The fact is religion is always both individual and social because human life is such. The development of these two sides, however, has been unequal. It reveals, roughly distinguished, three stages.

Primitive religion is primarily a group affair; it is concerned with the interests of the tribe, includes all its activities, and gives sanction to its customs. The individual accepts his religion from the group and shares in it as one of the group. There is more than solidarity of interest; family or clan is one in a realistic sense. Thus Achan's sin is the sin of his whole clan, and all are put to death because of Achan's deed.[4]

At the next stage religion becomes more individual. The sense of the individual human personality and its independent life and worth is a relatively late achievement. The Hebrew prophets and the Greek Stoics showed the first clear appreciation: it was the work of Jesus to bring out fully the significance and sacredness of human personality. But just as religion has an outward movement, tending to externalize itself in form and institution, so it has an inward movement also. It impels man to turn from the external, whether in visible things or unthinking custom, and to ask as to inner

[2]*Religion in the Making,* pp. 15, 17, *passim.*

[3]*The Psychology of Religious Experience,* pp. 168, viii, 280, 359. The position is more carefully put in *Religion,* pp. 38–40.

[4]Jos. 7:16–26.

meanings and spiritual values. It brings the soul into immediate and personal fellowship with God. That is seen in the great spirits, with their seeking, testing, questioning and affirming. The great forward movements in religion have undeniably had their social backgrounds and have involved mighty social forces, but their centers of creative power have been individuals, great spirits for whom the invisible world had once more become vividly real. They have exhibited religion as the highest development of the human soul, as its freest and fullest life.

The final stage is not a mere swing of the pendulum back to the social; it is a new level to which both individual and social are raised and where these complete each other.[5] This follows as religion becomes ethical and inner. Christianity best illustrates this. Here the worth of the individual comes to full expression and each achieves his own life in personal fellowship with God. At the same time the social significance of religion becomes clearer and richer and the corporate side of religion reaches a new level. The God with whom the soul has fellowship is the God of love and righteousness. They who seek him must find him in the lives of men; his Spirit is most fully present in the fellowship. They who would share his life find that his Spirit can be had only as it is lived out in the common quest for the highest. So the supreme task of the individual is to contribute to the group and the highest life of the individual is found through the group.

In practice religion tends to move to one extreme or the other. The group emphasis may take the form of stress on the ecclesiastical organization, with ritual, sacraments, priesthood, and traditional teachings. It is often the home of a deep and sincere piety, but it tends likewise to unthinking conformity, to emphasis on externals, and to the repression of

[5]"Religion as a sense of the whole is the most individualized of all things, the most spontaneous, undefinable, and varied. *For individuality signifies unique connections in the whole.*" John Dewey, *Human Nature and Conduct,* p. 331.

freedom in the individual and of progress in the group. In the end the social aspect itself suffers because the institution rather than the fellowship tends to become the end, and because the group cannot rise higher than the elements that constitute it. A like danger appears when an extreme emphasis is placed upon social goals and obligations. Here men fail to see that religious dynamic is being lost, that satisfaction of the inner life is being missed, and that these come only as man lives in faith and personal fellowship with the Eternal. The social program itself thus fails of success through bankruptcy of spiritual resources.

The one-sided concern for the individual and inner may be equally disastrous. High religion is social just as all human life is. Language, literature, science, art, industry, moral ideals, and religious faith, all are social products. Only the group can achieve and express the highest in man; only through the group can God give to man most fully. The New Testament relates the work of the indwelling Spirit normally to the group. When religion is ethical it cannot remain merely individual. If God be the Spirit of truth and justice and good will, then he cannot be found apart from human fellowship; the life from God can be received only as it is shared. The religious life must always have this double movement: back to solitude, to meditation and worship; forward to expression, to service, to human fellowship and co-operation.

Whitehead says, "Religion is what a man does with his solitariness." That is right as far as it goes; in the final decision man knows himself as standing alone over against his world and God. But the solitariness belongs only to that moment, not to what went before to make that moment possible, nor to what must follow if there is really to be religion. For no man ever came in strict solitariness to that knowledge of himself and his world which makes possible the religious decision. And to decide for religion is to surrender that solitariness for a life of fellowship with God and man, a fellowship apart from which man cannot achieve life. "Nobody is anything except as he joins himself to something. You cannot be a whole unless you join a whole. This, I believe is religion."[6] Religion is thus not merely what a man does *in* his solitariness, but what he does *with* his solitariness.

The tension between individual and social is unusually strong today, especially in political-economic-international life where the conflict threatens chaos. An extreme nationalism opposes its individualism to world unity, while within itself it emphasizes the corporate and represses the free life of the individual in the determination that everything shall be subordinated to the totalitarian state. In the democratic states, on the other hand, individualism asserts its independence of authority and social control just when co-operative action and devoted good will are increasingly demanded. Democracy in particular faces a life and death struggle at this point. To maintain itself against totalitarian aggression and to meet the new economic conditions, it must emphasize solidarity of life and secure a greater unity of social control and action. But equally it must conserve the freedom of the individual and recognize his welfare as the ultimate concern of the state. To eliminate these tensions is neither possible nor desirable. It is the task of religion not to remove them but to reveal by its principles of solidarity and good will and reverence for human personality, and by its power at once to build the social order and to fulfill human personality in the spirit of love, how each aspect is needed and finds its completion in the other.

III. RELIGION AS ACTIVITY AND REST

In some measure the attitude of submission and trust and rest belongs to all religion, though it is most evident on the higher levels. There are different elements involved in this attitude: reverence and awe before the Holy, dependence in the presence of power, submission of will to that which has

[6] B. Bosanquet, *What Religion Is*, p. 12.

the right to command. And when God is seen clearly as goodness as well as power, then religion means rest and quiet of soul. The authentic voice of religion sounds this note again and again. "In returning and rest shall ye be saved," says an ancient prophet, "in quietness and in confidence shall be your strength. He that believeth shall not make haste."[1] "Come unto me and I will give you rest," is the word of Jesus. "In his will is our peace," says Dante, in what has been called the greatest single line in literature.

But the contrasted aspect of religion is just as obvious. Religion gave Dante peace but sent him into exile. The word of Jehovah meant rest to the prophet, but it also meant a fire burning in his bones so that he could not keep quiet. We read of Jesus' word: "Peace I leave with you"; but there are other sayings ascribed to him: "We must work the works of him that sent me"; "I came not to send peace but a sword."[2] Jesus called men to strenuous and persistent activity. It is a narrow gate and a straitened way that leads to life, and his condemnation falls on "the unlit lamp and the ungirt loin."

It has been a common error to push one or the other of these aspects to an extreme and thus to make of religion either a passive and fatalistic quietism or that pure "activism" with which some continental scholars have charged American Protestantism. Let us note first that it is the conception of God that is determinative here. For the religions of passivity, God is the great All in whom the separate self is to be absorbed; or he is the absolute Will, determining all, doing all, so that it is ours simply to accept what happens since "Allah wills it," or to await the salvation which we can neither hinder nor hasten. For activism, on the contrary, the living and transcendent God tends to be lost in the finite forces, while the human Atlas tries to bear the world upon his shoulders. The Christian concept of God calls for both aspects.

To begin with the side of rest: the source of rest in religion is faith in a God who is both power and goodness. Once

[1]Isa. 30:15; 28:16. [2]John 14:27; 9:4; Matt. 10:34.

we see this, revolt gives place to ready submission. We learn dependence upon him for life and help, and quiet confidence as we face the future; we "let our ordered lives confess the beauty of his peace." But the very attitude of trust and surrender has in it the spring of action; it leads of necessity beyond itself when once we understand the God whom we trust. He is the God of righteousness; yes, but it is righteousness in action. No passive submission will suffice here, but only an active sharing in the work of the divine Spirit which is creating an order of justice in the earth. He is the God of love; but again it is creative love, not something passively received and luxuriated in, but actively shared and leading man forth on the same road of sacrifice and service that God himself takes. He who seeks rest alone in religion will lose the rest that he seeks, and will lose that God who dwells not simply in the place of worship but where truth is sought in earnest toil and justice established in fierce conflict and men served in their need.

But activity by itself is equally self-defeating. The church of our day is a sad witness to this, trying to mobilize spiritual forces which do not exist, summoning to action when the spring of action is wanting. All great action comes from faith; confidence in the Eternal can alone furnish strength for the age-long fight, and only in fellowship of the spirit with God can man find the resources for fruitful service.

Professor Hocking has well characterized these contrasted attitudes: "On the one hand the peace of the hermit, the silence of the forest, the exaltation of sacrifice, the mightiness of simplification and unity, the joy of self-abandonment, the calm of absolute contemplation, the vision of God. On the other hand, the variety and stress of life, the zest of common ends, the mastery of means, the glory of infinite enterprise, the pride of creativity and self-possession."[3] He declares that we must choose both. But that need not be done, as he suggests, in mere alternation; for the highest activity will lack

[3]*The Meaning of God in Human Experience*, p. 427.

the spring of power if there be not a continued dependence and trust, and we cannot find peace apart from the world of work and the God who works "even until now." Here once more is the principle of polarity in the opposing pull of these calls to rest and action and in the completion of each in the other.

IV. RELIGION AND ETHICS

The question of the relation of religion and ethics may well be taken up here for the light which the principle of polarity throws upon it. The discussion of the elements of activity and rest has already brought us into this field, for, roughly speaking, the one suggests ethics and the other religion. Whatever else religion includes, its center is the idea of a God upon whom we are dependent, to whom we owe devotion, from whom we await help. Just as clearly ethics is concerned with man: with the goods of human life and the principles of action which govern their attainment. True, there enters into ethics the right, with its imperative obligation which implies a Beyond. Yet the moral imperative involves human autonomy; it is man's free choice that admits it as authority. As religion is oriented to God, ethics is oriented to man. Ethics sets its hope on man, his responsibility and activity. Religion stresses man's dependence on the deed and gift of God: "By grace have ye been saved through faith; and that not of yourselves, it is the gift of God; not of works, that no man should glory."[1]

Further, ethics apparently has its independent roots in human experience; men find their ideals of right and wrong without necessary reference to the idea of God, and develop high conduct and character without belief in God. Indeed, ethics seems to take a position of superiority in relation to religion. The greatest single advance in man's religious development came when nature religions gave way to ethical religion, that is, when man's moral insights forced a change in his concept of God and of the religious life. Here is the

[1]Eph. 2:8, 9.

enduring debt that we owe to the Hebrew prophets, who saw that God must be more and not less than the highest that man knew of justice and mercy, and that no religious service could suffice which did not include the "do justly and love kindness."

But this statement of contrast is but part of the truth. There is a certain tension here, but it is within religion and not between religion and something outside. To see this we must take religion and ethics on their highest level. Ethics points to God. Moral experience is one form of the experience of God. It is God whom we know in the growing insights of righteousness and love; we perceive in these not simply human ideals but something essentially divine, something holy to which we respond with reverence and awe. Only thus, indeed, have they the right to command. The great prophets did not think of using ethics to correct religion; these moral insights were a form of religious experience, a real revelation of God.

And religion involves the ethical. God is goodness, not simply power; he invites trust, not merely submission. True, on the lower levels this trust is mixed with question and fear; the gods need to be won from indifference, or placated in their anger. But there is always something that gives ground for expectation, and in higher religions it issues in the deep conviction that goodness and power are one. And as the idea of God thus involves the ethical, so faith in God brings a moral demand reaching its highest in the Christian insight that man must be like God in truth and love, and must serve his fellow man.

The idea of salvation is the one place where the ethical might seem to be excluded, for the central idea of salvation is that of a deed and gift of God. Yet here too it is required. On the lower levels, of course, this is not apparent; indeed, it is one of the insights most slowly achieved. That may be seen even in Christian groups. There is a sacramentarianism in which physical means are supposed to work spiritual results. There is the non-ethical conception of a compelling divine power, as in the doctrine of irresistible grace. And apocalyptic theories indicate a salvation that is to come by some divine compulsion acting without relation to the historical-ethical process. Yet the Christian teaching and its implications are clear. The religious emphasis is on God and his gift, but the gift is personal and ethical; eternal life is quality, not duration, and its quality is moral. And such a gift from God is possible only through an active response from man. Man's insight must answer God's revelation, his obedient trust must meet God's gift, his active life must express the mercy and righteousness which God bestows by his Spirit. The Kingdom of God is both gift and task, *Gabe und Aufgabe*. "Work out your own salvation." "If we live by the Spirit, by the Spirit let us also walk." Only as we actively express the character of God are we sons of God.[2]

But that the ethical requires completion in the religious is equally clear. The great problem of ethics is not that of determining what are the highest human goods and what the appropriate action for their attainment; it is the problem of personal character and moral dynamic. How can the inner spirit of men be transformed? How can there be secured the enthusiasm for high ends, the inner devotion? How can morality be changed from a demand into a passion? And how can men be socially integrated, united in a fellowship of common devotion and co-operative action in which at the same time the individual personality shall come to its own? Religion does this and adds one thing more: it supplies a faith that gives to morality a rational ground and to men courage and inspiration to carry on. One can stand for the sacredness of human personality and its rights more confidently if one believes that the final reality of this universe is personal being and not impersonal energy. The ideals of ethics speak to us with a new power if we can believe that they are more than social tradition or individual preference or ab-

[2]Phil. 2:12, 13; Gal. 5:25; Matt. 5:44, 45.

stract notions, but are real and potent in the being of the Eternal. The social confusion and moral impotence of today find their surest explanation in a world-wide loss of spiritual faith. Without religion there can be no effective moral authority, and without moral authority there can be no social order except that of a militaristic autocracy.

V. PERMANENCE AND CHANGE IN RELIGION

Religion, like every form of life, is marked by permanence and change. The recognized conservative tendency in all religions has various grounds. It may be a matter of inertia or of the selfish fears of those in ecclesiastical position. More often its root is the same as that of the opposition to social change in general, that is, a fear that precious goods of life may be endangered. Naturally this would be strongest in religion because the goods at stake are the highest. One other reason is obvious. Religion is concerned with the divine; it seeks some point where the Eternal has revealed himself in the midst of time. When now it has found God in Bible or creed, in Church or sacrament, it feels that its certainty of God is imperilled by change. Moreover, it is easy to identify the divine with the forms that it has taken or the channels through which it comes. So the Bible becomes infallible and creeds unchangeable. The unlearned look upon the theory of evolution and historical criticism as products of the pit. A great Church declares not only the Bible but the Vulgate translation infallible, while a Protestant scholar like Barth discusses the Apostles' Creed in his *Credo* as if it were verbally inspired.

But the impulse to change, an unresting dissatisfaction, the spirit of independence and high adventure, and the eager search for truth belong equally to religion. Once more we are dealing with a polarity which marks all life. The two constituent aspects of evolution are continuity and change, the conservation of the old and the appearance of the new. Life is possible only as there is continuity with the past and constant adjustment to a changing present. That is as true spiritually as it is biologically. High religion is never static; it is not satisfied with any voice of the past, for its search is for the living God. It knows that we see now only in a mirror darkly, that no formula can comprise all truth, that the Eternal is more than all that has been won in human thought or deed. It knows the beatitude for those that hunger and thirst after righteousness. It is a pilgrim seeking a city. Its spokesmen have been the great centers of religious advance: Akhnaton and the Buddha, Amos and Jeremiah, Socrates, Jesus, Paul, Savonarola, Luther. They have always followed a vision that moved ahead. Almost inevitably they found themselves in conflict with Church and state. They were the heretics whom men cast out of the synagogue, but their God was the God of truth. To them the closed mind was disloyalty to God. Through them humanity once and again broke the hardening crust of custom and marked another advance.

This forward movement in religion may be noted at four crucial points: in the God in whom man believes, in the goods that he seeks, in the obligations that he feels, in the help that he expects.

(1) Fundamental in significance is the change in the idea of God. It can be indicated by the words unity, rationality, morality, personality, immanence. By unity: instead of many forces or spirits or gods, there is one God and so a world that is unitary and orderly. By rationality: instead of the strange and incalculable *mana,* or holy, there is reason and meaningful purpose. By morality: instead of a supernatural, or numinous, that is hostile or indifferent or arbitrary, there is a God of justice and mercy, in whom man can trust, through whom the values of life are secure. By personality: the cruder anthropomorphism goes but there remains a God with whom man can have fellowship and a world whose ground is spiritual and not material, a world in which man can be at home. By immanence: as purpose and goodness and power, God still transcends the world of the finite, but the old dualism is

gone; God is not exterior and apart, the Beyond is within and akin as well as above.

(2) In the goods that man seeks, the movement has been from the material to the spiritual and ethical, from the individual to the social, while at the same time making these goods inclusive of all that goes to further human life, as against anything narrowly religious or other-worldly.

(3) As regards the obligation that man feels, religion ceases to be offerings and sacrifices intended to placate God, or acceptance of correct belief, or observance of prescribed ritual. The emphasis falls on the inner spirit and attitude, and on the social expression to which this must lead.

(4) As to the salvation that man expects from God: the external and magical disappear; the help is not through rites that have a mysterious efficacy or by a divine power working from without. The spiritual world becomes one of order, which man must understand. Salvation demands right relation based on insight. God works as indwelling Spirit in and through the life of man, and all human life, social and individual, becomes the subject of redemption.

VI. DUALITY IN THE EXPERIENCE OF GOD

There is a duality, or polarity, in the experience of God. On the one hand the religious attitude is marked by awe, reverence, and fear. God is the Holy One, whose ways are above our ways as the heavens are above the earth. His judgments are unsearchable and his ways past finding out, and no one has been his counsellor. "Be still and know that I am God; I will be exalted."[1] God is *mysterium tremendum* in the words of Rudolf Otto, whose depiction of this aspect of religion in *The Idea of the Holy* has become classic. On the other hand is the deep conviction that he who is holy and other is also akin to us. Man says "Thou" to God; religion is a personal relation.[2] Prayer in some form is an

[1]Psalms 46:10.

[2]So even with Karl Barth, *Dogmatik,* I, 1, second ed., p. 214.

inalienable element of religion, and prayer involves a certain likeness and nearness of God. The Christian faith in a God of love incarnating himself in human life is the clearest expression of this.

In these two aspects of the religious attitude, there is a clear tension. Our sense of God's likeness and nearness and our trust in him are confronted and challenged by our awareness of his majesty and holiness and of our own finitude and sinfulness. We are constantly rebuked when we forget that difference. On the other hand, the soul that is bowed in awe and fear hears the summons to know and trust and to walk in fellowship with the Eternal: "Son of man, stand upon thy feet." "Come now, and let us reason together." "He that abideth in love abideth in God, and God abideth in him."[3]

In the highest expressions of religion, these attitudes interpenetrate; each is needed by the other and gives to the other its deepest meaning. Of what value were it to trust in God if he were not the God of majesty and power and holiness? And what were the worth of a God of power if he did not touch our human lives and relate himself to us? The danger lies in isolating one or the other. Modern immanentism tends so to stress the aspect of kinship and immanence that God is submerged in the relativities of the natural order and human effort becomes the sole hope of salvation. In thought this issues in some type of pantheism or naturalism, in both of which the personal, living God is lost. In practice there appears the drying up of the springs of vital religion, with the cynicism and pessimism which mark so many of the one-time liberals of our day. On the other hand, there may be such an emphasis on the transcendent and "totally other" God that the gulf between God and man cannot be crossed, and God remains both distant and unknowable.

A consideration of concrete religious expressions will show how the two aspects are joined in a way in which the very tension between them becomes the spring of the highest faith.

[3]Ezek. 2:1; Isa. 1:18; 1 Jn. 4:16.

We see this in Psalms 90 and 95 and Isaiah 40 and 55. It is the clue to Paul's discussion in Romans 8 to 11. These passages about divine power and absolute foreordination, isolated and turned into dogmatics, have led to the extremes of hyper-Calvinism; yet taken as a whole, with an appreciation of their religious motivation, they are a profound expression of this bipolarity in the experience of God. "What then shall we say to these things? If God is for us, who is against us? O the depth of the riches both of the wisdom and the knowledge of God! how unsearchable are his judgments, and his ways past tracing out!" More profoundly moving and even more clearly illustrative is the account of Jesus' praying in the night before his death. The facing of an end that seemed the clear way of duty and of God's will while yet so terrible, the "thy will be done" joined to the "Abba, Father," show at once the tension of religion and its highest expression. It is out of this experience that the faith springs for which God is both far and near, or, in Boutroux's phrase, "the Beyond that is within."

Pertinent to our whole study are Friedrich Heiler's words: "The alternation of childlike speech and mystical silence, of prayer and meditation, of 'Thou' and 'He', of "personalism' and 'impersonalism', gives to the soul's communion with God a constant tension and an inexhaustible fruitfulness. The living God is both *Deus absconditus* and *Deus revelatus,* the God who dwells 'in light unapproachable' and who becomes visible in human form, the impenetrable darkness of mystery and the bright light of revelation, the all-consuming fire of wrath and the helping, saving, self-giving redemptive love. For that reason true communion with God must include the polarity of personalism and impersonalism, and the life of devotion must move back and forth between the confident 'Thou' of prayer and the awed 'He' of contemplation."[4]

[4]*Das Gebet,* 5th Ed., Appendix, p. 617. *Cf.* W. R. Matthews, *God in Christian Experience,* pp. 25–28.

Chapter Four

THE NATURE OF THE CHRISTIAN RELIGION

IT SEEMS a hopeless task to secure any agreement on the question: What is Christianity? Catholics differ from Protestants, Protestants among themselves, and some of the deepest differences cut across denominational lines and are indicated by such words as fundamentalist and modernist. The difficulties involved are only the more apparent when we ask about the standard to which appeal is to be made. Is it the Bible as a whole, or the New Testament, or the teachings of Jesus? Is it the ecumenical creeds, or some other historic confession? Is it church council or pope? Or shall we depend upon the inner light, the witness of the Spirit, or critical reason?

But the question, however difficult, cannot be shirked. First it has great practical importance. The Church of today faces two inescapable questions: What is our message and task? And how can we unite our forces? The latter is just now especially urgent, when the totalitarian state threatens the very existence of the Church, and prevalent paganism offers a sharply competing philosophy of life. But Christian unity cannot be secured by mere exhortation or by setting up programs of common action; we must face honestly the differences in our understanding of Christianity. Loyalty to conviction is too high a quality of the spirit to be set aside for mere "practical" reasons. And as to the message, the weakness of organized religion today lies largely in the fact that it has no clear common word to speak to a day in which paganism is vocal and aggressive. But that again means the question of what Christianity is.

For the study of theology the matter is of equal significance. Theology aims to set forth the truths of the Christian religion. Clearly the answer is determined by our conception of Christianity. In one sense it is true that a man's whole system of theology is his reply to this question, and so we cannot easily answer in advance. But too often the theologian assumes a point of view at the beginning that is determinative for all the rest and yet is not discussed. The very least that can be done is to set forth fairly the principal forms in which this question has been answered and to state frankly one's own position.

In the end the answer will rest with a personal decision. Historic Christianity is a rich and varied fact. It has had diverse elements in it at every period from the beginning and it has changed in history. Neither historical study nor logical argument can determine objectively and for all just which period of its history is to be made normative for all the rest, or whether there is any such objective and unchanging standard. The position here taken is: (1) that the varying interpretations of Christianity can be brought under a few main types; (2) that the principal difficulty comes from assuming that Christianity is an institution with one unchanging form which is given in some objective and absolute standard; (3) that it is, rather, a spirit and a way of life, rooting in central conviction and having expression in a fellowship which because of its vitality assumes varying forms and develops in history; (4) that our conception of Christianity should be inclusive, rather than exclusive, and that strict uniformity is not the great desideratum. Whether this position commends itself, only a detailed study will show. The important matter is not so much to establish a conclusion, as to make plain the situation and give the materials for individual decision.

There are two ways in which we can approach this question. The traditional way has been to inquire as to "the rule of faith," that is, to seek first for a norm, or standard of authority. The argument was simple: Christianity is a revealed religion. In it God speaks to men and God's word is decisive. What we need to do is to find where that word is given; then we shall know what Christianity is. But this method has already jumped to a conclusion which we cannot allow. Those who speak thus assume that this word of God to man is a sum of teaching coming to us in some objective and absolute form, whether in Bible, creed, tradition, or the voice of the Church. They hold, that is, to an externalistic or institutional theory of authority. But this idea of some fixed authority, objectively embodied, is itself a part of the question at issue. We shall use then another approach: first, historical, studying the beginnings of Christianity and the forms of its later development; second, critical, considering the varying interpretations offered today and seeking to reach a conclusion for ourselves.

I. CREATIVE FORCES AND CONSTITUTIVE ELEMENTS IN EARLY CHRISTIANITY

In turning to the beginnings, we are not looking for some original and authoritative form of Christianity; that would be to prejudge one of the crucial questions, the place of growth in the Christian religion. We may well ask, however, what the creative forces were which gave rise to Christianity and the distinctive elements which entered in, before we consider how it received its present form, or forms.

1. The central creative force in the rise of Christianity was Jesus. This assertion does not rule out the influence of its *milieu,* religious, social, economic, and political, or the many and diverse elements that entered into its development such as Jewish apocalypticism and legalism, the mystery religions and other cults, and Greek philosophy. But Christianity was no mere syncretism. It possessed a marked individuality from the beginning and was strongly conscious of its own distinc-

tive character. From the first its members felt themselves as one throughout the Roman world, with a single loyalty that marked them off from all other cults and provoked frequent anger at their exclusiveness. The background of syncretism, as E. F. Scott has pointed out, is always the assumption that different cults are of equal standing,[1] but Christianity rested upon the passionate conviction that the eternal God had spoken to men in Jesus Christ. The plain historical fact is that there appeared at this time a great flowering forth of religious faith and spiritual power, and the evidence of the New Testament is indisputable that its creative source was Jesus. The composers of the New Testament writings differ among themselves—compare Paul's expectation of an apocalyptic kingdom to be established by the speedy return of Jesus with the emphasis of the fourth gospel on the eternal life already present in the hearts of men. But all unite in their confession of utter dependence upon Jesus. They do not mean some Christ dogma or some hero-savior myth, nor do they have in mind primarily his teachings or example; rather it is Jesus himself, his word, spirit, life, deed, death. Through him they feel themselves new men in a new world. "If any man is in Christ, he is a new creation: the old things are passed away, behold, they are become new."[2]

2. If we now inquire more closely we shall find five elements in primitive Christianity, all of which are vitally related to Jesus.

(1) There was a conviction, a faith. They shared, of course, the common Jewish belief in the one living God. The new thing was that this God "at the end of these days" had spoken unto them in his Son, but this meant everything. Their faith was in "the God and Father of our Lord Jesus Christ," and in that faith the world and life and death and things to come all had become different.

(2) Primitive Christianity was a way of living. There is

[1]E. F. Scott, *The Gospel and Its Tributaries,* p. 275.
[2]II Cor. 5:17.

a certain quality of life which marks this early movement whose distinctive character is not to be mistaken. There is no mystery as to its source; it was the spirit of Jesus, at once as dominating ideal and as contagious power. With its emphasis on spirit and attitude, it transcended the morality of law, yet it was neither vague nor impractical; it was as definite as the personality of Jesus himself. It is significant of the pervasive power of this spirit of Jesus that the best representation of it is from the man who did not really "know Christ after the flesh."[3] It meant a new way of living with God in which reverence, awe, and devotion before the holy One were joined with the love and trust of sons living in fellowship with their Father. It meant a way of living with men: reverence for men as men and a spirit of utter good will.

(3) Religion was not merely a way of living but a way to life; that is, it was life as a gift and not simply as a task, it was a religion of redemption. That was the fact which underlay all else: Jesus had brought life to them, not simply new ideas or ideals. They experienced this in two ways. First, Jesus brought them into a fellowship with God which of itself was the power of a new life: "God was in Christ recconciling the world unto himself."[4] They remembered words of Jesus about the forgiving father and the wayward son, and the prayer in which he taught them how to come to this Father.[5] Second, the new life came to them as a new spirit, a new kind of life within themselves. They thought of it as the Spirit of God given to them, or as the spirit of Christ living in them. They had reached that high stage where religion and ethics become one in the freedom and power of a new life; the spirit of Jesus was at once the life to be lived and the life that God gave.[6] God was a presence, not simply a distant power; religion was a life here and now, not simply a future hope.

(4) This first Christianity was a fellowship. To say

[3]See I Cor. 13 and compare with II Cor. 5:16.

[4]II Cor. 5:19. [5]Luke 15:11–32; Matt. 6:9. [6]Gal. 5:25.

Church is misleading for we inevitably carry back into that word the later ideas of organization and authority. It was not something made after a plan; it was not the result of prescription. There is a striking absence of what the later Church emphasized: orders and authority, prescribed ritual and binding creeds. Not by forces working from without but by inner forces, cohesive and life-giving, was this fellowship created. Men came together by an inner compulsion; a common Lord, a common faith, devotion to a common task, the inspiration of a common hope, and a common spirit of good will united them.

(5) There was, finally, a hope, ardent, confident, thrilling. In substance this went back to the great prophets; because they believed in one God, the God of power and goodness, the prophets hoped for a day when God should overthrow evil and establish righteousness and peace in all the earth. This was the kingdom of God, better translated, the rule of God. The proclamation of this coming kingdom was at the heart of Jesus' message. The framework of this hope was apocalyptic; but the Jewish time-form must not make us overlook its substance. The early Church lived in the glad conviction that sin and suffering and oppression, ignorance and hatred and unbelief, were under sentence of death, and that a new world was coming in which God alone should rule.

At all of these points Jesus was creative and constitutive. Through him they saw God; in him they had found life; his spirit was their supreme rule; he was their bond of fellowship and their ground of hope.

It is from this standpoint that we must answer the question: Did Jesus establish the Church? Confusion arises here largely from ambiguity in terms. If you mean by "Church" the ecclesiastical institution, and if by "establish" you mean a specific deed initiating such an organization and looking forward to its role in history, the answer is no. The synoptic passages cited in support of the contrary view, Matthew 16:18 and 18:17, are too slight a foundation for a contrary conclusion. Both are under critical suspicion and the second obviously reflects a later situation, with a long established institution dealing with matters of Church discipline. Jesus, like his first followers, expected the coming of the Reign of God and the overthrow of the existent order in the near future. There is no place here for the traditional conception of the formal founding of an historical institution. Yet there is another aspect to the matter. Jesus was more than a voice crying in the wilderness, or a leader with a group of friends. His concern was, like the prophets, with Israel; only, Israel did not mean for him a racial or political unity. It meant the people of God, a spiritual Israel, the remnant, summoned now in repentance and faith to prepare for the coming day of judgment and deliverance. This new Israel was already present in the company of those who had heard the good news. Jesus told them (see the Sermon on the Mount) how to live in the spirit of the coming age. He sent them forth to issue the same summons. They thought of themselves as the true Israel, not as something wholly new and different. Yet they were in fact the beginning of a new fellowship, of the historical Christian Church; and of this Church Jesus was the real founder.[7]

II. THE INSTITUTIONAL DEVELOPMENT OF CHRISTIANITY

It has been the common error of almost all branches of Christendom to seek in the primitive Church a ground for their particular creeds and ritual and forms of organization. But, as B. H. Streeter has said, "To understand the history of early Christianity, we must begin by eliminating from our minds the traditional picture of the Twelve Apostles sitting at Jerusalem, like a College of Cardinals, systematizing the doctrine, and superintending the organization, of the Primitive Church. They had more urgent work to do. The day of

[7]R. Newton Flew in *Jesus and His Church* presents the relevant material from a conservatively critical standpoint.

Judgment was at hand; their duty was to call men to repent. . . . In the meanwhile the most vivid fact of present experience was the outpouring of 'the Spirit.' "[1] Doctor Streeter here indicates the focal points of interest around which the early Church moved: the apocalyptic hope with its obligation of calling men to repent and believe and the experience of a new life from God which demanded expression. The determination of orders and creeds for the Church of future ages does not fit in with a community for which "the hammer of the world's clock was raised to strike the last hour."

But the course of history did not bring the expected end, and the Christian fellowship had to shape the forms in which its life was to be expressed and its work done. Every great religion begins with some new and creative experience of spiritual reality, usually in the person of its founder; but a religion that is historical and social must create forms in which to express and maintain itself. We may call this the institutional side of religion, using that term in the broad sense as including doctrine and ritual as well as organization. The principal aspects of this institutional development were three.

1. The Christian movement early faced the need of interpreting its faith for itself and formulating its message to others. Further, confession became a part of the common worship, converts had to be instructed, truth had to be defined as against threatening error, and the position of Christianity had to be made clear, first over against Judaism, later in relation to the culture of the Graeco-Roman world. So there appear successive expressions of the new faith: the words of Jesus, the preaching of the apostles, the letters of Paul to his scattered churches with other writings, the confessions used in worship, a new collection of Sacred Scriptures, and finally authoritative creeds.

2. A second development was that of sacrament and ritual. On the one hand were the requirements of social worship, de-

[1]In *The Primitive Church*, pp. 42, 73.

manding common forms; on the other was the need of expressing realities which could be set forth in symbol and rite as they could not be in mere word. Simple forms of worship there were from the beginning, probably borrowed from the synagogue. The Lord's Supper would seem clearly to go back to Jesus himself and baptism at least to the earliest years of the Church, whether taken from Jesus or carried over from John.

3. The third need was organization. The first fellowship was the creation of the Christian spirit; the early Church was a Church of the Spirit. It lived in the faith that the Spirit of God dwelt within it and that the Spirit gave both teaching and direction, doctrine and government. True, different offices and functions were needed: some were apostles, some prophets, some teachers. But that was a matter not of formal appointment but of special gifts, and the gifts were from the one Spirit that was shared by all.[2] In theory any one might receive any of these gifts at any time. Any one might have an admonition or a teaching to which, as to a word of the Spirit, the Church was bound to hearken. Paul has given us a picture of the result in practice.[3] Thus problems of worship, matters of discipline, material problems connected with places of worship and the care of the poor, requirements of teaching, all compelled a more definite organization, with selected leaders and delegated authority. So there began that development which issued at last in the Catholic Church, with a sacred priesthood in ascending ranks set sharply apart, having authoritative charge of discipline and of the sacraments as necessary means of salvation. There is no ground for the belief in a uniform and prescribed system of organization obtaining from the first. We have rather "an original diversity, a rapid evolution in response to urgent local needs, to be followed later by standardization up to an efficient uniform model."[4]

[2] I Cor. 12; Eph. 4:7–11. [3] See I Cor. 14.
[4] B. H. Streeter, *op. cit.*, p. 76.

III. THE INSTITUTIONAL CONCEPTION OF CHRISTIANITY

From the standpoint of this brief historic sketch we can better understand the different answers to the question, What is Christianity? Innumerable though they seem, they fall into two main classes; the dividing line is the varying emphasis put on the two aspects of Christianity here considered, the vital-spiritual aspect on the one hand, the institutional on the other.

The institutional conception of Christianity is represented not only in the Greek Orthodox and Roman Catholic Churches, but in different form has dominated a large part of traditional Protestantism. It would be utterly wrong to say that this institutionalism means the exclusion of the vital and spiritual. Alike in the message preached, in the fruits of labor, and in the piety of individual souls, one sees spiritual concern and spiritual power. It is the emphasis that is decisive. What is it that is stressed as the distinctive and divine element? The answers agree at one point: Essential Christianity is something objective and visible, established by a direct deed of God and as such absolute, infallible, and unchanging. As to what this essential and divine factor is, there is varying opinion; it is the Church organized according to divine prescription and given certain definite powers, the Bible as containing a sum of supernaturally communicated teaching, doctrines divinely revealed and set forth in certain creeds, or some combination of these elements.

(1) The Orthodox, or Eastern, Church sees as essential a definite body of doctrine, supernaturally revealed, and set forth by Ecumenical Councils. In discussions of reunion it demands "agreement in faith" expressed in the ancient ecumenical creeds.[1] With this, however, goes another conception, the mystical-sacramentarian. Both points of view were early represented in the conception of Christ. First, Christ was the

[1]See *The Reunion of Christendom,* edited by J. Marchant, chapter by Archbishop Germanos; and *E.R.E.,* Art., "Eastern Church," by Archbishop Porphyrios.

Logos, the Word, the Truth of God; second, in him were joined the divine and human natures and men were saved by a like union of the divine with the human effected through the sacraments. In the end ritual triumphed over doctrine; the creeds became part of the sacred ceremony and it was not necessary for the worshipper to understand them. Christianity is the Church with correct doctrine, sacraments, and priesthood, established by divine act; but the central fact is the sacramental system by which the human and corruptible may receive the divine and eternal and be transformed and saved. Recently a group of Orthodox theologians has stressed the mystical element, always present in the Eastern Church, relating it to the conception of the Church as a mystical body whose corporate life is the spiritual Christ. But the authoritative institution, the Church which God established in specific form with its necessary priesthood, sacraments, and creeds, is still the essential; and this institution is Christianity.[2]

(2) The Roman Catholic Church is inclusive; it takes in as divine alike Bible, priesthood, creeds, and sacraments. Its point of emphasis, however, is the Church. The theory begins with the Incarnation: Christ was God on earth with the threefold authority of prophet, priest, and king, that is, to teach, to save, to rule. This authority, absolute and infallible, was given to the Twelve with Peter at their head when Christ left the earth. Infallible teaching, supreme and absolute rule, and control of the means of salvation thus belong to the Church in the person of the successors of the Twelve, that is the bishops, with the Bishop of Rome at their head. The hierarchy and its authority are the crucial point, and this becomes clear in every expression of the attitude of the Roman Church toward other branches of Christendom.[3] As against

[2]See Sergius Bulgakov, *The Orthodox Church,* and Nicholas Arseniev, *We Beheld His Glory.*

[3]A clear and uncompromising statement is found in the encyclical of Pius XI, issued January 6, 1928, and finding its occasion in the Lausanne Conference. See also the chapter by Cardinal Bourne in *The Reunion of Christendom,* and *The Conversations at Malines,* Oxford Univ. Press, 1928.

the mystical emphasis of the Eastern Church, the Roman conception is legalistic.

(3) Protestantism brought a rediscovery of the personal and spiritual nature of Christianity. It emphasized the supreme significance of religion as a personal relation determined by God's forgiving mercy and man's response in faith. But from the first Luther accepted the ancient creeds as final, the initial freedom which he showed in relation to the Bible gave way in later Protestantism to a hard and fast theory of verbal inspiration, and the various confessions shared in this authority as *de facto* summaries of the truth thus revealed. To this also we may properly apply the term institutional. Though it was doctrinal rather than ecclesiastical, Christianity was here too conceived as divinely instituted in terms of something objective and fixed that was supernaturally handed over.

(4) It is not without value to ask the reason for the strong tendency toward the institutional conception of Christianity which history shows, a tendency that is the stranger when we realize that Christianity began as a definite protest against institutionalism, and that every renewal of its life, under such leaders as St. Francis and Luther and Wesley, has been a call back to the spirit. The reasons, however, are not far to seek. First, it is not easy to maintain the religion of the spirit, to live on the level where fellowship with God in trust and obedience, and fellowship with men in mutual reverence and good will, form a satisfying and controlling life. The religion of the son, though simpler, demands more than that of the servant. For most men the acceptance of an authority to which one can hand all decisions as to belief and conduct is far easier. Second, men want certainty. The authoritarian religions offer this in the simplest and easiest form. As regards truth they bring a fixed, objective authority claiming supernatural character and strict infallibility, "an authority in the form of a purely external and oracular guarantee of intellectul truth, an authority of which the effect, when once its claims have by an initial act of private judgment been

definitely acknowledged, shall be to exempt them from any further responsibility of a personal kind for the intellectual truth of the religious beliefs which they entertain."[4] As regards salvation, the "Catholic" type of institutionalism offers its sacramentarian system, with the appealing claim, especially in relation to the Eucharist, that here the divine is visibly and corporeally present and man may have absolute certainty that he is receiving God.

Underlying all this there is a particular conception of God and of his relation to the world which has worked strongly to support this position. The conception may be indicated by the words transcendence, dualism, and absolutism. It was operative in the minds of men especially during those formative periods in both Eastern and Western Churches when the accepted theology was being shaped. It is not a consistent conception, for various and differing elements entered in. For the Greek theologian God was essence, or substance; he was Spirit, pure, eternal, incorruptible, in sharp contrast with the human, the finite, and corruptible. For Western thought God was Ruler; he was above all else authority and power. But both conceptions worked to the same end. God stands over against his world and external to it; God does indeed sustain his world and work in his world, either indirectly through the natural order, or directly, but it is always as something entering from without. Here is an underlying dualism: man and God, natural and supernatural. Where man or nature acts the divine is absent, where the supernatural comes in the natural is superseded. God works by direct action and his deed is determinative, and when God acts the deed is perfect and final; it cannot be other since it is the deed of absolute power not dependent upon man or conditioned by man. Hence the Christian religion as a divine institution is absolute and unchanging.

Any criticism of the theory must not obscure the necessity of institutional forms or ignore the service rendered by the Churches which have stood for this position. These have

[4] A. E. J. Rawlinson, in *Essays Catholic and Critical*, p. 94.

sought to conserve the heritage of the past and maintain the historic continuity of Christianity. They have emphasized the corporate nature of religion as against a one-sided individualism. They have aimed at a worship that was rich and inspiring and that by its symbolism made the invisible real to men. They have stressed the more than human in religion, and sought to supply needed authority and certainty.

(5) The difficulties which the institutional conception of Christianity faces are obvious. There is the historical-critical difficulty. History nowhere shows the infallible and unchanging which this theory demands; Bible and creeds and Church all come under the law of growth and are relative to changing needs and forms of thought. The underlying conception of God and his relation to the world furnishes a similar problem. Nature and history are the sphere of God's action but in both his method has been that of development, and his entrance into human life is conditioned by man's response.

The final objection is in the name of religion itself. Some would say flatly, "When organization comes in at the door, religion flies out at the window."[5] In more discriminating fashion, Baron von Hügel, in his discussion of what he calls the "institutional-historical type," has pointed out what happens when the institutional side, legitimate in itself, becomes dominant. He speaks of the danger of materialization and absolute fixation, "a ruinous belief in the direct transferableness of religious conviction, . . . a predominance of political, legal, physically coercive concepts and practices," as against "spiritual sincerity and spontaneity and the liberty of the children of God." Orthodox Mohammedanism is the classical instance, "with its utterly analytic, unspeculative, unmystical, thing-like, rock-solid faith; its detailed rigidity and exhaustive fixity; its stringent unity of organization and military spirit of blind obedience, its direct, quite unambiguous intolerance."[6]

[5]Warner Fite, *The Platonic Legend,* p. 309.

[6]*The Mystical Element of Religion,* II, pp. 387, 388. *Cf.* also W. A. Brown, *Imperialistic Religion and the Religion of Democracy.*

IV. THE PROPHETIC CONCEPTION OF CHRISTIANITY

To this institutional viewpoint we here oppose what for want of a better term may be called the prophetic conception of Christianity. The marks of prophetic religion as it appears in the Old Testament and is consummated in Christianity include the idea of a personal God, transcendent and yet immanent, revealing himself in history and working out a purpose of righteous love; a conception of religion as through and through ethical, a morally conditioned relationship between God and man which involves right relations between man and his brother; the corporate expression of religion in a fellowship of faith and worship, of mutual love and common service (the Church); the goal of history seen in the rule of God on earth in a new humanity informed by his Spirit. The conception is historical, ethical, spiritual. So conceived, Christianity may be defined as the ongoing life of that fellowship which had its origin with Jesus and seeks its continuous inspiration and guidance in him, finding through him the God of its faith, the goal of its hope, and the way of life. On the divine side it appears as the redemptive deed of God, revealing and giving himself to men in Jesus Christ, and working through men by his Spirit. The idea of redemptive love is crucial here at every point: for the God in whom men trust, for the life which they are to live, for the power by which men are to be redeemed alike individually and in society.

God is central with the prophetic as with the institutional conception, but the difference appears when you ask where each of these views finds the divine presence and action. For the latter the central and constitutive divine element in Christianity is some writing or doctrine or institution established by God in definite and objective and complete form. For the former the divine is seen as the continuously creative Spirit, self-revealing, redeeming, coming to supreme expression in

Jesus, but moving forward from him in a new fellowship and in the creation of a new humanity. The institutional has its place, but it is as the creation of the Spirit and its instrument. The Church has its place, but it is the Church in terms of a fellowship informed by the divine Spirit, not of legally prescribed forms and authorities. Individual religion is not primarily adherence to an institution, acceptance of doctrine, or the use of prescribed ritual and sacrament; it is rather faith in this living God and a life in which his Spirit is received in humble dependence and expressed in active loyalty.

In Church history the institutional matters have always been the main points of interest and discussion: doctrine, sacrament, orders, and creeds. But the great religious spirits stand on the other side. For the Hebrew prophets the first thing was not temples and sacrifices, though they may not have been so iconoclastic as we sometimes think; it was the living God working out his ends in history, and religion as a summons to deal justly and love mercy and walk humbly with this God. Jesus put first the heart that said Abba, Father, and the life ruled by love of God and Man. Some would put Paul on the other side as the initiator of sacramentarianism and orthodoxy, substituting for Jesus and his way legalistic theories of atonement, schemes of magical transformation, and doctrinal speculations. But again and again, when Paul comes to his simple and matchless summaries of what is central and essential, his stress is on the personal, spiritual, and ethical. His faith is in "the God and Father of our Lord Jesus Christ"; men are saved "by grace through faith"; religion is "faith working through love."[1] Unfortunately, theologians have usually preferred Paul's peripheral speculations to his central convictions. Similarly the Johannine writings declare that "He that abideth in love abideth in God, and God abideth in him."[2] Not the Church and its sacraments, not an inspired set of writings, not a system of doctrine, but the conviction that in Christ the living God had spoken to them

[1] II Cor. 1:3; Eph. 2:5; Gal. 5:6. [2] I John 4:16.

and brought the way of life, this is the religion of the men of the New Testament.

All this does not mean an individualism that turns from the fellowship of the Church, nor a subjective mysticism that cuts loose from history, nor a vague emphasis on feeling that dispenses with definite conviction. Its specific character will appear if we consider in turn its historical quality, its distinctive ethos, and its central conviction, that is, its idea of God.

1. The historical character of Christianity constitutes an essential element in its nature and its strength. It is no affair of abstractions. God is no timeless Eternal nor is history meaningless change. It holds to a living and creative God, achieving his ends through history as seen especially in the person of Jesus, in the movement in Israel that led up to him, and in the movement which he inspired whose evidence and instrument have been the historic Church. Religion has its being and its strength only as it becomes concrete in individual and historical embodiment. And no religion has such wealth here as Christianity: in the person of its Founder, in its Scriptures, and in the rich materials of persons and events and writings produced in its later history. And here, especially in the person of Jesus, was its saving strength when there was danger that it might be dissipated in speculations like those of Gnosticism, or hardened into dogmatism or ecclesiasticism.

2. In his spirit Jesus is decisive for the distinctive ethos of Christianity which has an unmistakable quality alike as religion and morality. It is marked on the religious side by reverence and awe before the holy God, joined with liberating trust in his goodness and utter devotion to his will. The moral ethos of Christianity may be distinguished in thought from the religious; in fact, however, they are inseparable, and it is their unity as achieved in the teaching and spirit of Jesus which marks the supremacy of his religion. Here too is reverence for what is highest, for the personal as seen in man, in

oneself as well as in others, a reverence that roots in faith in a personal God. Here is good will which he must show who shares the spirit of the God of good will. Here is love that is unitive, redemptive, and creative, for such is the love of God by which we live.

3. This religion of the spirit involves a definite conviction and lives by this conviction. It believes that in the spirit of Jesus man knows the heart of the Eternal. The center of Christianity is not the Church, nor Jesus of Nazareth; it is the living God who has come to men in Christ. It is not only that the character of God is thus known, but that in the spirit and deed of Jesus men have found the redeeming and life-giving presence of God, showing his purpose for man, giving his life to man. "God was in Christ, reconciling the world unto himself."[3]

With this goes a definite conception of God and his relation to the world. God is not the spiritual substance of Greek theology, the immutable essence that is totally different from our corruptible finitude. He is not the monarch of irresistible power, as with Augustine and Calvin, working in pure transcendence. He does indeed transcend nature and history and man, as holy Spirit, as directing purpose, as sustaining and creative power; but the finite and the human are not alien to him. With all its need and sin, there is a kinship between humanity and God, as between the cosmos and God; not only is man *capax dei,* but even nature is in lesser measure. Since nature and human nature thus belong to God, God is conceived as working in immanent fashion, as indwelling in history and working his creative will of love in men. Christianity is not the entrance of an alien God from above, nor an institution handed down to man; it is God working in the

[3] II Cor. 5:19. *Cf.* also Paul Wendland, *Hellenistische-Römische Kultur,* p. 127: "The piety which Jesus taught and lived before men signifies the greatest simplification and the deepest spiritualization of religion. . . . Jesus carried the ethicizing of religion to its end, and secured the dynamic forces of religion for the full range of the ethical." Similarly A. Harnack, *What Is Christianity?* pp. 78–80.

historic stream of our life, manifest supremely in the life of our Lord, operative continually as indwelling Spirit.

V. CHRISTIANITY AS PROPHETIC OR MYSTICAL

1. The prophetic conception of Christianity needs to be constrasted not only with the institutional but with the mystical. This way has been taken by two distinguished scholars, Nathan Söderblom and Friedrich Heiler.[1] Here again the basic question is how we are to conceive God and his relation to the world. In the highest religion, says Archbishop Söderblom, there are "two main kinds of mysticism; the one originating chiefly in the sense of the Infinite, the other in the longing for the Ideal and in the striving for transformation: the one ultimately directed toward an impersonal goal, the other emphasizing personality."[2] Heiler's contrast is between the mystical and prophetic types of religion, but he means by mysticism the type which Söderblom contrasts with the Christian type. Their position, however, is essentially the same.

The common conviction of all religion is that there is a world of higher meaning and power in relation to which man may achieve the fullest life. The common concern of religion is to establish this relation and to win this highest good. How men think of God, and how men conceive this good, will determine how they seek God and how they live with him. For convenience in this discussion we will use mysticism,

[1]N. Söderblom, *Natürliche Theologie und allgemeine Religionsgeschichte; The Nature of Religion,* pp. 48–100; and especially the article, "Communion with Deity," *E. R. E.;* Fr. Heiler, *Das Gebet,* pp. 248–283 (also in English translation). See also C. C. J. Webb, *Pascal's Philosophy of Religion,* pp. 30–36; Chas. Gore, *Reconstruction of Belief,* pp. 74–132; and A. C. Knudson, *The Doctrine of God,* pp. 54–60.

[2]*E. R. E.,* III, 738. For this general distinction of two broad types of mysticism, see article, "Mysticism," *E. R. E.,* by R. M. Jones, as well as his *Studies in Mysticism;* J. B. Pratt, *The Religious Consciousness,* Chs. XVI–XX; and N. Söderblom, *The Nature of Revelation,* where he makes the distinction of personal and impersonal mysticism.

with Heiler, for the "extreme" or "pure" mysticism, and by no means exclude from prophetic religion that "milder" mysticism which is man's awareness of God and his conviction that he may have real fellowship with him. These are the two religions which in varying forms are making the strongest appeal to men today. Never wholly separated, often closely joined in individual men, they nevertheless show a significant contrast.

India and Greece are the two great sources of the mystical type. In the former it is represented by the pantheism of the Upanishads working in Brahmanism and Buddhism. In the latter it appeared in Orphism, came to high expression in Platonism, and continued its influence in neo-Platonism and in later Christian mysticism. Söderblom cites Lao-tse, Zarathustra, and Socrates as among the representatives of the second type; but its supreme expression has been in the Hebrew-Christian line, in the prophets, in Jesus, Paul, Augustine, Luther, and others.

2. For typical mystical religion God is the One, the Absolute, the impersonal, the pure being, the ultimate reality, the infinite. In the stricter forms he appears as the unknown God. As pure being, he stands unchanging over against all that is finite and limited; as timeless, he does not enter into the stream of history or the passing world of nature. And of him nothing determinate can be said for that would limit him. To ascend to him we must leave ourselves and this world behind; we must take the *via negativa*. In Meister Eckhart's word, he is "a not-God, a not-spirit, a not-person."[3] Mysticism therefore does not need history for the knowledge of God; the God whom it seeks is above history, and is not to be sought in what is really an alien realm. The idea of a historical revelation belongs to prophetism, not to mysticism. Nor is he to be reached through the social relations of life, whether in the common faith and worship of the group or in the fellowship of love and service; the mystic is not neces-

[3]See Heiler, *op. cit.*, pp. 259–261.

sarily indifferent to these but the search for God takes him beyond them.

The prophetic religion believes no less than the "mystical" in a transcendent God, a God who is more than this world in power, wisdom, goodness, and purpose; its emphasis on God as personal is, in fact, the best safeguard against the pantheism into which mysticism sometimes runs. But it does not seek God by leaving this world, nor find the clue to his nature by turning away from all that this world shows. (a) It believes that the highest which this world shows is the clue to God; it takes the *via eminentiae* rather than the *via negativa.* The highest here means that which is morally supreme, the greatest in meaning and value, that is, the personal and ethical. Thus the great Hebrew prophets found their clue to the nature of God in justice and mercy, known in moral insight and revealed in human life. So Jesus finds his clue in human fatherhood, and the Christian Church in the spirit revealed in a human life, that of Jesus of Nazareth. Its idea of God, therefore, is ethical and personal. (b) God is the supreme reality for prophetic religion as for mysticism, but the former finds that reality not in abstract being but in doing; Goethe's translation in his *Faust* of John's prologue would express its faith: "In the beginning was the Deed." In the highly significant Old Testament phrase, it believes in "the living God." God is creative power, shaping purpose, directing providence, redeeming love. (c) It believes in the perfection of God, but the perfection is not that of abstract, impassive, changeless being; it is the perfection of life, of an active, creative, self-giving good will. (d) Nature and history are thus for God not spheres of indifference nor alien realms; they have a real significance. They may be considered as the necessary spheres for the expression of his love, that love which cannot but share the life which has its fullness in God. Thus the idea of a historical revelation and redemption is vital to prophetic religion. God is the revealing and redeeming God. (e) The being of God is thus determinate, not abstract. It is being that has a definite quality and meaning, it is being that is in relation.

3. The contrast of the "mystical" and prophetic types appears most clearly when we consider their respective conceptions of the religious life in relation to such matters as the idea of the good, the way of attainment, and the conception of evil. (a) Mystical religion finds its good in that which is above and beyond this life, in peace and rest, in a union with God in which the self disappears and the common relations and activities of life are negligible or absent. The good which it seeks is apart from or opposed to those goods which come through the activities and relations of this world. (b) The way to the highest good also involves this turning away; it is salvation through negation. The ethical has, indeed, a certain place; it is useful as a preparation, and with the mystics who have been most influenced by the Christian spirit, it has a positive meaning, for they use it as a test of the genuineness of the mystical experience. But the highest experience, the real good, the mystic's salvation, is union with the God who is above and beyond all this; and this union with the divine essence must come through illumination or rapture. (c) The evil that is to be overcome, with the mystic, is not primarily sin as wrong moral spirit or attitude; it is the separation of the finite, the changeable, the corruptible from the infinite, the unchangeable, the eternal.

Prophetic religion is affirmative, alike as to the goal and the way. It knows the evil; it is, indeed, vigorously dualistic, but along the ethical line. (a) As to its idea of the good, man's own personal life is to be fulfilled, not denied. Humanity's social life also is to be redeemed and completed in a coming kingdom of God. It is not *kulturfeindlich.* It knows that man's social life, like his individual life, needs transformation, but it sees in the daily task and the relations of friendships and the gifts of earth real goods and divine meanings. (b) The way of salvation is quite as sharply contrasted. For mystical religion it is a union of substance in which the personal self is lost; for prophetic religion it is a fellowship of persons in which the real self is achieved. For the former it is *unio substantialis,* for the latter *unio filialis.* The decisive matter for prophetic religion is a vital fellowship that is ethically conditioned; men are to be children of their Father in the spirit of good will.[4] The decisive words are faith and love, or, in Paul's pregnant phrase, "faith working through love."[5] In both we have the active expression of the will of man, of human personality at its highest. That will appears as confident trust on the one hand, on the other as a positive obedience receiving and expressing God's spirit of creative good will. It is thus through and through ethical. Here, too, the goal is life through union with God, but the union is that of a personal and ethical fellowship with a personal and good God. To pray, "Our Father; thy will be done; forgive us as we forgive," this is prophetic religion. Reverence and awe and utter dependence are here but with the recognized demand of moral loyalty and oneness of spirit. The way of salvation, therefore, is very simple in contrast with the numerous rules and exercises which are usually indicated in the mystical type. To love God and one's neighbor, in faith to give oneself utterly and confidently to God, in love to live out loyally the life of God, these suggestions of Micah and Jesus and Paul are typical. They do not require the training of the adept nor the machinery of ecclesiastical institution; they do not require men to leave their common vocations and they can be practised in the midst of other activities. On the other hand, they make the most searching demands, for they probe the depths of man's spirit and claim the whole reach of his life. (c) Finally, the evil that is to be overcome is ethical. The ground for man's separation from God is not any metaphysical difference between eternal and finite, nor primarily a matter of knowledge; it is sin: the fear that will not trust, the selfishness that denies love, the self-will that refuses loyalty.

[4]Matt. 5:38–48. [5]Gal. 5:6.

4. It is clear that Christianity, in its distinctive expressions and its most significant leaders, belongs on the side of prophetic religion and is its highest exemplar. The mystical influence has, of course, entered in very strongly and its union with the prophetic is seen notably in such a leader as Augustine. Theology has been influenced by the mystic's conception of God, coming through Platonism and neo-Platonism, the God who is conceived as pure spirit, incorruptible essence, transcendent, opposed to all finite. Its influence in the idea of salvation appears in that stress on the mystic way which makes subordinate the ethical, social, and historical, and in sacramentarian theories. One may recognize a degree of this with Paul himself and admit the influence of Hellenism. But this is not distinctive of Christianity and when the crucial test comes, Paul stands definitely for the ethical-personal-historical; he is Hebraist, not Hellenist. The mystical is independent of historical Christianity and could express itself as well in other forms. Mysticism, indeed, cuts across the lines of all religions. "We cannot honestly say," admits Evelyn Underhill, "that there is any wide difference between the Brahman, Sufi, or Christian mystic at their best."[6] That must be regarded, however, not as the virtue of a more universal sort of piety, but as the limitation of a religious way that cannot do justice to the highest ideas and demands.

But while Christianity as a prophetical religion stands over against this extreme mysticism, it has a definite place for mysticism in the larger sense. So conceived, mysticism involves a threefold conviction: that there is an Other, a Beyond, an Ultimate, a "mysterious" which does not appear on the surface of this everyday world and which sense and reason of themselves cannot apprehend; that this Ultimate, God, can be known in some immediate fashion and not merely by inference; that there is a relation with God, a union of spirit and self which is more than thought and deed, in which in some way the divine enters the finite as transforming pres-

[6] *Essentials of Mysticism,* p. 4.

ence and power. These three elements appear in Christianity: a sense of the presence of the Holy; a call to "know God," not simply to know about him; the experience of an indwelling God (Holy Spirit) and of a life transformed by this presence. Here Christianity shows an immediacy, a depth, an emotional "tone," a feeling-awareness, a certainty, and a dynamic, which in this broader sense we may call the mystical element. Yet all this is within the framework of prophetic religion; the mystical enters in but it is not a higher and independent category, not a plane on which the personal-ethical-rational is left behind.

Chapter Five

THE FINALITY OF THE CHRISTIAN RELIGION

CHRISTIANITY claims to rest upon a divine revelation. Its followers have declared that it is original, absolute, and final. We need to consider these claims, ask their meaning, and inquire whether Christianity can assert uniqueness among the many religions of the world and finality in a universe of constant change.

I. AS TO THE ABSOLUTENESS OF THE CHRISTIAN RELIGION

For traditional theology the problem of the absoluteness of Christianity is very simple. The transcendent and almighty God works his will by direct action. When he gives men the Bible or establishes the Church, the result is absolute and inerrant. Christianity is thus lifted above the stream of time, above the conditioned and relative. What is overlooked here is the fact that God cannot enter the stream of time except in definite and conditioned relation to history, and that truth can come to man only as an element in conscious experience and as related to human life. For Christian faith Jesus Christ is God's supreme word of revelation. But Jesus passed through the stages of physical, mental, and spiritual growth, confessed limitations of knowledge, and voiced truth in the thought forms of his age. The divine is not a tangible, thing-like substance, thrust down from some upper level; it is the life of the Spirit realized in human experience, that is, in human insight and thought, in ideal and devotion. The divine, therefore, must always be relative for us, relative to man's apprehension, to his stage of development, to his response. So the New Testament speaks of our seeing through a glass darkly, of growing up, of not yet having attained, of being guided into further truth. Absoluteness in this sense is not a demand of religion or an implication of Christian faith.

In another sense, however, religion does demand the absolute, and that is because it demands the divine. It does not think of its ideas or attainments as absolute; only the epigones feel the need of making this claim, and it is with them that the theories of verbal inspiration and infallible Church arise. But faith does demand God, and that means the absolute. One may even say, where there is no absolute there is no religion, for religion is man's conviction that there is a final power on which he depends, a final good for which he must strive, a highest to which he owes utter loyalty if he is not to be wholly untrue. Other demands of life are relative, a matter of less or more; religion means all or nothing, "the utmost for the highest." The authentic note of religion speaks clearly here in Jesus. Men may call it arrogance or delusion, as Nietzsche did, but Jesus could do no less. He made on men an absolute demand because he brought absolute reality. He brought the highest, and he summoned men to leave all and give all.

The issue is clear when we turn to the opposing position, with its pure relativism and humanism. There are in this position elements of truth that we must recognize. There is Kant's insight that all knowing is a human activity, man's own ordering perception and shaping reason. There is the fact of the functional significance of religion, that religion springs from human need and maintains itself as a minister to human life. But relativism leaves out of account or flatly denies the other member of this relation, that higher world of spiritual reality the belief in which is at the heart of religion. A consistent expression of this position is to be found in *The Philosophy of the As If,* by Hans Vaihinger,[1] where God is one of various useful fictions whose assumption is justified by the practical needs of life. When this stage is reached we have come not merely to the twilight of the gods, but to the twilight of all religion.

II. AS TO THE UNIQUENESS AND ORIGINALITY OF THE CHRISTIAN RELIGION

For traditional theology the answer to this second question was likewise very simple: Christianity is true, other religions are false; Christianity is original and unique because it came direct and perfect from the hand of God. This answer, too, is untenable. The Old Testament itself reveals a larger point of view, especially in the prophetic writings. It sees the one God of all the earth, concerned with righteousness and not with differences of nationality, interested in all peoples and moving in all history. The New Testament points even more clearly the same way. Christian thought must hold not only to the one God of all men, but to the one indwelling and illuminating and redeeming Spirit of love and truth that has everywhere and always wrought in men. As God is one, so truth is one and righteousness is one. Wherever they are found, there men may see God.

Further we must recognize the continuity and interrelation of all man's cultural life, including religion. The stream of history is one; there is no one current that we can separate from the rest and call sacred, or supernatural. Christianity confessedly roots deeply in the religion of Israel. Israel herself throughout her history had been under many and varied influences and mediated these to Christianity. The latter, even in its earlier development, not merely took terms but inevitably ideas and forms from the Graeco-Roman world in which it lived, and has been similarly affected ever since. If God be one, everywhere seeking to reveal and give himself to men, and if man be one, everywhere the same in his funda-

[1]As translated from the German, *Die Philosophie des Als Ob.*

mental needs, then we should expect analogies in all religions, common ideas such as those of revelation, salvation, sacrifice, and communion with the divine.

1. In our earlier discussion we found the distinctive nature of Christianity not in its institutional forms, in doctrine or organization or code or cultus, but rather in a conviction concerning God and the way of life which had its abiding inspiration and direction in the person of Jesus. Our question then is as to the significance and originality of Jesus.

The whole matter has been put in the wrong light by being turned into a dispute as to whether Jesus set forth any doctrines that were strictly new. History does not move in that way; her first principle is continuity. No advance is ever made except as related to what went before; Jesus stood definitely upon the faith of his race and especially upon the teachings of the prophets. Just as erroneous is the assumption that religion can be summed up in ideas. Jesus' avowed purpose was not to give a new teaching but to summon men to repentance and faith and to bring in a new life on earth. Irenaeus gave the right answer back in the second century: "He brought all newness in bringing himself."[2] The modern theory of emergent evolution offers a suggestive idea here. What it shows us is a process which we can describe but cannot really explain. The whole development of life depends upon this process of making new wholes, in which elements are joined together to form a new unity not by way of mere addition, but in such manner that a

[2]See A. Harnack, *Dogmengeschichte,* I, 71: "It is the person, the deed of his life, that is new, and that creates the new." See A. Deissmann, *The Religion of Jesus and the Faith of St. Paul,* p. 150. *Cf.* the comment of a modern Jewish writer, Rabbi H. G. Enelow, in his *A Jewish View of Jesus,* p. 18: "Wherever we find true personality, we have originality. Supreme personality is greatest originality." Elsewhere he quotes from Hazlitt: "This is the test and triumph of originality, not to show us what has never been and what we may therefore very easily never have dreamt of, but to point out to us what is before our eyes and under our feet, though we have had no suspicion of its existence, for want of sufficient strength of intuition, of determined grasp of mind, to seize and retain it." P. 15.

new and higher life appears with qualities that the closest study of the individual parts would not have suggested. We have been told again and again that Christianity is a syncretistic religion, and we have had pointed out to us the origin of this sacrament and that doctrine. If we look at it as a whole, however, we see rather a great creative synthesis and the personality of Jesus as its beginning and its abiding center.[3] The first Christian century was an age of deep religious interest and great religious confusion. The most diverse elements had been brought together in the Roman world. Universalism and syncretism marked the time. It was their refusal of this easy-going tolerance that brought suspicion and enmity to the Christians. The facts seem contradictory, the explanation is simple. Jesus was the creative center of this new movement. Christianity was no sum of addition, no chance confluence of diverse tides of religious thought and life, any more than it was the product of a given social milieu. With that insight which is the final secret of his own being, Jesus saw for himself the truth of God and life and used the rich heritage of his people's past. And all this came to a new creative expression, first in his own life, then in his teaching, then in that life which he was able to create in others. Even a slight acquaintance makes plain, first the unity of his message, then the unity of word and life in himself. He is neither a quoter of authority nor a collector of wisdom.[4]

2. If now we look at the heritage which he left, we see

[3]This vital difference between syncretism, and a creative synthesis through which a qualitatively higher level of life appears, is just what emergent evolution stands for in insisting on the difference between a mechanical addition which combines without effecting anything new and that organization into a new whole which brings a higher emergent level. See C. Lloyd Morgan, *Emergent Evolution*, pp. 6–9.

[4]"The Jewish scholars," Wellhausen once commented, "say that everything that Jesus says is in the Talmud. Yes, everything, and much more besides. How did he manage to take the true and the ethical out of this rubbish heap of legal scholasticism? Why did no one else do it?"

how all the old truths gain power and meaning because of what he chose, what he omitted, and what he made central.

(1) We note first what he did to the idea of religion. (a) He gave humanity a religion of the spirit. He found religion identified with the externals of ceremonial and rules of behavior. He called men to see the significance of the inner spirit, the higher righteousness. Yet the spirit, the reverent trust which he emphasized, the loyalty to the highest, the absolute good will, did not mean mere subjectivism or passivity; it summoned men to the highest activity. (b) He gave men a religion that was ethical through and through. His God was ethical, not abstract essence or sheer power or even highest sovereignty first of all, but righteousness and love. Fellowship with this God was ethical; its supreme demand was that men should share the Father's spirit of good will. The test of religion for him was not observance of ritual, or feeling, or correct ideas. And his idea of salvation was ethical; it was the life and help that came to men as they turned, repentant and trustful, to fellowship with such a God. No salvation without repentance and obedience and moral likeness! (c) He made religion universal. It had always belonged to some given place and people. Nationalism was both the strength and the limitation of Judaism. The religion of Jesus is for man as man.

(2) If we turn to the great concepts that underlie his teaching, we shall see again their simplicity, unity, thoroughgoing ethical character, and universality of appeal. One conclusion is made clear by the centuries that have passed: if any spiritual faith can maintain itself in man, it will be this faith. The heart of it is his idea of God. It is no conclusion of philosophy, to be overturned some time when its premises are shown false. It is no inheritance of tradition unthinkingly accepted. It is a faith that dares to believe that the highest that man knows is supreme in the universe, and that man must live in the light of that highest. His God is transcendent in power and goodness, calling men to reverence and awe; he

is immanent as the ever-working God of redeeming love, calling men to trust and surrender. He is personal and man may have fellowship with him; yet the center of religion is never man but always God, always the God that is above man, the power to be trusted, the good that summons to obedience and calls to achievement. Supremely significant is his idea of God as redemptive good will. "The rabbis," says Montefiore, "attached no less value to repentance than Jesus. . . . They too welcomed the sinner in his repentance. But to *seek out* the sinner, and, instead of avoiding the bad companion, to choose him as your friend in order to work out his moral redemption, this was, I fancy, something new in the religious history of Israel."[5] And Jesus regarded this attitude and activity on his part as representing the spirit and deed of his Father.[6]

Equally significant is his idea of man. Stoicism offered the highest conception of man in the Graeco-Roman world; it transcended the limits of race and even of sex, and called for an equal regard for all. Yet it drew its lines in another way. It was intellectualistic and aristocratic; it could recognize the wise man in a slave, but for the mass of men, not wise, not strong, but unfortunate and wretched, it had no word. The eye of Jesus was just as keen for the realities of life. He was no sentimentalist, but he did see more deeply than the noblest of the Stoics; he saw the inner motive and ultimate possibilities. He condoned no evil but he believed in the power of the good. For him every man in his truest nature and in God's intention was a son of God; therefore every man was sacred as man. And he believed in men; in his reverence for humanity, in his passion for justice, in his faith in men, in his summons to a common service for a common weal, Jesus is the deepest spring of the best that we mean by democracy. The teaching of Jesus is the foundation of the highest social idealism of our day.

Of vital importance in his teaching is the goal of human

[5]C. J. Montefiore, *The Teaching of Jesus,* p. 57.
[6]Luke 15.

life, set forth in threefold aspect. He offers fulfillment for all the needs and hopes of men, recognizing the individual in his own right; he holds up a social hope, a kingdom of God which means a new humanity; he includes the life beyond. His word for all three is life, and in them he presents a lofty and inclusive hope as well as a commanding summons.

3. So far we have considered simply the teaching of Jesus. But neither the nature of Christianity nor the significance of Jesus can be rightly determined unless we take account of his influence upon others, the forces that he released in the world, and the experiences and insights of his followers, especially of the first generation.[7]

It has been repeatedly urged in recent years, in denial of the originality and uniqueness of early Christianity, that it was simply one of the many mystery cults of that age, and that it is to be interpreted in the light of these religious movements which were so characteristic of that time. Our knowledge of the mystery cults is meager; their special lore and peculiar rites were restricted to initiates and little has come down to us from this period. Common is a deep sense of the evils of life, a longing for deliverance, the faith in some deity, or hero-god, the belief that a certain mystical-emotional communion with this god is possible, and the stress upon rites of purification and sacrament through which this union with the god is achieved and by which immortality is assured. Very common is the thought of this hero-god as one who died and rose to life again.

There are obvious points of likeness not only with later Christianity but with Paul: the sense of evil, the concern with redemption, the idea of a dying and risen Lord (kyrios), the belief in mystical communion, the use of sacraments, a certain dualism of world-view, and the union of followers in cult groups as against religions which included whole peoples. But such analogies of form are common in religion; the

[7]See P. G. S. Hopwood, *The Religious Experience of the Primitive Church,* and F. C. Porter, *The Mind of Christ in Paul.*

crucial matter is as to the content. It is sufficient here to state certain main contrasts. (a) Early Christianity held, with Judaism, to a thorough-going monotheism; Jesus was not a hero-god, but one through whom the living God had come to men. The concern of the mystery cults was not with God but with this or that divine hero. (b) Jesus was a historical figure, whose spirit, teaching, and life stand forth in clear and unmistakable individuality. The central figures of the mystery cults are vague in outline and either mythical or of unknown origin. (c) Ethical elements, though distinctly subordinate, are not lacking in the mystery religions, especially in the later stages; rites of purification and discrimination in choice of candidates are in point. Celsus, indeed, suggested their ethical superiority to Christianity which, he said, receives "every one who is a sinner, who is devoid of understanding, who is a child."[8] But it is at this very point that the superiority of Christianity appears. In it the ethical is not preliminary or incidental but a central and constant demand; and the redemption that it offers is no mere deliverance from such natural ills as change and death, but the power of a new life by which to meet these high demands. Hence it dares to invite, not the selected few, but the many, not just the wise and virtuous, but the simple and sinful.

III. THE FINALITY OF THE CHRISTIAN RELIGION

Can we regard Christianity as the final religion? The objections lie at hand: If Christianity as we actually have it in Scripture and creed and Church is always something relative to the historical and human, to man's apprehension in thought and realization in life, then must it not be partial and imperfect? If it be something here in time, must it not show constant change? Does not the history of Christianity reveal such change from the beginning, and is not such progress what we desire? Does not the final mean the static, and so

[8]Origen, *Contra Celsum,* Book 3, Ch. 59.

mean death? Are not the open mind and loyalty to truth at the very heart of high religion, so that we must repudiate the claim to finality in the very name of religion?[1] In answer we must examine more closely what is involved in the Christian position.

1. It has been a common mistake to seek finality for Christianity in the wrong place, that is, in its institutional forms of expression, in creeds, moral codes, organization, and ritual; this would, indeed, mean a static finality and a closed mind. But these are all interpretations and expressions of religion. For Christianity as a prophetic religion, however, the dominant category is personal and vital, not institutional. It knows how imperfect its life is, how faulty the empirical Church, how far its formulae are from expressing the truth of the infinite God. But its conviction is that the personal and living God, infinite and eternal, has spoken to men in Jesus Christ. Our knowledge about this God is not absolute, but we do know this absolute God. In Jesus Christ we have heard his word to us, have found the way of living fellowship with him, and have seen his will for our lives.

2. It is a mistake to think of development, whether in nature or history, as merely ceaseless change. The law of life is rather a double one, that of change on the one hand, of continuity and conservation on the other. An age-long movement reaches a definite achievement with a certain finality. There is still movement, but it is along other lines; the achievement becomes a permanent gain and the stage is set free for other needed work. Thus, as has been suggested by H. F. Osborn and others, man came to the end of his development as a psycho-physical organism with the Cro-Magnons, perhaps two score thousand years ago. In his natural endowment the man of today is no whit his superior; human advance since then has been in the cultural field through social

[1]So in Schiller's lines:

Welche Religion ich bekenne? Keine von allen,
Die du mir nennst. Und warum keine? Aus Religion.

heritage. In the apprehension and creation of beauty the Greeks reached certain goals that have not been passed. There are insights in the field of ethics which, though age-old, retain their place; we still recognize the value and authority of truth and justice and mercy. Despite opposing forces the monogamic family, reached long since in human development, will remain an abiding social institution.

In like manner Christianity represents definite and final insights in religion. Jesus made religion through and through ethical and supplied to ethics the motive force of religion.[2] "It is the distinction of Jesus," writes Havelock Ellis, "that he has, for us, permanently expanded the bounds of individuality. What a supreme work of art we already possess in the Gospels! So that now when I open and turn over with reverent joy the leaves of the Gospels, I feel that here is enshrined the highest achievement of Man the Artist, a creation to which nothing can be added, from which nothing can be taken away."[3] So if we turn to his conception of God, his idea of man, or to the ideal of life as seen in his own spirit, we find again what seem like final insights. "The finality of Christ and of what he imparts," says H. R. Mackintosh, "can justly be called in question only when a loftier fact than holy love has come into view."[4] When we look at the movement of thought of the last nineteen centuries in relation of these basic ideals, the trend is forward toward the position of Jesus rather than beyond him.

3. Such finality does not exclude growth but demands it. No religion can be final which is not a growing religion. The

[2]*Cf.* Adolf Jülicher: "Jesus hat die Versittlichung der Religion bis zum Ende geführt und der Sittlichkeit im ganzen Umfange die religiösen Triebkräfte gesichert." In *Kultur der Gegenwart,* I, 4, p. 61.

[3]Quoted by Edwin Mims, *Adventurous America,* p. 262.

[4]*Types of Modern Theology,* p. 215. See also the suggestive discussion by N. Söderblom, *Natürliche Theologie und allgemeine Religionsgeschichte,* pp. 82–86, and that of Sidney Cave, in *The Future of Christianity,* Jas. Marchant, ed., pp. 17–25.

finality of Christianity lies in a life of fellowship with God by faith and with men in love. As such it is a great creative experience, and advance in knowledge and insight are of its very essence. Here quiet confidence and daring venture go together.

Historically the Christian religion has approved itself as final by this very capacity for growth. It has constantly taken over and assimilated new truth while at the same time maintaining its identity. The cynical saying, *Plus ça change, plus c'est la même chose,* may be used here in tribute instead of criticism. As Archbishop Temple has said: "This is one of the distinctive characteristics of Christianity, that whereas all other religions have tended to stereotype the conditions in which they originated, because only in those conditions could their requirements be obeyed, Christianity has been a fermenting principle of change in every society into which it has come. This is primarily because it is centered not upon a formula but upon a Person, and its regulative principle is not a code but a Spirit." What is needed for progress, he says, is change with constancy of direction. "This is the constancy that the Gospel gives us. Our starting-point is fixed: it is the creative love of God. Our goal is fixed: it is the realized Kingdom of God. And our way is fixed: it is found in Him who said, 'I am the Way.' "[5] Christianity has always kept a forward look. It believes in an indwelling Spirit who is to guide into larger truth. Despite recurrent lapses, it has made loyalty to truth central in the religious attitude. It has believed in a living God, continually working in the world. And the truths that it has taken up have not only found room in the Christian faith but have gained in that faith their richest expression. We may agree with Bishop F. J. McConnell that the uniqueness of Christianity includes a unique power to use everything that is usable. "Everything of the true and good and beautiful will get a better chance to show truth and goodness

[5]*Jerusalem Meeting of the International Missionary Conference,* Vol. I, pp. 378, 379.

and beauty after it has been converted to Christianity than it ever had before."[6]

It is in this connection that we can best consider the problem that has been raised for many by the apocalyptic element in early Christianity. It is not so easy to determine the actual teaching of Jesus at this point. The longer apocalyptic discourses attributed to him furnish an outstanding illustration of the influence upon the gospel account of the thought and life of the later community out of which these writings came. But that he expected in the immediate future the end of the age and the saving deed of God by which his rule was to be established on earth, that this expectation was shared by the early Church, and that primitive Christian thought and life were profoundly influenced by this hope, this is hardly to be disputed. Can we then accept as valid and final a religion whose central hope was not fulfilled, and whose ethical teaching seems to have been an *ad interim* affair designed for the brief time before the end?

But here again we have an illustration of Christianity's unique significance. Within that apocalyptic framework was the belief in the one living God and his saving purpose of love, and the summons to repent of sin and live in the spirit of this God. "The ethical teaching of Jesus," says C. H. Dodd, "is 'interim ethics' for those who expect that the world will shortly come to an end, but it is absolute ethics for those who have experienced for themselves the end of the world and the coming of the Kingdom." It springs "from its roots in the very constitution of the Kingdom of God, as determined by the nature and character of God himself, the loving God and our Father. The one universal ethical principle is that which is revealed in God's free grace to underserving men in offering them the blessings of his Kingdom."[7] The

[6]*Human Needs and World Christianity,* p. 217. *Cf.* Kirsopp Lake: "Christianity has changed more than most religions because it has had a higher and intenser vitality." *The Religion of Yesterday and Tomorrow,* p. 7. See also E. F. Scott, *The Gospel and Its Tributaries,* pp. 290–291.

[7]In *A Companion to the Bible,* T. W. Manson, ed., p. 379.

finality of Christianity is seen here once more in the validity of its central faith and its capacity to receive new truth and make the needed change in the form of its expression.

IV. SOME PRACTICAL CONCLUSIONS

From this discussion there follow answers to two questions that press urgently on the Church today.

1. What of the relation of Christianity to other faiths and to the work of missions? Christianity is a religion of inclusion, not of exclusion, and wherever it finds truth and love there it sees God and rejoices. But the open mind does not mean a mind without convictions, and the Christian believes that in Christ there has come a revelation of the living God. He takes it humbly; it was not his discovery. He does not point to himself; he is not offering men western culture or Anglo-Saxon achievement. But believing this he cannot but speak, and having this possession he cannot do less than offer to share. Albert Schweitzer writes from his hospital in Africa: "It is unthinkable that we civilized peoples should keep for ourselves alone the wealth of means for fighting sickness, pain, and death which science has given us."[1] Can we do less with the spiritual than we have with the physical? The practical attitude involved in this may be expressed in three words, appreciation, witness, and cooperation: appreciation of truth and life wherever found; witness to the revelation of God that has come to us; cooperation everywhere with men of good will to serve and save mankind. Such cooperation must be at the farthest remove from domination or from the effort to impose on one land the forms which Christianity has assumed in some other. The test of a universal Christianity is whether Jesus can really become "The Christ of the Indian Road" and of every other road.[2]

2. Our discussion has its meaning also in relation to the

[1]*Out of My Life and Thought,* p. 227.

[2]See A. E. Taylor, *The Faith of a Moralist,* II, 97; and *cf.* E. Stanley Jones, *The Christ of the Indian Road,* and *The Christ of the Round Table.*

urgent question of Christian unity. In the solution of that problem the underlying issue is the difference in the conception of the nature of Christianity. In the three decades, from 1910 to 1938, there were held seven notable ecumenical conferences, three of them meetings of the International Missionary Council, two of the Faith and Order Movement, two on Christian Life and Work. It has become increasingly clear through these gatherings that differences in organization, ritual, and doctrine are not insuperable obstacles either to Church union or to Christian unity. Illuminating also is the report of a commission appointed by the Archbishops of Canterbury and York, entitled *Doctrine in the Church of England,* showing the wide divergence in doctrine within the unity of this great communion. What these world gatherings have made plain is that the greatest single obstacle arises from what we have called the "institutional" conception of Christianity, that is, the idea that certain forms which historical Christianity has taken, particularly in terms of doctrine, organization, and rite, are directly instituted of God and so have absolute authority and unchangeable character. When that conception obtains and communions differ as to what these absolutes are, then an impasse is reached. The situation must be frankly recognized and then we must proceed to consider, not simply detailed differences as heretofore, but this underlying question as to the essential nature of the Christian religion. We must see that the alternative to an externalistic absolutism is not relativism and indifference in relation to matters of faith. Christianity is more than an emotional mood or a moral intention. It roots in a deep conviction out of which all else comes forth: that the eternal God has revealed himself in Jesus Christ, who is alike God's word to man and God's saving deed for man. In him we know what God is, what man should be, and how man may have the saving help of God; and he is the center of that fellowship, the Church, in which it is God's will that men should be united.

Our study has made clear one other matter vital for the life of the Church. There is a diversity which is as desirable as division and conflict are undesirable. For all life is under a principle of polarity, whose double pull and consequent tension become a spring of action and the source of the richest life. The tendency in our divided Christendom is to take one aspect or interest, and not merely to lose the wealth of this double movement but to rest in relative stagnation. Here we find the stress upon individual liberty and experience, there upon the corporate life and institutional control and expression. Now we have the emphasis on the inner mood, now on the outer expression. The mystical is set over against the rational, the ethical against the doctrinal. Freedom and authority are seen as alternatives. The obvious need is for an inclusive fellowship which shall have room for all these types of life and thought, which shall continually challenge each group with the demand of the contrasted way and thus enrich each part as well as avoid the stagnation of life and thought into which a one-sided expression always tends to sink.

V. A SUMMARY

A summary statement is here in place which will seek to define Christianity particularly in relation to other religions. In so doing it will help us to keep in mind the three questions with which religion must deal and by the answers to which each religion must be judged: (1) What is Ultimate in the universe? (the question of God); (2) What is that relation to the Ultimate by which man may have life? (the way of salvation); (3) What is the supreme goal or good of life? (the question of obligation).

1. Christianity is a personal-ethical monotheism: the Ultimate is spirit, is person, is one, and is good.

As against all polytheisms and dualisms it believes in one God. Our world is universe, not multiverse, cosmos, not chaos, and all things come under one order, rational and ethical. It recognizes the fact of evil but it stands against all dualisms in which two original forces are arrayed against each other in a struggle of uncertain issue—light against darkness, mind against matter, order against chaos. Equally it stands against the naturalistic speculations for which God is one aspect among others, one force among many, or himself the possible issue of something more ultimate.

This God is personal-ethical. Person and purpose and creative will are here involved. He is person, not abstract idea or impersonal force or order or essence. He is good, but the goodness is dynamic and creative, not remote and static. Here Christianity stands with the Hebraic faith as against Graeco-Indian religions.

This God is both transcendent and immanent, ultimate and intimate. As person and purpose and holy he stands above his world; but in personal relation and creative purpose and self-giving goodness he is immanent in his world and in intimate relation with it. So Christianity stands equally opposed to the pantheisms and naturalisms in which God is lost *in* the world, and those absolutisms and dualisms through which he is lost *to* the world by the gulf that separates him from the finite and changing.

2. Christianity is a religion of redemption, but its conception of salvation is definitely determined by its concept of God. God is not a mysterious essence, imported into man by potent sacramental rites and thus redeeming man from finiteness and corruption. God is not abstract truth or idea, and thus redemption is not by mystical intuition or philosophical insight or esoteric knowledge. God is not an indifferent or autocratic power to be won over through ritual or sacrifice. He is not a Monarch, dealing in rules, offering rewards for obedience, or demanding a suffering substitute when this has failed. He is not an impersonal order to be discovered by research and utilized through adjustment. In a word, Christianity is not sacramentarianism, gnosis, ritualism, legalism, or naturalistic humanism.

Because God is good the Christian way is that of mercy, God's free gift of himself in forgiveness and life. Because he is personal he gives that life through personal fellowship. Because he is ethical the life that he gives is one of love and truth and righteousness, and as such it can be received only as it is lived out in relations with men. Because he is indwelling, creative, living God, this salvation is not a violent irruption from without but is achieved in the historic movement, and is this-worldly as well as other-worldly. Because it is historical and inclusive, this salvation is both social and individual, coming in and through a divine-human fellowship and moving toward that Kingdom of God which is the rule over all life by the Spirit of love and truth.

3. The distinctive nature of Christianity is seen in its concept of the good life. In its conception of the world, it is not negative; it stands over against the asceticisms, world-denials, and world-flights, for example, of the religions of India, and is world-affirming, life-affirming, life-creating. But it is equally opposed to all secularism; it brings a transcendent Good in which the finite finds at once its master and its fulfillment.

It is absolute ethics, not relative. Our knowledge is relative, whether it concerns basic principles or practical applications; but the good that has its being in God is itself unchanging, waiting for our slow vision and achievement. And so the absolute is not arbitrary, and we see at length that his will is our life and peace. The ethics of authority is at the same time the ethics of freedom, divine heteronomy with human autonomy. For the demand that comes in such absolute fashion appeals to the inner conviction of right and truth; and the religion which brings the demand gives with it the inner spirit, the life that is freedom, whose action springs from within. Thus as a spiritual ethics it goes beyond the most exacting legalism, claiming the inmost thought and attitude with the outward deed; but as a religion of the spirit it gives what it demands.

Paul summed up that demand in the simple but inclusive phrase: "faith working through love:" in relation to God, faith, the response of utter trust and absolute loyalty rooting in inner conviction; in relation to men, love, a good will that is creative, inclusive, unconquerable.[1]

4. More briefly we may say: (1) Historically Christianity is the ongoing life of that fellowship which has its origin and its abiding inspiration and guidance in Jesus. Christianity is Christ as the revelation of what God is and what man is to be. (2) With reference to its central conviction, Christianity is the religion of redemptive good will; it believes in a God of creative good will, in the life of good will as the way for men, in the redemptive power of the Spirit of good will working in and through men, and in the final triumph of that spirit in a coming Rule of God.

[1]See Gal. 5:6, and *cf.* Matt. 5:43–48.

Part Two

THE PRESENT-DAY SETTING OF RELIGION

Chapter Six

RELIGION AND THE NEW WORLD OF SCIENCE

I. CONCERNING TIME AND THE ETERNAL

RELIGION is the life of the Eternal in the midst of time. Time and the Eternal are the two foci about which it moves. Its first concern is with the Eternal; here is the differentia of religion, this faith in an unseen world which is at once ultimately real and infinitely good. But it is just as truly concerned with time, with the finite world in which man lives, by which his life is conditioned, within which the saving help of God must work.

The tendency of religion, however, has been to disparage if not to denounce the world of time. Sometimes the reason has been philosophical: so with the religions of India, which have all followed in a measure the Brahmanic conception of the material world as mere appearance, as Maya, a magic show; so with "metaphysical" mysticism which finds salvation only as all that is concrete and visible is left behind while the soul embarks upon the flight whose goal is the losing of itself in the Eternal; and so with that dualism which finds above us a world of the spirit, perfect and unchanging, in which alone the true and the good are found, while this changing world appears as of dubious reality and worth, if not wholly evil. In Christian thought two streams of influence in particular entered to destroy for men the significance of time and the visible. The earliest was apocalypticism, coming from popular Judaism. It saw this age as evil and hopeless, at best a more or less unmeaning preliminary for the eternal age which was already at the door. There was no hope for this age and no help in it; and there was nothing that man could really do except to be faithful and to wait for the day of the Lord to bring its supernatural deliverance. The second influence was the dualistic trend; Hellenistic and oriental rather than Jewish, it led to the disparagement of all that belonged to man and time and earth, sometimes tending even to consider the material as such to be evil. This was supported by the doctrine of the corruption of all nature, as well as of the human race, which ensued upon the fall of man.

But there were other influences operative in Christianity, springing from its basic character as a prophetic religion. For its faith was in a living God who worked in history to bring his ends to pass, a God for whom man was a responsible being, a moral personality living in decision and action. Time and history were thus given meaning and value. What Christianity involves at this point is illuminated by contrast in Albert Schweitzer's *Indian Thought and Its Development,* where we see how religion in India was never able to escape world-negation or do justice to the ethical and historical on the basis of its own principles.

In the transition to the modern age other powerful factors came into play and helped to bring about an extraordinary change. The contrast with medievalism can be put in the phrase: the modern man discovered this world, or, one might say, discovered himself and his world. There was a breakdown of authority; man became less certain of the reality of heaven and the threat of hell. Science not only awakened a new interest in this world, but brought a new ideal of knowledge, experimental and certain as against the authoritarian or speculative. Life in this world had been a meager and hard affair, in which man stood helpless over against nature and his fate; now the new science brought a sense of power, the promise of control, and a prospect of endlessly increasing comforts and pleasures, which was substantiated by the results of industry and trade. The growth of democracy brought a new sense of freedom and of the possibilities of social change. Men no longer accepted the *status quo* as a finality. With this went the change from a static to a dynamic and developing conception of the world, alike of nature and of society. The Darwinian theory of biological evolution was the center of interest, but far more important was the way in which this general viewpoint permeated every aspect of thought and life. Man's world was no longer a static affair but a place of incalculable forces, of incessant change, of momentous possibilities. Modern man had "discovered time."

Religious thought was inevitably affected by all this. Religion became more inclusive in its interests and more constructive in its attitude toward everything that concerned this world, whether scientific, social, or historical. The whole matter of the relation of God to the world came up for fresh consideration. That was evidenced by the discussions, continued to this day, of the relation of natural and supernatural, and, especially in recent years, as to a Christian philosophy of history. The pendulum swung from a dualistic transcendence which denied significance to history and the human scene to a stress on divine immanence and human effort which tended to eliminate the Eternal. One fact, however, is clear: Religion must take account of this changed world. For religion is life and life consists in relations, and these relations include not only God but the world. God is not simply a Word spoken from above, or a power entering from without, or the one-time Creator of the universe; he is in his world and in the movements of our time as action working for human redemption, as truth waiting to be discerned.

As regards this changed world which forms the setting for religion, three broad aspects present themselves for our study: (1) the world of nature, especially as interpreted by modern science; (2) the social scene as indicated by such words as industrialism, democracy, communism, and fascism; (3) the world of thought. The last named will be considered in connection with other discussions; our interest here will center in the first two points.

Our day is often called the age of science. The term is becoming less fitting as those problems of social and individual life press upon us which science as such cannot solve; nevertheless it would be hard to over-estimate the influence of science upon the modern world. It has changed our world picture, it has powerfully affected our world view, it has put into man's hands forces of incalculable power, and through invention and industry it has profoundly modified every phase of human life. We must, therefore, construe this subject of religion and science very broadly, considering the total effect of science on religious faith and life.

II. THE OLD WORLD PICTURE AND THE NEW

1. It is necessary to distinguish here first of all between world picture and world view. By the former we mean a picture of the physical universe built upon science, by the latter a philosophy, a view of the world and life. Clearly it is our world view (*Weltanschauung*) rather than our world picture (*Weltbild*) that counts most. On the other hand it is true that religious thought in the Bible and in traditional theology had as its background a definite world picture, that this picture influenced the content of thought, and that it is still embodied in the imagery of current belief and worship.

Recall this older world picture. For it this vast universe was but a few thousand years old. It had come complete from God's hand. The earth was its center. Above it stretched the fixed dome in which the heavenly bodies moved. Man, the special creation of God, was to rule the earth, and sun and moon were made to give him light and mark his sacred days and seasons. Above him in the blue firmament was the abode of God from which he looked down upon man. Three names mark epochs in the making of the new world picture. In 1543 a Polish monk, Copernicus, published his *De Revolu-*

tionibus Orbium Coelestium and forever dethroned the earth and man from their erstwhile central place. In 1686 Newton gave forth his *Principia Mathematica* and suggested the picture of a universe in which a single reign of hard and fast laws determined every event. In 1859 Charles Darwin produced his *Origin of Species.* A fourth epoch is marked by the new physics. Here no one name or event stands forth, but one thinks of relativity, a four-dimensional space-time world, the quantum theory with its wave-mechanics, and the departure of the old atom. We will first look at the main aspects of the new world picture, so far as a layman can formulate them, and then at some items of deeper significance.

(1) First of all, the new universe is inconceivably vaster, alike in terms of space and time. The writer of Genesis pictures the creation of the earth with its attendant sun and moon; then, almost as an afterthought, dismisses the rest of the universe with the word, "he made the stars also." How different the universe we envisage! Our sun is a million times larger than the earth, yet itself but one of fifteen hundred million suns that compose the galactic system. Beyond this stretch other systems, galaxies and supergalaxies which astronomy cannot number, though we read of a million "island universes." For measuring this greater cosmos we have had to devise a new yardstick, the light year; our unit is the distance that light, moving at the inconceivable speed of 186,000 miles per second, will travel in a year. Our nearest star is four light years away, but the nebula in Andromeda is so far distant that the rays by which astronomers see it today left their flaming source a million years ago, while other nebulae are estimated to be a hundred and forty million light years away.

(2) A second feature is the idea of a unitary order pervading all the universe and including all happenings. Traditional religion conceived of two distinct frames of order: the natural order in which things behaved according to their nature as originally created by God; the supernatural order,

the world of God's action as seen in creation, revelation, incarnation, special providence, miracles, and redemption. In this second sphere men were not to seek for "natural" causes; the only explanation was the will of God and his deed. Modern science sees one order in all the universe. Newton advanced that position when he showed that the law of the heavens by which the planets moved in their paths was the same as the law by which an apple fell to earth. Darwin pointed out this order in the sphere of the evolving forms of life, for the theory of evolution is simply the effort to find a unitary order in change. In psychology men sought to show that there was a like order which could be stated in terms of laws and which included the most significant and individual aspects of our inner life, not omitting religious experience itself. Religion, which had so commonly sought God in the exceptional and inexplicable, was now challenged to show where in such an all-inclusive order there was any need of God or any room for him.

(3) The idea of evolution affords the third significant aspect of the modern world picture. Used in the broad sense, evolution involves the two principles of continuity and change: everything that is must be understood as the result of a process in which change has been constant and yet always in relation to what went before. The general idea is as old as Greek philosophy. It was Darwin's service to give this general principle support in a specific field, that of biology, to marshal a multitude of concrete facts, and to interpret these facts so as to indicate the method or mechanism of this change. His epoch-making work exerted a wide-reaching influence. (1) It transformed a general idea into a scientific theory of assured standing. (2) It conspired with the new interest in history to produce a "genetically minded" age, whose consuming interest in origins and development is applied to every field, to biology and Bible, to astro-physics and chemical elements, to nature and history. (3) Philosophically it led men less cautious than Darwin to suppose

that here was a key to unlock all the problems of thought, that to trace the "evolution" was to supply the explanation. (4) It furnished a strong support to a naturalistic philosophy of the mechanistic type. For the factors which Darwin used in the description of evolution seemed to be purely mechanical: variation that was heterogeneous and fortuitous, without purpose or direction; over-production and hence a struggle for existence; the survival of those possessing the fitter variations; conservation of such variation by heredity, and so the origin of new species. Friends and foes alike drew this conclusion. Thus James Sully, in his article, "Evolution," in the ninth edition of the *Encyclopedia Britannica,* could define evolution as a "natural history of the cosmos, including organic beings, expressed in physical terms as a mechanical process."

The general effect of this broader movement upon traditional religion was especially evident at two points. (1) It seemed to cut the ground out from under the belief in a Creator. Men had believed in a static universe, complete from the beginning, which thus required a Creator God to bring it into being; but here was a theory showing how all things had gradually evolved. (2) With the passing of the Creator God there seemed to disappear all certainty, all validity and authority of truth and ideal. Only one thing seemed certain and that was that everything changed. Social institutions, moral standards, sacred Scriptures, Christian doctrines, all were a part of this ceaseless flux through which they had come, in which they in turn would disappear.

In this general situation there have been marked changes. The theory of evolution itself has been profoundly modified by the scientist, and the first easy-going deductions have been sharply criticized by the philosopher. We have come to see that what is unique in truth and life remains unique no matter by what road it comes, that evolution has helped us toward a tenable conception of divine creativity, and that it has thrown light on the dark question of evil. Yet there is no problem of natural science or social life, of ethics or religion, whose study is not profoundly affected by our realization that whatever is has come to be through ages of continuous change.

2. More significant than any particular results was the entrance of the scientific spirit and the use of the scientific method. To keep the open mind, to observe concrete facts, to test every hypothesis by experiment and further observation, this was the new way. The appeal to fact was to displace all theories or conclusions based on general principles. Nothing was to be accepted on authority, however high its claim, or to be based upon tradition, however ancient and sacred. For many the ideal for the scientific method was furnished by physics, with its exact quantitative measurements, its possibilities of controlled experiment, and its reduction of all happenings to a scheme of mechanical events, the action and reaction of physical forces. Hence biologists, psychologists, and students of the social sciences vied with one another in finding in their fields something that could be reduced to measurement and set forth in statistical tables and graphs, so that they too might be "scientific."

3. Perhaps the greatest influence of science on the new age was through its practical applications. At the threshold of modern history Bacon had envisaged this with his dictum, "Knowledge is power"; he thought of science in terms of the control of nature which it would give. The actual results went far beyond what Bacon dreamed. It is easy to overestimate the influence of science upon the common man. Scientific truth is disseminated slowly despite the numerous "Outlines." Still slower is the progress of the scientific temper, with its rigid impartiality and its concern for concrete fact; witness the methods and the success of propaganda during the first World War and its resurgence today. Opinions still seem more the result of visceral than of mental activity, and unscrupulous leaders take full advantage of this. Curiously enough, the very word "Science" has become a label for the

object of a new idolatry; and we see a new authoritarianism taking the place of the old and securing unquestioning acceptance of opinions by pronouncing such words as "scientific" and "modern." But what really impresses the common man is the tremendous practical difference that science has made in his every-day life. It has lifted age-old and intolerable burdens from his back; it has given him power over the forces of nature and has made a commonplace of goods and comforts and conveniences of which his father could not dream. Indeed, one scientist has said flatly: "Human progress grows out of measurements made in the sixth place of decimals."[1] It is this of which the common man thinks when you say science, and this that has given natural science its popular prestige.

III. SOME NATURALISTIC CONCLUSIONS

What affected religion most, however, was not the world picture but the world view which was supposed to follow from the new science, a philosophy of naturalism with accompanying agnosticism, relativism, and secularism.

1. Naturalism is the effort to make natural science do service as a philosophy. It is an illegitimate conclusion drawn from a legitimate method. Impressed with the results of science, it assumes that the only valid knowledge is that of the natural sciences and the only reality the world which science studies. Natural science rightly limits its field to the space-time world as discerned through the senses. It excludes all that cannot be observed by its instruments, subjected to its measurements, or subsumed under its order (natural laws). To use the illustration of J. Arthur Thomson, it employs a net with a wide mesh and is not concerned with what slips through. It does not, for example, regard the individual as such or deal with the world of value. The beauty of sunset or rainbow is not a matter for the physicist as physicist studying the refraction of light, nor the character of an individual

[1] R. A. Millikan, *Science and the New Civilization*, p. 165.

as citizen or friend for the physiologist and chemist studying the action of hormones. Religion, on the other hand, lives by the conviction, not only that there is another world, a world of the spirit, a world of persons and ideals and values, but that this world is supremely real and that in it the source and meaning of our cosmos are to be found.

2. Agnosticism means literally nescience, or ignorance. It is the theory that we can have no knowledge of ultimate reality. Strictly it is as much against materialism as against theism. To the common mind, however, it means that our only real knowledge is that of the physical world as given by natural science; if men will they may have religion for their dreams and inner longings and moments of emotion, but there is no knowledge in religion. And not only the insights of the saint must be discarded, but all that has come through poets and philosophers, through lovers and friends.

3. Relativism has seemed to many to be a necessary conclusion from the universal application of the principle of development. However imperfect this world of the finite and changing might be, the men of yesterday commonly held to faith in something absolute as a frame of reference and a standard of judgment. There were absolute standards of ethics by which to judge human conduct, absolute ideals by which to measure such social institutions as family and state, and an absolute God who was the seat of authority and the home of perfection, just as there was, until Einstein, an absolute frame of reference in Newton's space-time world in relation to which the position and movement of the heavenly bodies could be defined. For the modern man all this seems to have yielded to the one law of change. "Whirl is King, having driven out Zeus."[1] Nothing is certain except the endless succession. Nowhere do we reach any final meaning or authority. The world has no longer any ultimate source or any clear end. Religious faith and high human hopes both disappear. Religious beliefs, moral ideals, and social institu-

[1]See Walter Lippmann, *A Preface to Morals,* Part I.

tions are alike wanting in ultimate standards; they are merely a part of man's effort to live by adaptation to the shifting scene.

4. Secularism is a philosophy of life resting upon the theory of naturalism. If the visible world, the world of space and time, is alone real, then we must seek in that world the goods with which to satisfy our desires and the means by which to attain them. We are using "secular" here to mean "a way of life and an interpretation of life that include only the natural order of things and that do not find God, or a realm of spiritual reality, essential for life or thought."[2] In practice it has had tremendous support from the applications of modern science, from the sense of power over the world which these have brought, and from the multiplied material possessions and comforts which have come with the machine age. Russia is an illustration of an avowed secular culture, officially adopted by the State and systematically promoted; but every land knows this temper. The secularist would put his case as follows: Before the age of science, the life of man in relation to this world was marked by ignorance and hardship. With poverty, toil, and sickness as the common lot, man turned for compensation to another world and sang "Jerusalem the golden, with milk and honey blest." Standing helpless before the forces of nature, he looked to God and supernatural powers for saving help. The modern man, thanks to science, is neither ignorant nor helpless. He needs no compensatory other world and no supernatural aid. The conquest of disease and poverty lies in his own hands, and the satisfying goods of life are present and waiting. And as there are no higher goods or forces, so there is for the secularist no authority except the rules that are effective in gaining his ends and the conventions that are needed for social life.

[2]Rufus M. Jones in *The Jerusalem Meeting of the International Missionary Council,* I, 230. The entire chapter might well be read in connection with the chapter from Lippmann cited above.

IV. THE NEWER TRENDS IN SCIENCE

We have considered the world picture brought by nineteenth-century science and the world view which some men built upon it. But science did not stop with the nineteenth century, and we must consider some of its newer trends and the direction in which they point.

1. We note first the movement in physics that looks away from a mechanistic interpretation of the world. The science of the nineteenth century through various basic concepts seemed to give strong support to a theory which made of nature a great machine. There was first the conception of the atom as the ultimate, indivisible, unchanging particle of which all being was composed. There was the theory of the conservation of energy and correlation of forces: energy might change its form, as in motion, light, or heat, but no energy was ever lost and none could be added. There was the idea of cause operating mechanically in action and reaction according to a law of rigid necessity to which everything was subjected. Newton's world of space and time furnished the framework, and Darwin's theory of evolution suggested that these mechanically operating forces could explain all changes in the world of life as well. In such a universe there seemed to be no place for purpose or freedom, no chance for anything new and higher to appear, no creative activity, no soul, no God. With this scheme of rigid necessity, if one could fully know the world at any given moment, that is, the position and velocity of all the mass-points of which it was composed, he could fortell every coming event to the end of time. "At the beginning of the twentieth century," writes W. C. Dampier, "the majority of men of science held unconsciously a naïve materialism, or inclined to the phenomenalism of Mach and Karl Pearson, or the evolutionary monism of Haeckel or W. K. Clifford. . . . Evolution has become a philosophy, indeed to some men almost a creed."[1]

Present-day science seems to be cutting the ground out

[1] *A History of Science,* pp. 445, 556. *Cf.* Bernhard Bavink, *Science and God,* pp. 8–11.

from under this idea of nature. First of all modern physicists recognize that science cannot know the nature of ultimate reality, some of them tending to the phenomenalism just referred to. "Science has nothing to say as to the intrinsic nature of the atom. The physical atom is, like everything else in physics, a schedule of pointer readings. The schedule is, we agree, attached to some unknown background."[2] That is, we have the readings of measuring instruments but we do not know what is being measured. Eddington himself thinks of this background as "something of a spiritual nature of which a prominent characteristic is thought," and Jeans would agree with this. That, of course, is their opinion as philosophers, not their conclusion as physicists, but in any case the old materialistic "billiard ball" conception of matter is left behind.

Just as significant as the changed concept of matter is the changed idea of causation. The older view pictured a world of mechanistic determination, where every event was the necessary result of some force acting upon it as irresistible cause. There is, first, the changed conception of cause. The old idea of compulsion, says Bertrand Russell, must be given up; the so-called necessity means simply "that there is some general rule . . . according to which events such as A are followed by events such as B." The laws of science are summary descriptions of the order of such happenings, and are practically always "quantitative laws of tendency."[3] C. Lloyd Morgan, discussing the modern conceptions of causation, declares that "science has simply to observe behavior and sum it up in 'laws,' or suitable equations. All reference to force as an explanatory agency is barred from science because valueless." He would distinguish causation, as thus used in science, from the idea of causality, by which he means the ultimate interpretation of the universe as this is sought by philosophy.[4]

But not only does modern science content itself with de-

[2]A. S. Eddington, *The Nature of the Physical World,* p. 259.
[3]*Philosophy,* pp. 115, 144. [4]*Emergent Evolution,* pp, 276–296.

scription and refuse to use the idea of cause, it seems inclined to reject what previously was a basic presupposition, that there is a rigid necessity in the physical world, an inevitable and necessary order, which would make it possible for us, like Laplace's World Spirit, to predict all future happenings if we only had sufficient knowledge of the present. Now we are told that there is a certain indeterminateness that is basic in nature. The laws of nature are "expressions of probable tendencies, . . . concerned, not with individual molecules, atoms, or electrons, but with statistical averages only." We cannot tell when a given atom will explode, though we can predict how many atoms in a milligram of radium will disintegrate in a minute; nor can we determine when a particular electron will fall into a new orbit and therefore radiate. All this may be a matter of ignorance some time to be overcome, but "present tendencies point the other way. The principle of indeterminacy seems to introduce a new kind of incalculability into nature. . . . The work of Schrödinger and Bohr indicates that there is an uncertainty in the nature of things."[5]

Bernhard Bavink, whose monumental work on *The Natural Sciences, an Introduction to the Scientific Philosophy of Today,* has passed through a number of editions and has been translated into English, explains this more fully. The mechanistic conception of the physical world is a prejudice derived from our observation of *macroscopic* processes, that is, the behavior of things in the mass. The conclusions are accurate enough in this field. On the macroscopic scale we may assume that the "laws of nature" hold without exception. True, it is a matter of statistical averages, like the actuarial tables of the life insurance company; but since trillions upon trillions of molecules are involved, the item of "chance" practically disappears. So we can make the same technical use of science as in the past. Yet "it appears possible that all natural law may be reduced to the calculation of probabilities."

[5]W. C. Dampier, *A History of Science,* p. 473.

In any case we cannot apply to submicroscopic processes within the atom the ideas that we have taken from macroscopic processes, any more than we can expect the statistics of an insurance company to reveal just when and how specific fires, suicides, and accidents will occur in the future.[6]

The strongest influence against a mechanistic determinism, however, has come from biology rather than physics. Biology furnishes us the principle of organicism which looks at the whole instead of component parts, and an idea of development which shows us a plastic universe undergoing a real qualitative change, a change in which there appears what is actually new. Both of these look directly away from a mechanistic-materialistic conception, in which there can never be real change or real creativity but only a mechanical rearrangement of elements present from the beginning. Finally it gives the idea of purposiveness, of a movement towards ends, which is against the conception of the chance results of blindly acting physical forces. We must consider more carefully these newer scientific concepts and the nature of the world picture to which they point, taking up first the idea of organicism.

2. There is an increasing tendency today toward an organismic, or organicistic, conception of nature. It is the effort to understand our world by looking at wholes instead of merely at parts. The older method of science laid the emphasis on analysis: the way to find the real was to analyze until one reached the ultimate particles of which things were composed. The error was that of a false simplification; it assumed that there was nothing real except these ultimate particles, or atoms, and that all the rich and varied forms of being, crystals and cells, the soul and society, men and stars, were simply aggregations of atoms in different combinations or patterns. But the real world of our experience is something wholly dif-

[6]These items and quotations are taken from Bavink's *Science and God*, pp. 80–82, a more popular report on the new science, especially physics, and its bearing on religious thought. His discussion of contingency is especially interesting.

ferent. It is a world of concrete wholes, of distinct individual beings marked by endless variety. The term organicistic does not imply that all being is organic in the biological sense, but the word seems to express the facts better than any other term. A biological organism is always more than the sum of its parts. It has a life as a whole, a distinctive character and way of behavior. Instead of the parts accounting for the whole, we have to look at the whole to understand the parts. Each part has its function in relation to the whole; what it really is can be understood only as we look at the whole, and its true life is achieved only in relation to the whole.

It becomes more and more apparent, in every department of study, that only as we look at these unitary wholes, with their peculiar qualities or modes of behavior, can we understand our world as it really is. The physicist is no longer concerned with the atom viewed as an indivisible unit but rather seen as a unique whole, a system of constituent electric particles. The living cell of the biologist is another unique whole whose nature cannot be described by any chemico-physical account of how its component particles behave. It is the great service of form psychology (*Gestaltpsychologie*) to insist that we can only understand human behavior by looking at the subject as a whole reacting meaningfully to a total environment. The sociologist knows that man as pure individual is an abstraction; human life is possible only in social relations, as part of a social whole. A distinguished entomologist, W. M. Wheeler, asserts the same on lower levels: "There is something fundamentally social in living things. . . . There are no truly solitary organisms. . . . Indeed, the correlations of the social—using the term in its most general sense—even extend down through the non-living to the very atom." All classes of elements show an irresistible tendency "to cohere and organize themselves into more and more complex emergent wholes."[7]

[7] *Proceedings of the Sixth International Congress of Philosophy*, pp. 40, 41. See also his *Emergent Evolution and the Development of Societies.*

What this means for a philosophical interpretation of our universe has been especially developed by Jan C. Smuts and Alfred N. Whitehead, each in his own fashion. Smuts is especially rich in scientific materials and illustrations. He coins the word holism from the Greek. For him the world process is one of evolution, and evolution may be described as the formation of increasingly complex, significant, and inclusive wholes. Whitehead uses the terms prehension (that which is grasped, or brought together, in a unity), concretion, spatio-temporal unity, or event, to indicate these organic wholes.[8]

On all these various levels, physical, chemical, biological, psychological, and social, each concrete whole, in turn, must be seen and understood in relation to a larger whole. That means more than to say that each whole has an external environment or is part of the cosmic whole. It is more than a matter of ecology. Rather, each being, whether atom or cell, man or star, is organically related to its world. By this relation its emergence into being and its behavior are conditioned. This organic relation is in time as well as space; in Whitehead's terminology, each being is an "event" in the cosmic process. Smuts uses the word field to describe this space-time setting, after the analogy of the magnetic field. He, too, emphasizes the time aspect, and declares that in the structural unity of any given whole the push of the past, the activity of the present, and the pull of the future all meet.[9] So we reach the idea that the cosmos itself is an organic whole, a living universe, to use the title of one of Principal Jacks' works. We have said that it was cosmos, not chaos, universe, not multiverse; but this involves more. "Nature is not a collection of dead and dried *disjecta membra,*" but "the interwoven body of living, creative, progressive unities and

[8]See Smuts, *Holism and Evolution,* and for Whitehead *Process and Reality* and especially his *Science and the Modern World,* Chapter IV of which gives perhaps the simplest statement of his position for the lay reader. A popular exposition is given by Dorothy M. Emmett in *Whitehead's Philosophy of Organism.*

[9]*Holism and Evolution,* pp. 111–116, *et passim.*

syntheses," says Jan Smuts.[10] Does not that, however, point to a unitary Spirit as the source and seat and direction of this unified life?

3. The idea of creative, or emergent, evolution is closely related to this organicistic conception, and has furnished empirical data for its development. It sees a process in which there is a formation of wholes, and with these wholes the emergence of something new, something qualitatively different. Evolution thus is creative, or emergent. The old mechanistic naturalism saw in all life's varied forms nothing but the chance rearrangement of atoms in shifting and complex patterns. There could, therefore, be no real creativity, no appearance of anything new. Lloyd Morgan, who originated the phrase emergent evolution, describes evolution as a progress in emerging levels: on one line that of atom, molecule, crystal, the other line being organic and moving from the cell to the mind. At every stage, as Morgan points out, the significant feature is a new kind of relatedness—new terms in new relations. The entity thus emerging has both new qualities within itself and new properties, or modes of behavior, in relation to other entities.[11] The significant elements in the concept of emergent evolution would seem to be: (1) evolution is epigenetic, that is, there is a supervening of something really new, and that, too, in ascending levels; (2) the new is unpredictable; no knowledge of the constituent elements indicates the nature of that which is to "emerge"; (3) the appearance of the new is always in connection with the formation of new wholes, so that "association may be regarded as the fundamental condition of emergence";[12] (4) each supervening higher level rests upon and includes in itself the preceding levels. Thus water in its nature and behavior is wholly different from the hydrogen and oxygen of which it is composed; no knowledge of the latter could possibly enable the

[10] *Op. cit.*, p. 329.
[11] C. Lloyd Morgan, *Emergent Evolution*, pp. 19, 35.
[12] W. M. Wheeler, in passage quoted above.

chemist to predict the nature of water before it appeared; its appearance comes through the association of these chemical elements in a certain manner, forming a new whole. Even more striking are the illustrations on higher levels, as, for example, with the living cell, a rational being like man, or human society in its many group forms.

4. The idea of purposiveness seems to go inevitably with this organismic conception. That does not necessarily mean the old idea of design and a Designer; but there is a growing recognition that we cannot adequately describe the world as we know it without the use of terms that indicate ends, and means related to ends. The idea of organism always involves that of function, the activity of the part in relation to the being and well-being of the whole. It implies a purposive activity in self-maintenance through constant and changing adjustment; and there is a similar relation of each whole to larger wholes. Further, the idea of emergent evolution suggests a general trend of development toward higher levels.[13] In biological evolution there seems to be increasing place given to the idea of orthogenesis; instead of haphazard variations, aimless and mostly useless, there seems to be evolution moving in some direction.[14] Hobhouse suggests as the total result of his study of evolution the idea of a "development of harmony which constitutes the gradual realization of a conditioned purpose.[15] Joseph Needham, as biochemist, insists upon mechanism as the only principle of investigation even in biology, but he recognizes that this cannot set forth the total reality and welcomes Whitehead's philosophy of organism with the central place which it gives to values.[16]

L. J. Henderson, professor of biological chemistry at Harvard, has carried this idea of purpose in nature down to the inorganic realm in his two volumes, *The Fitness of the*

[13] L. T. Hobhouse, *Evolution and Purpose*, pp. 11, 12.

[14] G. T. W. Patrick, *Introduction to Philosophy*, pp. 121, 122.

[15] *Evolution and Purpose*, p. 370.

[16] See his chapters, "Organicism in Biology" and "Anaxagoras," in *The Sceptical Biologist*.

Environment and *The Order of Nature*. Needham calls this "the most important contribution to the philosophy of biology since Wilhelm Roux's *Programm.*"[17] The physical universe, Henderson holds, is so uniquely and extraordinarily adapted to the production and development of life, that we can only conclude that one purpose lies back of the whole. He points out first the qualities that a living organism must have and the kind of environment necessary for its life. He considers then the nature of the physical order and its extraordinary fitness for this purpose. His conclusion is that "The fitness of the environment results from characteristics which constitute a series of maxima—unique or nearly unique properties of water, carbonic acid, the compounds of carbon, hydrogen and oxygen, and the ocean—so numerous, so varied, and so nearly complete among all things which are concerned in the problem that together they form certainly the greatest possible fitness." He declares that there is not one chance in millions of millions that this combination should occur as a mere accident. The conclusion is that we have here an *order,* an order that looks to an end. "Matter and energy have an original property, assuredly not by chance, which organizes the universe in space and time." The whole evolutionary process, both cosmic and organic, is one, and the biologist may now rightly regard the universe in its very essence as biocentric."[18] In his second volume, *The Order of Nature,* Henderson points out that these elements and compounds, with their peculiar properties, "are favorable not merely to life as we know it; they are favorable to any mechanism, to any possible kind of life in this universe." "This collocation of properties," then, is "in some intelligible sense a preparation for the processes of planetary evolution," that is, "they unaccountably precede that to which they are unquestionably related."[19] The universe thus shows for Henderson

[17]*Op. cit.,* pp. 198–205.
[18]*The Fitness of the Environment,* pp. 272, 276, 308, 312.
[19]Pp. 6, 192.

not only purposiveness (*Zielstrebigkeit)* and adaptation (*Zweckmässigkeit*), but a purpose which works through the mechanism of the physical and yet does not originate in this.

5. More significant still is the increasing realization that this organic interpretation of the world involves an immanent organizing principle or tendency. The eighteenth-century scientific scheme, says A. N. Whitehead, provided no organic unity for the world whole, and showed nothing in the nature of things why things should come together in physical relations or why living bodies should emerge. But that is just what we find in nature, not particles of matter in aimless motion, but everywhere, from simplest atom to stellar system or living organisms, an immanent principle or tendency which unites in patterns or configurations or working unities or living wholes. That is widely recognized under various names. So William Patten writes on *The Grand Strategy of Evolution,* making basic the principle of co-operation, or mutual service, "the extension of harmony in activity." Michael Pupin calls it a principle of coordination.[20] With Jan Smuts, as we have seen, it is the principle of "holism," a "whole-making tendency which works up the raw material, or unorganized energy units of the world, utilizes, assimilates, and organizes them, endows them with specific structure and individuality, and finally with personality, and creates beauty and truth and value for them."[21] Whitehead's term is the principle of concretion. The appearance of the organic or structural is not a chance affair or incidental; the essential order of nature is its character as "the locus of organisms in process of development." "Space-time is nothing else than a system of pulling together of assemblages into unities."[22] Wilhelm Wundt had long before used the suggestive term, creative synthesis.

[20]The concluding lecture of *The New Reformation.*

[21]See *Holism and Evolution,* p. 108, and *passim.*

[22]*Science and the Modern World,* pp. 104, 102.

V. THE INTERPRETATION OF THE NEW WORLD PICTURE

What does this new world picture mean for our world view? Even in presenting the newer trends of science we have found it impossible to keep this question out and a whole library of discussion has come forth to show the interest in this problem, an interest shared by scientists, philosophers, theologians, men of letters, and men of affairs. We must guard here against two dangers. First, we must not let our conclusions outrun our premises. Thus, to recognize creativity in the evolutionary process does not imply a personal Creator, to deny an exclusive mechanical causation does not prove moral freedom, and to repudiate the old materialism does not permit us to conclude our particular idealism. Second, we must not let our respect for the scientist's work as scientist lead us to accept his conclusions when he philosophizes; modern physics is one thing, the idealism of Jeans and the mysticism of Eddington are another.

Yet the fact remains that the newer science has given us a world picture hostile to the old materialistic-mechanistic view and distinctly more favorable to religion. Religion, we must reiterate, has its own roots. Poet and artist, saint and seer have always known a world of spiritual reality and have never asked permission of science to believe in it. But it is significant that today science itself points in this direction. The world is no longer mere *Kraft und Stoff,* energy and matter, endlessly working but always to no end, showing only ever shifting patterns of that which itself remains always the same. The universe has become a living whole. There is order in it, but not that of rigid determination; rather, from the atom upward there is a certain indeterminateness that increases in significance and becomes in man a rational and moral freedom. There is real creativity, the appearance not only of what is new but of higher levels of being; and the movement suggests a certain purposiveness. To religious thought there is presented a world which can no longer be interpreted merely by the categories of matter and force acting in mechanical causation. To religious hope it indicates a scene where man's creative effort seems to find not only opportunity but a supporting movement. How is modern reflective thought interpreting the newer science?

Our first task is not to demonstrate that the newer science requires or permits faith in God, but simply to review the different conclusions that have been drawn. The crucial fact that must be faced in the new world picture is that of creative evolution. We may apply to the cosmos as a whole the words of a distinguished biologist when he speaks of "life that is upon a new adventure, life that is transforming into what did not before exist, life that is rising to heights not before reached."[1] What is the meaning of this movement? What is the nature of the creative power here at work? Broadly speaking, we may distinguish three tendencies among present-day writers in the interpretation of this process. All three repudiate the old materialistic-mechanistic naturalism. All recognize the three main levels of emergent evolution: matter, life, and spirit. But one of these finds its principle of sufficient explanation at the first level, the physical, one at the second, that of organic life, and the third at the highest level, the ethical-personal.[2]

1. The first of these positions we may call the new naturalism. The first mistake of the old naturalism was its effort at reduction. The world of our common experience is rich and varied; to it belong lifeless things, living creatures, the rational, spiritual being. The old naturalism tried to reduce it all to one level of being and happening. The spiritual became biological, biological processes in turn were explained in chemical and physical terms, and the whole was reduced to

[1]H. S. Jennings, *The Universe and Life,* p. 65. Jennings, however, repudiates all suggestion of a directing Power or antecedent Purpose. It is life "moving in directions not laid out beforehand."

[2]The meaning of these three levels is succinctly indicated by a modern scientist: "The fundamental concept of physics is that of magnitude, of biology the whole or form, that of the moral sciences value." Bernhard Bavink, *Science and God,* p. 153.

the material and mechanistic. We may take Professor Roy W. Sellars as an exponent of the new naturalism. He recognizes this error and repudiates it. The new emergent evolution helps him to this. "The newer naturalism recognizes levels and differences. It is both humanitarian and naturalistic."[3] Being is not an inert substratum; it expresses itself not only in extendedness and change, but in togetherness, life, mind.[4]

But in the end the remove from the old naturalism does not seem so great, despite the idealistic humanistic interest which the author reveals. That appears at two crucial points. (1) The source and explanation of the world is to be found purely at the lower levels and in no sense in the higher. "Man becomes entirely a creature of time and space. Back of pomp and circumstance, back of love and beauty and tragedy and happiness, lie—matter."[5] (2) After all that is said about higher levels and the recognition of the new and different, mind or spirit is not different in nature from the biological or material. Mind is "a physical category"; it means "the nervous processes which find expression in intelligent conduct." "The new naturalism," we are frankly told, "is a new materialism."[6] "The brain in its organic setting of muscle and gland is the mind."[7] The two positions, of course, hang closely together. As Sellars personally recognizes, it is science itself that has destroyed the old materialistic-mechanistic naturalism; its empirical data "force the thinker to construct categories corresponding to them."[8] That is, you cannot

[3]*Evolutionary Naturalism,* p. 341.

[4]*The Philosophy of Physical Realism,* pp. 3, 4. For his conception of religion see his *Religion Coming of Age.*

[5]*The Philosophy of Physical Realism,* pp. 1, 6.

[6]*Evolutionary Naturalism,* p. 300; *The Philosophy of Physical Realism,* p. 3.

[7]*Contemporary American Philosophy,* Vol. II, p. 278. Note the recurrent ambiguity or double meaning. The brain is muscle and gland, and then it is more than, and muscle and gland are the "setting."

[8]*Evolutionary Naturalism,* pp. 19, 302.

longer deny the realities that must be described as mind, consciousness, intelligence. But the new naturalism is determined to avoid giving these categories any real place in interpreting the cosmos. Its distinctive mark, as with the old, is the effort to interpret the world as to its origin and ultimate nature in terms of the material and not the spiritual, that is, in terms of the lowest categories which the world shows rather than the higher.[9]

So we see two errors of the old naturalism repeated. (1) Despite contrary assertion there is the error of reduction; the spiritual (consciousness, mind) is treated as incidental to the material, as "function" or as "internal feature." Mind is a "physical category." "Any psychical fact is a quality of a nervous complex when functioning synthetically."[10] (2) Description passes for explanation. The new science describes the organismic trend in nature and the conditions under which the higher levels of life and mind emerge, as we have already noted; but what is the meaning of this organizing trend? Why does the higher appear under these conditions? Whence does this higher come? Here is the old naturalistic error, the proposal to limit all knowledge to science and "to make the institution of science serve also as the institution of philosophy."[11]

To do justice to this newer naturalism, one other point needs emphasis: its "matter" is not the old matter. It is no inert substratum. It expresses its "nature" in life and mind. It functions as life and intelligence. The "rise of higher levels" rests upon and carries out the "potentialities" of the lower

[9]"The principle of all hypotheses which may be described as naturalistic is that of taking the lower elements in the universe as the most significant, as truly real, and attempting to give some account of the higher elements, such as consciousness, in terms of these supposed more elementary factors." W. R. Matthews, *Studies in Christian Philosophy*, p. 92.

[10]*Evolutionary Naturalism*, p. 316. *Cf.* p. 300. This is an interesting example of a verbal solution which leaves the real question just where it was before.

[11]R. B. Perry, *Present Philosophical Tendencies*, p. 45.

levels.[12] It is important to see here the advance in the new naturalism but at the same time its weakness. Must we not apply here the comment of Perry: "Everything can be claimed for matter, just in proportion as matter is not identified with anything in particular."[13] In other words, you can explain everything by matter, if you import into matter everything that is to be explained.

Samuel Alexander is a distingushed illustration of this effort to use the lower categories of being, together with the idea of emergent evolution, to explain the cosmos.[14] The higher levels are recognized, God himself being that high level which is waiting to be realized. But God is not the explanation of the process; he is at the end, he is its product. "The world actually or historically develops from its first or elementary condition of Space-Time, which possesses no quality except what we agreed to call the spatio-temporal quality of motion." What we have is the emergence of new qualities, as "new complexity of motions comes into existence." But, as with Sellar's matter, here old terms have new meanings. Alexander is not dealing here with time but with Time, and capitalizing a term changes its meaning apparently. Space-Time, we read, is "animated"; Time is "the mind of Space, . . . the generator of qualities, the principle of motion and change."[15]

The new naturalism, then, marks an advance upon the old. It recognizes, nominally at least, qualitative differences, the emergence of what is really new and higher in the levels of mind and spirit, and the qualities and values that go with these. But closer inspection shows its instability and inadequacy. If it admits these higher levels, how can it account for their appearance, or with what right does it leave them out of account when it interprets the universe? So it wavers between

[12]*Evolutionary Naturalism,* Ch. XIII.

[13]*Present Philosophical Tendencies,* p. 69.

[14]In his Gifford Lectures of 1916–1918, on *Space, Time and Deity.*

[15]See *Space, Time and Deity,* Vol. II, pp. 45, 47, 48, and the chapter contributed by Dr. Alexander to the volume *Science and Religion.* (Scribners, 1931.)

two positions: first, trying to get something out of nothing by deriving the spiritual from the material, or space-time, world; second, ascribing to matter or space-time such qualities and activities as wholly change their nature or make of them an indefinite somewhat which can do anything that is needed in the philosophical exigencies of the situation. The new naturalism seems to have moved part way along the road; it must go further if it is to find a ground that will adequately explain what is high as well as what is low, and the process by which this higher came to be.

2. The second group of thinkers finds the principle of explanation on a higher level, that of the organic. Creative evolution, we have seen, involves two elements, continuity and change. The new naturalism puts its main stress upon continuity; the "organicistic" view seeks to do justice to the element of change. "Qualities are to be noted and registered but accepted without pretence of accounting for them," writes Alexander.[16] But while we cannot account *scientifically* for the emergence of higher levels, a real interpretation of our cosmos must go further. The men of the second group seek an adequate ground or explanation for the facts which nature shows. They take the principle of organicism and use it to interpret the cosmos as a whole. This is most fully developed by Whitehead and Smuts.[17] The ultimate energy working in the universe does not operate mechanically or blindly. It is a shaping or fashioning power that tends to inform the ceaseless flux, constantly organizing what is individual and disparate into increasingly significant wholes. Empirical study reveals

[16]*Space, Time and Deity,* II, p. 74.

[17]Note works referred to above. H. N. Wieman, following especially the lead of Whitehead, has sought to develop this in a philosophy of religion. See his *Religious Experience and Scientific Method* and *The Wrestle of Religion with Truth.* An interesting criticism of Smuts' standpoint has been written from the Roman Catholic position, pointing out its basic congruity with theism as well as its failure to reach this. See *A Roman Catholic View of Holism,* by Mgr. Kolbe. The "new naturalism," of course, also uses the idea of organicism.

this trend as fundamental in the universe; we must ask what it means for a philosophical interpretation.

This position is distinctly more favorable to religion. The higher values of life find a creative source in something that is basic in the universe, and there is therefore ground of hope for their survival. A religion based upon this position would show the forward look and the adventurous and creative spirit which belong to modern theism. Neither Smuts nor Whitehead, however, reaches the idea of a personal God. The creative movement inheres in an impersonal principle or an abstract order. There is room here for a religion of aspiration and devotion but not for one of personal fellowship. Nor is it clear that this organizing tendency or aspect of the cosmos implies basic control or ultimate victory. We might call this position naturalistic idealism. It is idealistic because the higher values of life are not viewed as an inexplicable by-product of forces moving on a lower level, but as grounded in a higher activity operative in the universe. It is naturalistic in its overstress on the data of natural science while failing to give due weight to the highest levels of human experience in interpreting the meaning of the whole.

3. There remains then a third possibility in our interpretation of the cosmos: not only to include the third and highest level, but to find at this level, that of the rational and ethical, of persons and values, the clue to the understanding of the whole. This is done by what we may call the new theism. The new theism is empirical; it concerns itself with concrete facts. It would include all the data of the lower levels—the material-mechanistic and the organicistic. But it insists that a true empiricism must take account of *all* the facts. It recognizes in far greater measure than the old theism the meaning of nature, that is, of the space-time world. It recognizes that man roots in this world, physically and psychically; man is organic to nature. But if that be true, if man with his reason and values, with his moral ideals and religious insights, be an integral part of this organic whole, then this whole has a different character. Then the rational and ideal and personal

must be seriously taken into account in any adequate interpretation of the universe. The new theism accordingly insists that the lower cannot account for the higher, that the higher is the key to the whole. So the ultimate ground of the whole must be rational and ethical.

The influence of the new knowledge, however, is seen in the way in which this new theism conceives of the relation of God to his world. The organicistic conception is especially suggestive and influential in shaping the form of the new theism. It still holds to a transcendent God. God is more than an impersonal process of active forces and evolving forms; he is the sustaining energy which moves through all, the conscious purpose which directs, the goal to which it tends, and the eternal Goodness which the finite good is seeking to achieve. But the new theism sees the relation of God to the world as something much more intimate and vital. It turns away from the externalism which set God over against this world as a force operating from without, and from the absolutism which emphasized sheer power working its ends directly and irresistibly. It finds Creative Goodness at work in the world, but that work is done slowly, through long processes of growth and at the cost of toil and struggle. It recognizes God as conditioned or limited in his creativity. Some see this limitation or hindrance as something imposed by the nature of the visible world itself, viewed as a given fact which is not itself capable of further explanation. Others find the ground for such limitations or conditions in the nature of the creative-redemptive process itself; creation they see as achievement by the finite as well as the deed of the Eternal, as demanding a world with a certain spontaneity and autonomy instead of an inert substance shaped by compelling force. The whole discussion shows a certain *rapprochement* between the idealistic and the naturalistic interpretations. The dividing line between inorganic and organic is wearing thin, as is that between matter and spirit. The conception of "Nature" is becoming far richer, more vital, more charged with high meanings.

The newer views that have emerged might be called the new supernaturalism and the higher naturalism. The new supernaturalism not only drops the old dualism and externalism; it has a positive appreciation of the world of nature. Not in spite of nature but in and through nature, the higher spiritual levels have come; and only in intimate relation to this natural world, the world of food and toil, of pleasure and pain, the world of inflexible order, bringing at once tragedy and opportunity, limitation and freedom, can the world of the spirit come to fruition in our human life. In similar fashion the higher naturalism, emphasizing the oneness of all being, must see clearly the reality of its higher levels as new and different, must realize that science can describe the order of becoming but not explain the source of being, must recognize that our cosmos is an organic whole, not a chance conglomeration, and must see that the true understanding of this whole is to be found on its highest levels, not its lowest, in the end to which it moves, not in its crude beginnings.

But while the dividing line is wearing thin, it is still there. The new naturalism, or naturalistic theism, does not arrive at a personal conception of God. It does not make adequate use of the data offered by moral and religious experience as giving us the most significant guidance to the nature of ultimate reality, or give an adequate basis for the moral and spiritual life.[18]

[18]The present situation is interestingly illustrated by J. B. Pratt in his volume, *Naturalism.* He asserts that naturalism is his own position, but these lectures are a systematic criticism of what that term has traditionally meant. His own naturalism is an emphasis on empiricism as against speculation and authoritarianism, and a protest against dualistic supernaturalism. But he wants an empiricism that will embrace the spiritual with the material, and a Nature that includes purpose, mind, and consciousness. There does not seem to be a great difference between this "naturalism" and the new theism. The new supernaturalism here described is to be distinguished from the current neo-supernaturalism which stems from the continental theology. A position similar to that here taken is found in E. E. Aubrey's *Present Theological Tendencies,* pp. 191–205.

Chapter Seven

THE SOCIAL SETTING OF RELIGION

It is not the problems raised by science and philosophy that most directly affect everyday religion, whether as faith or as practice, but the social setting. By that is meant here man's total associated life in its institutions, activities, and ideals, with special reference to political and economic relations. This group life was never so complex, so inclusive, or so profound in its influence as now. Its relation to religion is apparent, and especially to an ethical religion like Christianity. An ethical religion does not simply ask about God, but about man and his needs, about the goods which man seeks, the ways of their attainment, and the relations between man and man. But it is just these questions that concern us in economics, politics, and other forms of social life. Inevitably there will be conflicts here as religion asserts the supremacy of its ideals. At the same time man's social experience and ideals will affect religion, as the history of religions abundantly shows.

Our concern will be primarily with the effect of the social setting upon religion as life rather than as faith. We may well note, however, that such doctrines as those of God and salvation are affected by the experiences and patterns of the social life.[1] That would naturally follow from the character of Judaism and Christianity as prophetic religions, for their distinguishing mark has been to find the clue to the nature of God in the highest ideals exemplified or suggested in human life, and to insist that salvation must be ethical and social.

I. INDUSTRIALISM AND CAPITALISM

It is hardly possible to overestimate the significance of the rise of modern industry for the human scene. It lies back of our chief social problems, with the defense of privilege on the one hand and the demand for economic opportunity and security on the other. It constitutes an invisible government that often wields the real power behind forms of democracy. And far more than is realized, it shapes the ideals and institutions of our cultural life, including religion, education, and recreation.

In the rise of this system scientist, inventor, engineer, entrepreneur, and financier are the great figures. The scientist discovered to us the laws of nature, that is, the ways in which its forces act. Inventor and engineer made use of that knowledge. They harnessed the forces that had remained unused during the million years of man's habitancy of this globe, during which he had bent his back to hard burdens and won a pitiful return. Slowly the economy of poverty yielded to that of abundance. New and unlimited forces were available.

[1]That this has been over-emphasized by some writers should not prevent appreciation of its truth. The idea has been especially developed by Shailer Mathews. See his article, "Theology and Social Psychology," *The Journal of Religion,* July, 1923, and his volumes: *The Atonement and the Social Process, The Growth of the Idea of God,* and *Christianity and Social Process.* It involves, however, a neglect of other significant aspects to say flatly: "The patterns of theology are the patterns of social experience." See article cited, p. 342. *Environmental Factors in Christian History,* edited by Professors McNeill, Spinka, and Willoughby, offers suggestive material. It is in honor of Shirley Jackson Case whose *Evolution of Early Christianity* and other writings represent the more radical viewpoint here.

Mass production of necessities and comforts followed, making them available for increasing numbers, while technical development offered new forms of satisfaction in travel, amusement, and all kinds of comforts and luxuries. Meanwhile masses of population were gathered in congested cities to meet the demands for labor, the control of industry became more absolute and more narrowly centered, and workmen in increasing numbers were separated from the means of production in land and tools and became more and more dependent.

Capitalism is the form of economic organization under which this was carried on. Obviously enormous funds were necessary for the creation and administration of the new instruments of mass production, transportation, and exchange; but the distinctive feature of this capitalism lay in the fact that ownership and control were in the hands, not of the state or some other organization of the social whole, but of private individuals and associations operating under competition and for profit. It is about capitalism in this sense that controversy wages today, particularly at four points. Has it functioned as it should in relation to the distribution of these vastly increased goods? Is such concentration of possession and power desirable? Have its social costs been too great? Has it been the most efficient means of production, or do financial crises and conditions of unemployment indicate that it has broken down and needs either revision or displacement?

Our concern is not with the merits of this system, but with the kind of environment that it has created for religion and the way in which its powerful and permeating forces have conditioned faith and life. The evils to which we must point are none of them absolutely new, but all of them have so developed under capitalism as to furnish a setting strongly inimical to high religion. They cannot be discussed but only indicated, nor can we here consider whether they could be eliminated under a reformed capitalism or would disappear under some other system. Our task is simply historical.

Capitalism has centered power, through financial control even more than through ownership, in the hands of a small group, without development of either adequate means of control by the state or a sense of responsibility on the part of capitalists. Such power tends to produce in its holders arrogance, isolation from their fellowmen, hardness of heart, and ruthlessness. In business, as in state, such power seems to put human nature to too great a strain. In others it is apt to beget uncertainty, fear, and often subserviency and servility.

Its distribution of goods has been glaringly unequal. The Brookings Institute states that in the United States in the "prosperity" year of 1929, nearly twelve million families, forty percent of the population, belonged in one of three classes: starvation, poverty, or the upper range of poverty. At the one extreme this has brought temptations of self-sufficiency, class spirit, pride, selfishness, luxury, dissipation, callousness to human need; at the other it has tended to engender envy, bitterness, and hatred. It has excluded men from full access to the higher values of life; in the varying stages of insecurity, unemployment, and poverty, it has demoralized the spirit and character of men even though they were not left to starvation.

Emphasizing constantly the material goods of life and the power over others which money secures, it has promoted materialism and dulled the sense of the spiritual and the aspiration for higher things. The common and avowed hedonism of today has a close connection with this situation.

In its frank appeal to the motive of individual advantage it has inevitably fostered selfishness as against a due regard for others, and in its basic principle of competition it has tended to turn the world of work into a field of war. The workman competes for a job, the merchant for trade, the manufacturer for his market, and the last step is the arraying of nation against nation, while employer and employee face each other in a struggle over the division of their product. With the close of the period of industrial expansion, the nature of modern industry as a peace-time kind of war becomes more and more evident. It appears in the force that is employed as labor demands its right to organize over against the long organized capital, and the force tends to become violent. War justifies all means; so in business we find misleading and misrepresentative advertising, the labor spy and the *agent provocateur,* and the exploitation of the investor by "high finance." The development of selfishness and callousness is inevitable and is furthered by the increasingly impersonal character of industry. How many men, individually gracious and kind and even generous, are caught in the machine, driven by the demand for profit, which is the life blood of the system, and compelled to be "hardboiled," and to exploit men in this industrial warfare in the same ruthless way in which in war the military machine deals with men.

And finally we must note that war becomes more and more the inevitable result of such a system. For the chief protagonists in the fierce industrial warfare of today are no longer individuals or corporations but nations, nations striving for food and raw materials and markets, fighting with tariffs and currency manipulation, the older imperialisms holding on to their early gained advantages, the less privileged demanding their place in the economic sun and finally appealing to arms to enforce their demands. How can you have a competitive industrial system without involving the nations, and how can you expect nations to disarm so long as their very life is contingent upon self-assertion within such a competitive system?

Men of religion often forget that it is the ideals and activities and ends of the world of work that claim the major attention of men six days in the week and usually reach into the seventh. We need not discount the advantages that industrial development has brought in human welfare, nor overlook the fine qualities of many who have worked under this system; but we must recognize the fact that in the principle of competition on which it builds, the motive of individual advantage to which it appeals, the awards of power and possession which it holds up as the ends for which men are to strive, our economic order is distinctly to be contrasted with Christianity. Is it any wonder that "in such a society Christianity is gasping for breath?"[1]

II. THE NEW NATIONALISM

The development of the nation-state is, with the rise of industrialism, the most obvious feature of modern history. It followed inevitably upon the breakdown of the earlier and looser unity that had been secured in the western world by empire and Church. It was not a return to racialism for the new states were composites of various racial strains. These more compact and unified political entities were an obvious necessity in the new economic and political situation.

The development of internationalism, coming later, was not as such a conflicting movement. The forces behind it in important respects were the same: the presence of common interests and dangers, and the need of finding effective expression of this common life and effective means of common action. The new common interests, cutting across all lines of national division, included communication, travel, manufacture and trade, as well as the more distinctly cultural concerns of science, art, education, and religion. So there developed instruments such as the League of Nations, the World Court, and many non-political agencies. Internationalism has been hampered by inertia, ignorance, prejudice, selfishness, and fear. So far as it has been motivated by ideals of the solidarity of human interests, of cooperation, and of a common concern for peace and justice, it has been an expression alike of democratic faith and Christian ethics; it is simply the application of these principles to the widening sphere of man's associated life. On the other hand, much of the international activity in the way of conferences, pacts,

[1]E. Stanley Jones, *Christ's Alternative to Communism,* p. 32.

leagues, and courts has been simply due to the pressure of obvious danger. "The devil was sick, the devil a monk would be." And the difficulty of the new internationalism lay right here: men wanted the advantages of the new way without surrendering the special privileges of the old. The spirit of humanity had not been transformed. At the close of the first world war the western powers wanted the peace that would come through disarmament, but of other nations not of themselves; they wanted to put an end to the era of conquest and exploitation, but they wished likewise to freeze the *status quo* and assure themselves of what they already possessed.

Nationalism presents two broadly distinguishable underlying conceptions. The one is quite congruous with the international point of view. For it the state is one among various social institutions in which the common life of men is expressed and by which their common interests are served. Modern conditions have greatly increased the functions of the state and its importance, especially on the economic side. But ideally the state is simply the larger community, whose relations are basically human and personal. Ethically considered it should maintain essentially the relations shown by the family. Its function, as with the family, is to guide this larger life in respect of those interests where common action is needed, realizing, however, that it has no higher ends to serve than just these human concerns in which all share alike.

The new nationalism as expressed in the extreme form of the fascist or Nazi state sharply differs from this first conception. Its essential features seem to be the following: (1) The state is not a means toward human welfare, but an end for which human beings are means; it is a superentity, sometimes mystically conceived and with a racial emphasis. Power and glory are its goal, and to share in these is the citizen's highest privilege. (2) It is an autocratic state, whose absolute authority resides simply in the will of the Leader or his representatives. (3) It is a military state, depending upon force, or threat of force, not only in relation to other nations but to its own subjects. (4) It is totalitarian. Here it differs strikingly from the imperialisms of history which never even attempted this. Rome was satisfied, in the main, if order was kept, taxes paid, required military service rendered, and threatening subversive movements suppressed. Politics (only one party and that under rigid control from above), industry (including labor, management, and returns to capital), education, recreation, radio and press, and all sources of information are under absolute control in this new autocracy. The Church is to be strictly subordinated to the state, which sharply limits its freedom to preach and denies its right to give instruction to its youth and to carry on its youth organizations. There is a virtual enslavement of the spirit; the state determines what men can know, and how they shall think and feel.

The effect of this upon religion appears at two points. First, and most obvious, is its bearing upon the Church, which seems to face the alternative of compromise or extinction: either to give up its central function of proclaiming freely and fully the truth of God and training its youth in the Christian way, or to suffer elimination. The indirect effect is one that works more slowly but penetrates more deeply. The totalitarian state, whether fascist or communist, cannot rely simply upon the compulsion of external force with its people. It pays this unwilling tribute to the new age and the democracy which it scorns, that it knows it cannot rule its people without consent of mind and support of spirit. With no scruple as to method in regard to suppression or propaganda, and with skillful use of every dramatic device, it takes over the total training of its people almost from infancy. And its concern is not simply with health, knowledge, and technical skill, but to determine faith, ideals, and devotion, making them one for the whole people. In actual fact, it is trying to supplant the Christian religion with a type of neo-paganism. With the older generation its success can be only partial—the early Christian training still remains. But it is a different matter with youth, and one must seriously ask what a generation of such inclusive and intensive regimentation of the spirit will bring about.

To realize the significance of all this for religion it is necessary to note the radical opposition of the Nazi-fascist ideology and ethos to that of Christianity. It represents a frontal attack upon the Christian faith and way and the most direct assault which the Church has met since its first persecutions. The elements of any pagan philosophy of life are threefold, corresponding to the three great questions which man raises: as to the highest good which he is to seek, the supreme power which he is to trust, and the final rule for his life. For paganism, the good is material, the power is force, the rule is self-interest; and this represents fairly the compound of secularism, militarism, and national selfishness for which this movement stands. That does not mean that it has no place for idealism and devotion; it has, indeed, demanded and secured these in large measure, especially from youth. It asks men to endure hardship, to forget individual interests in the thought of the nation, to sacrifice on the altar of unquestioning obedience to autocratic power the treasures of freedom for which generations had struggled. But all this is in relation to the individual; the state itself is "beyond good and evil," and in relation to other peoples, as to minorities within itself, it knows no law of God or truth or justice or mercy, only its own will and the measure of force it can command. And all this, so far as it succeeds, means to just that extent the corruption of the spirit of the people. As to its ideology, it will suffice to point out two aspects. One is its concept of man, seen not merely in its crude racialism, engendering pride, arrogance, scorn, and cruelty toward others, but in its underlying conception, including its own people, which sees men as property and instruments of the state, unfit for self-government and having no essential rights as human beings.

In this total situation, then, it is not just democracy that is at stake; it is Christianity. That is recognized by the fascist-

Nazi leaders. "We or they," Mussolini puts it, in words taken by Hamilton Fish Armstrong for the title of a volume of penetrating discussion. And Hans Keerl, head of the Reich Ministry for Church Affairs, said in an address to Protestant and Catholic Church leaders: "The primacy of the state over the church must be recognized. The primary assumptions of the state as we have it today, expressed in race, blood, and soil, must be inviolable for the church too. . . . The question of the divinity of Christ is ridiculous and unessential. A new authority has arisen as to what Christ and Christianity really are–Adolf Hitler."[2]

The fascist states are important for our consideration because they represent such large population areas and because they show what the new nationalism means when carried to its logical conclusion. It is, however, equally important to recognize that the spirit of the new nationalism extends far beyond fascist realms. It is seen in nationalistic pride, in growing racial prejudices, in the violation of civil liberties, in the effort at economic self-sufficiency and the raising of economic barriers against others, and in growing militaristic establishments and militaristic spirit. More particularly it appears in the assumption of an ultimate supremacy of the state where there may be conflict with moral conscience or religious faith, and in the development of "patriotism" as a quasi-religious cult. The exploitation of this point of view by certain economic groups and privileged classes, as well as by individuals seeking personal advancement and power, adds to the danger, and repeats the pattern of fascist countries. Looking thus, not just at Japan and Germany, but at the total western world, Laurence Housman declares that, "Nationalism is far more the religion of every nation than Christianity. . . . In the world today, Christ has been made the parasite of nationalism. . . . If we go on making each nation a God–Christianity will die of it."[3] And John Foster Dulles, writing after

[2]See *From U-Boat to Pulpit,* by Martin Niemöller, p. 217.

[3]*St. Martin's Review,* April, 1931. Quoted by Edward Shillito in *Nationalism, Man's Other Religion.*

the second world war began, says: "To great masses of mankind their personified state is, in effect, their god; it represents the supreme object of their devotion; its power and dominion are, to them, sacred, and to subtract therefrom is akin to sacrilege."[4]

III. COMMUNISM

It is not the theory of communism as such that we consider here, but simply the significance for religion in Russia of the Union of Soviet Socialist Republics. It is of interest to us because we have here another totalitarian system, which seeks to shape not merely state and industry, but the total thought and life of these peoples, because it includes one eighth of the earth's surface and one tenth of the human race, and because we have here a social experiment that is profoundly affecting the thought and life of other lands.

The first fact to be noted is the well known anti-religious attitude of the Soviet leaders. Religion, we are told, is an opiate, deadening the minds of people to the injustice against which they should revolt, making them submissive when they should be revolutionary, diverting them from the real tasks of earth by directing their thoughts to heaven, bidding them rely upon supernatural forces when they should be turning to science and machinery and engineering, and operating through an institution (the Church) that is allied with autocracy and exploitation. The second fact is the avowed secularism of Russian communism. That does not mean necessarily materialism, for its leaders are concerned with higher human values. But neither the values which they consider nor the forces to which they appeal have any place for religion or a spiritual philosophy of life; and this secularism, that sees life purely in terms of the finite, is systematically inculcated in a system of education that includes old and young. The propaganda is directed against all religion, including the most lib-

[4]"The Church's Contribution Toward a Warless World," *Religion in Life*, Winter, 1940.

eral and socially minded, so that the new generation as a whole is alike anti-religious and ignorant of what the Christian religion is. A third feature is the denial of freedom, as, for example, in religious education and in political organization. No dissenting political organization is permitted here any more than under fascism; the control is autocratic. Finally, there is the frank acceptance of the method of force, not only in the initial revolution but in the continued suppression of all dissent and in ruthless "liquidation" of individuals, groups, and classes that stand in the way of the movement or of the leader in control.

It has often been pointed out that the anti-religious attitude of the Soviet Government must be understood in the light of the anti-social character of the pre-revolution Russian Church and its identification with the old czarist regime. And it may be argued that, in principle, communism involves no necessary hostility to religion and has, indeed, a kinship with Christian ethics in its ideal of a common good, its emphasis on the principle of cooperation, its denial of racialism, and its goal of economic justice. It is our simple task, however, to deal with the actual situation. And here we note, particularly since Stalin's control, the increasing approximation to the other totalitarian regimes in terms of nationalism, imperialism, and militarism, with a consistent pursuit of power politics and the total disregard of the rights of smaller nations. Thus fascism and communism force us to a like conclusion, that autocracy, whatever its avowed aims may be, is destructive of the highest social values, and that totalitarianism is necessarily in direct conflict with Christianity.

As with fascism, Russian communism has a certain religious quality; quite consciously, apparently, the leaders are furthering ideas and activities which might serve as a substitute for religion. There is a distinct messianic faith, a half-mystical belief in communism as the bringer of the new earth. There is a call for sacrifice and absolute devotion. There are sacred scriptures which must not be questioned and an authorized interpretation whose acceptance is equally required. It has new processions in place of the old, and Lenin's tomb is here although the miracle-working bones of the saints are discarded. In this whole situation Christianity has little chance for actual presentation to the thought of the people, not to speak of acceptance.

Modern industrialism, fascism, and communism, all three, though in varying measure and in different fashion, represent conditions unfavorable to Christianity. But while the movement of events in the twentieth century has heightened this conflict, it did not create it. That conflict between the social order and the Christian ideal has been here through the centuries. If now it has been brought out more sharply, that may be in part because we see more clearly what the Christian religion really means. In his wide-ranging volume of personal experiences, Pierre van Paassen tells of a conversation with the veteran French colonial administrator, Marshal Lyautey. How would you have dealt with a man like Jesus if you had been in Pilate's place, he inquired of this former governor of Morocco. Pilate did right, came the answer. Pilate's task was to maintain the *pax Romana;* what else could he do? "In that kingdom of which Jesus dreamed and spoke there was no room for Cæsar, or for Pilate, or for the princes and mighty ones. . . . If Jesus' ideas had been translated into reality, not only in Judea, but in the world at large, . . . I do not think *nous autres Français,* we would be in Morocco now, or the British in India."[1]

IV. DEMOCRACY

The term democracy is not used here with the limited reference to political institutions, but rather as representing a social faith, or philosophy of society. It involves a definite conception of man, of his nature and rights and obligations, of the nature of society, its proper ends, and the instruments

[1] *Days of Our Years,* pp. 144–149.

needed to secure these ends. As such it represents the most notable development of social thought in modern history.

The older social philosophy was based on ideas of privilege and power and permanent status that made it aristocratic, autocratic, and static. The common man was viewed politically as subject, a being to be ruled, economically as property or tool, a creature to be used. Whatever one may think of the present-day resurgence of autocracy, or of present-day capitalism and its organized privilege, the long view of history shows a steady, though slow, movement toward another position. It began as long ago as the Hebrew prophets and rooted in their idea of God. For them he was not ultimate essence or abstract idea or order, as with the Greeks, nor impersonal being as with Indian mysticism; he was personal, ethical being and as such akin to man. His supreme concern was with justice and mercy, and he included the humblest and poorest, "the fatherless and the widow." The same idea and its implications for life became even more clear with Jesus. With this went a new evaluation of the common man, who outweighed the whole world of things, for whose treatment God called kings and rich men to account; and a new confidence in man, whom God called to high loyalty and summoned to stand upon his feet that the Eternal himself might reason with him. It takes generations for such ideas to penetrate mind and imagination, and still longer for them to shape conduct and institutions. But the long view shows a profound change which has affected the institutions of family, state, industry, and religion. Opposed in most respects to capitalism and fascism, it constitutes one of the most important though often intangible elements in the present-day climate of religion.

How shall this social philosophy be designated? We cannot use humanism, despite the verbal fitness of the term, for this has always had a limited meaning. In the Renaissance humanism was more literary, concerned first of all with the classical studies, *litterae humaniores,* and the revival of the classical outlook upon life, with no social-ethical implications. The modern forms of humanism, too, are limited in scope and differ widely in meaning. One type is cultural, following the classical tradition. A second is more philosophical, a pragmatism that looks to F. C. S. Schiller, William James, and John Dewey. A third represents the effort to find within this pragmatist position a religion of social idealism on a naturalistic, or non-theistic basis. Humanitarianism is even less adequate. For while it seeks to soften cruelty and mitigate evils, it does not meet the basic issue of social justice or proceed creatively, and it often becomes mere sentimentalism. Liberalism is too vague a term, too much lacking in content of positive principles, and too much tied up in popular thought with passing economic, political, and religious theories. Harold J. Laski in *The Rise of Liberalism* has pointed out the connection of social liberalism with the rise of capitalism, and its meaning as the claimed right of a rapidly growing middle-class group to produce at the lowest rate and sell at the highest price without restraint from state regulation or from the demands of labor. Thus liberalism meant individualism and freedom meant the exploitation of the weak by the strong.

The best single term that remains is democracy, used in the broad sense indicated above. There is difference of opinion as to the instruments by which the ends of democracy are to be reached, but its principles can be briefly stated. The first two are most generally accepted as the basic elements of the democratic ideal, but the validity and necessity of the others grow increasingly apparent.

1. Human personality is sacred. The test of all social measures and the concern of all society must be the welfare of men—not of an institution, whether Church or state, not of a class or a group, noble or Nordic or superman, but of men as men. As Kant declared, man is always to be treated as an end, never as a means. We may recognize realistically the wide differences among men, individual, racial, in native endowment, and in social function; but the common hu-

manity which unites is more significant than all that divides.

2. The highest good includes freedom and can be achieved only by the way of freedom. In other words, it is both end and means. It involves the discovery of truth instead of the passive acceptance of the opinion of others, the vision of good and the setting of goals, some share in plan and direction, not only of the individual life but of the associated life, and in industry as well as in the state. It is man's right in all the important aspects of life to live as a rational being and not as a robot. Such freedom does not eliminate self-discipline; as rational freedom it demands it. The principle of leadership is not excluded, nor the need of delegated power, nor the necessary limitation of individual action by the rights of others and the requirements of the common life. It does mean that freedom is itself a good, an essential element in the life of a rational, moral, self-respecting being, and that its loss is not compensated for by safety of person or security of job.

3. Democracy involves confidence in man and in the power of truth and right as ultimately decisive; it is an idealistic faith. That does not mean a romantic idealization of human nature. It does not mean mere "self-expression" in education, or the assumption in politics that the voice of the people is the voice of God. The evil of the individual and the follies of the masses are before our eyes. Humanity is in the making. Political and industrial democracy involves nothing less than the training of a whole people. But democracy holds that individual and group can thus be trained, that men are susceptible to rational and moral appeal, and that, with education and free and full discussion, we can better trust ultimate decisions to the whole group than turn absolute authority over to some one or few holding their place by the chance of heredity, by skill in amassing wealth, or by ruthlessness in seizing power.

4. Democracy involves the idea of social solidarity and the principle of obligation. At this point it is clearly opposed to the individualistic conception of the old social liberalism,

both political and economic.[1] But human life is group life. The principle of organicism, running through nature, comes to its fullest expression in human society. True, men must never be mere tools, even for the group; but the life of the individual is achieved only in the life of the whole, and for that life all must work together. The obverse of every right is a duty, of every privilege a responsibility. Freedom itself is not possible without self-rule, nor achievement without devotion to the common end.

5. Democracy brings a new principle of authority. Whether in politics, ethics, industry, or religion, it is the repudiation of the old principle of external, or autocratic, authority. It stands for autonomy, for self-determination. In religion and ethics it means the free faith of an inner conviction, the free expression of a transformed inner spirit, the free choice of a supreme devotion: "I delight to do thy will, O my God; yea, thy law is within my heart." In industry it is the demand not only for a fair share in the proceeds of production, but for a voice in determining conditions and a right to some control of its instruments. In politics it is the demand that the rule of government shall be founded upon the decision of the people reached by discussion and resting upon intelligent conviction. Yet there is still need of authority. Little recognized by the mass, it becomes increasingly clear that autonomy, for the group as for the individual, does not mean the *creation* of the law, the *nomos,* but rather its discovery and its free adoption. The opposition is not to authority as such but to that which is imposed without conviction and assent. The voice of the people is not the voice of God; the will of the

[1] "The watchwords of the nineteenth century," says A. N. Whitehead, "have been struggle for existence, competition, class warfare, commercial antagonism between nations, military warfare." He ascribes this to an exclusive attention to one aspect of the doctrine of evolution, and to the construing of the struggle for existence into a gospel of hate. (*Science and the Modern World,* p. 288.) The temper is rightly indicated here but its background is more economic and political than philosophic and scientific.

majority may mean the worst of tyrannies. By law is here meant, not the rules created by government, but those eternal principles of truth and justice which are necessary bases of human life and are grounded in the very nature of the universe itself. To discover these, to choose them freely, to seek some expression of these in institutions and law, this is the task of democracy, and it is the only way of social salvation. Without a common authority thus discerned and chosen, there can be no security, no freedom, no rights for the individual. Thus the recognition of a common higher authority in international relations is perhaps the crucial problem for the race today, the alternative to which would seem to be a common destruction as the result of our present anarchy. The democratic, or free, way of life is never possible for society without spiritual authority. Authority thus conceived conditions and completes the idea of freedom. There can be no real freedom without submission to authority. Such submission involves that constant self-rule, that persistent discipline and restraint which is perhaps the weakest single point with individual and group in the practice of the democratic way of life.

If we inquire as to the progress of these ideals, the present day exhibits a clash of contending forces and a strong reaction against political democracy. The situation, however, demands analysis if we would understand it. (1) The forms of political democracy, or at least of current parliamentarianism, seem to be unequal to that task of economic planning, or are assumed to exclude the centralized and flexible control which is being more and more demanded of the state. But deputed and centralized power is not inconsistent with democracy. The test is whether that authority rests upon a grant by the people, is used for the advantage of the people, and is ultimately responsible to the people. (2) We are told that democracy has failed because the people are ignorant, incompetent, and indifferent, and so have allowed the control to pass to an invisible government of party bosses and privileged groups. But the fault lies here in the imperfect conception of what democracy is and demands. The *forms* of social organization never solve human problems; they only offer the opportunity of solution. The road of democracy is a long road and a hard one. It makes high demands on the people; it asks for self-control, intelligence, and unselfish devotion. It involves the training of a people in spirit as well as in mind. Political democracy must join the realism with which Christianity sees men as they are, to Christianity's faith in what man can become, and in the forces of truth and justice and good will. And we must make plain the democratic goal: not individual "liberty" in a ruthless fight for wealth and privilege and power, but a cooperative effort in devotion to social justice. (3) Democracy as a social faith, like every ideal conception of life including religion itself, is suffering from the anti-idealistic and anti-humanistic forces of our time, from the prevalent cynicism, scepticism, and despair, and the repudiation of spiritual values and authority. The immediate source of this may be found in the first World War, with its demoralizing influences and its stimulus to militarism and nationalism; but the deeper roots of it must be sought in a growing secularism and in an economic order that emphasizes the competitive strife for individual advantage, a system whose nature and consequences are not changed when the competing units become groups or nations or even international blocs. (4) Whatever the present situation, humanity that has once envisioned these ideals and tasted these goods will not permanently surrender them. What we see, indeed, is the insistence that democracy shall be extended to another and even more important field. The demand for economic justice is the expression of the very essence of democracy as a social faith; it is the insistence that the social order is here for men and not men for the social order, that the economic system shall minister to men and not exploit them. There is hardly a country today in which profound changes are not taking place looking to these ends, or in which the power of these ideals is not at least being recognized by the lip service that is paid to them. Fascism itself, the antithesis of democracy and the foe of high religion, got into power both in Italy and Germany on the plea of such service to men.

What is even more necessary today is to see the dependence of our democratic hopes upon the moral ideals and spiritual forces of high religion. No one can read the prophets, the gospels, and Paul without recognizing the close kinship between the basic ideals of democracy and the ethical side of Christianity. Here, indeed, is where democracy got its underlying beliefs as to freedom, justice, solidarity, cooperation, and above all the sacredness of human personality.

But there is more than moral kinship here; there is an indication of the necessary foundations of democracy. The threatened bankruptcy of modern democracy is due, not so much to imperfect institutions, as to a loss of faith and a failure of spiritual resources. Religion, wrote James Bryce in the closing chapter of his *Modern Democracies,* "has been for the finer and more sensitive spirits the motive power in the past. Governments that have ruled by Force and Fear have been able to live without moral sanctions or to make their subjects believe that those sanctions consecrated them, but no free government has ever yet so lived and thriven: for it is by a reverence for the Powers Unseen and Eternal which impose these sanctions that the powers of evil have been, however imperfectly, kept at bay and the fabric of society kept together." And in the *New York Herald Tribune* for Dec. 17, 1938, Walter Lippmann writes on "The Forgotten Foundation": "What separates us from the totalitarian regimes is our belief that man does not belong to the state." Our fathers said "that man belonged to his Creator, and that since he was, therefore, an immortal soul, he possessed inalienable rights as a person which no power on earth had the right to violate . . . The treatment of human beings as things, as the mere instruments of power and ambition, is without a doubt the consequence of the decay of the belief in man as something more than an animal animated by highly conditioned reflexes and chemical reactions. For, unless man is something more than that, he has no rights that any one is bound to respect, and there are no limitations on his conduct which he is bound to obey. . . . Perhaps the ordeal through which mankind is passing may be necessary. For it may be the only way in which modern man can recover the faith by which free and civilized people must live." Democracy has come out of a spiritual faith; can it survive without it? Is there a direct correlation in our day between the decline of democracy and the loss of that faith?

Part Three

THE KNOWLEDGE OF GOD

Chapter Eight

KNOWLEDGE, REVELATION, AND TRADITION

IF RELIGION be man's life as lived in the light of God and by the help of God, then the question of how man may know God is of supreme importance. The problem here envisaged, it should be noted at the very start, is not that of grounds for belief in God, nor is it that of knowing about God; it is knowing God, and that has a peculiarly significant and vital sense for religion. On the other hand, the effort to treat the problem of religious knowledge as something that can be separated from the general problem of knowledge, whether by appeal to revelation or to some special mystical sense, is mistaken. In order to define our problem, then, we must first ask what we mean by knowledge and how knowledge is possible.

I. SOME THEORIES OF KNOWLEDGE

1. The simplest answer to our question is that of naïve realism, the common-sense position. Knowing is a direct apprehension of the world as it is. The senses are open doors, as it were, through which the world of sight and sound comes in. Knowing means a one-way traffic; the mind simply arranges what it thus receives.

2. Criticism gives a second answer, and Kant is its great representative. It was Kant's great service to analyze what was involved in knowing, and to make clear that strict realism had not even envisaged the problem. Knowing is never a

passive affair, not even when I look at this book. It is a creative activity, and I enter in at every step to shape the process. It is a two-way road: the world without beats upon sense and understanding, but I supply the forms of space and time in which I perceive this world of things, as well as those thought relations in which I think things together and make the world one.

3. Scepticism is the easy conclusion that some draw from this. If knowledge is my creation, what right have I to assume that my ideas correspond to the world without? So we are forever shut up within ourselves and knowledge can at best be only of appearances. That will be true of the material world as of the spiritual.

4. Idealism seeks to transcend this difficulty. Knowledge, it says, is indeed my creation, but it is real nevertheless. For the world and I are akin; it is not a wholly other world of things, but is of the same kind of being as myself, that is, a world of idea, or spirit, or personality. In any case, I find in myself the clue to the real world, and I can know it because we are akin. Here knowing, with some at least, tends once more to become a one-way road, only this time it is from within outward.

5. Here, however, we are met by a theory which would rule out this whole discussion as futile and irrelevant. That is the position of instrumentalism, the left-wing pragmatism sponsored by John Dewey. For him this debate about knowledge as correspondence between my ideas here and the world out there is an unreal issue. The concept to which Dewey's thinking is oriented is that of life; his philosophy, one might say, is biologically minded. The great words of traditional philosophy were reality and knowledge. Its great questions were: What is ultimate Reality and how can we know it? Dewey calls this the spectator conception of knowledge. He begins with the conception of man as furnished by biological evolution. Man is a creature who has developed and maintained his place through a long experience of active and suc-

cessful adjustment to his environment. Knowing is a part of the process of living, of an intercourse with the world in which the whole man is engaged and not simply his intellect. Our ideas are simply plans of action. Their significance is prospective and practical (in relation to future action), not retrospective and theoretical (as a sum of conclusions gained in the past). The test of ideas is how they work in solving the problems of living. Knowing is just "responsive behavior," distinguished from other responses by "the part played in it by anticipation and prediction." "Knowledge is the act, stimulated by this foresight, of securing and averting consequences."[1] Our task then is not to contemplate ultimate Reality, the perfect Being that we may call the Absolute, or God, but to consider the "intelligently thought-out possibilities of the existent world which may be used as methods for making over and improving it."

II. CONCERNING KNOWLEDGE AND THE KNOWLEDGE OF GOD

1. The plan of our study excludes detailed criticism of these viewpoints and permits of only a brief constructive statement. We may first summarize our position in regard to knowledge:

(1) Knowing is not a special activity or "faculty" of man; it is an aspect of the total process of living. Life at every level, from amoeba to man, is a matter of relations, relations that require constant action and adjustment. The world acts upon man; man acts upon the world. In this ex-

[1]*Creative Intelligence,* by John Dewey and Others, p. 61. This chapter on "A Recovery of Philosophy" and the little volume on *Reconstruction in Philosophy* form the best introduction for an understanding of Dewey's general standpoint. In *Human Nature and Conduct, The Quest for Certainty,* and *A Common Faith* we have works especially significant to the student of theology. *The Philosophy of John Dewey,* edited by P. A. Schilpp, gives the most thorough critical survey and includes a comprehensive closing statement by Mr. Dewey.

perience man comes to know his world. If he did not he could not adjust himself to it, and could not survive. We may call this the knowledge of acquaintance. It is the kind of knowledge that is most common in life and most significant. This acquaintance by active intercourse is the way in which a farmer knows soil, seed, sun, and rain, in which the carpenter knows plane and wood, in which a man knows his friends. In knowing, as thus vitally conceived, the whole man must participate; sense perception, reason, æsthetic appreciation, moral insight, spiritual awareness, and the activities of heart and will, all must enter in. This knowledge of acquaintance does not exclude the mind but demands it. It is not something passively received nor a matter of unthinking response. So far as it is really knowledge, it demands reflection and interpretation, and issues in the effort at expression in ideas. It is the capacity for this that has lifted man above all other creatures.

(2) Such knowledge is not absolute. Our ideas are not copies or reproductions of the world without; that is not what knowing means. But it is real knowledge. It is something more than the working arrangement of the instrumentalist. We do really know what our world is. For it is in their behavior that things are truly known; a thing is what it does. There is much about water that I do not know. The physicist will not say what its ultimate nature is. Yet I do know water by the way it behaves; I know it as solid and liquid and vapor, as life-giving and at times life-destroying, as seen in cooling drink and rainbow's beauty.

(3) It is a mistake to think that we have a direct knowledge of the physical world while our ideas of the spiritual world are a mere guess or unfounded wish. There is no knowledge of any kind without the mind's work of interpretation. "Sensations are not parts of any knowledge. . . . They are stimuli to reflection and inference."[1] Of the scientists who reflect at all upon this ultimate problem, some hold that physics gives us no knowledge of ultimate reality; all

[1]John Dewey, *Reconstruction in Philosophy*, pp. 89, 90.

would agree that our results are expressed in symbols which are not simple copies or models of the real, as some thought at an earlier time. Eddington has said: "In comparing the certainty of things spiritual and things temporal, let us not forget this—Mind is the first and most direct thing in experience. . . . And if today you ask a physicist what he has finally made out the ether or electron to be, the answer will not be in terms of billiard balls or flying wheels or anything concrete; he will point instead to a number of symbols and a set of mathematical equations which they satisfy. What do the symbols stand for? The mysterious reply is given that physics is indifferent to that; it has no means of probing beneath the symbolism."[2] But if the scientist, *qua* scientist, can go no further, that need not represent our total position. Schrödinger, the great physicist, is reported once to have said: "Sometimes very valuable results are obtained when we don't know what we are talking about."[3] Would it not be truer then to say as religionists and scientists: In our active intercourse we deal successfully with our world and are convinced that we know it, physical and spiritual, though our symbols, alike in science and theology, at best can only set forth in part what the world of our experience means?

Yet my knowledge is not less true knowledge because it is subjective, because these are *my* percepts and *my* ideas, and because in shaping them I have used analogies from my own experience. What else could I use? No man can jump out of his skin, and the man of science no more than the man of religion. All our thinking is necessarily anthropomorphic. That is as true when we think of things as when we think of God. "The idea of causation is derived from the experience of human exertion. . . . If science is to avoid every suggestion of anthropomorphism, it must be dumb. Does not the word 'law' sin in the same way as cause? And energy?"[4]

[2]*Science and the Unseen World,* pp. 37, 30.
[3]*New York Times Book Review,* June 24, 1934.
[4]A. Wolf, *Essentials of Scientific Method,* p. 111.

(4) The great error against which we must constantly guard is that of an artificial separation. We have seen the error of intellectualism: separating the knowing process from the total process of living. Here we must emphasize the even greater error: separating man from his world. We first set man over against his world and then attempt the impossible task of bridging the gulf between man the knower and the alien world that stands over against him, between subjective idea and objective thing. The gulf is one that we have made: in real life every man feels himself one with his world in intimate knowing and living relation. Man is organic to his world. That is why we need not be frightened by the bogey of anthropomorphism; man can use the analogies of his own experience in interpreting his world because he and his world belong together in one organic whole. The evolutionary viewpoint has long since made us familiar with the kinship of man and his world on the chemico-biological side. What we are slower to see is that man as rational, moral, and religious being is also organic to his world. If, for example, his very blood is witness to the fact that the sea was once his habitat,[5] then his relatedness on the higher levels must also be recognized. And if his spiritual nature has developed in a like process of interaction with his world as has his physical, then his knowledge on both these levels will be something real, a part of that total life process of the organic whole.

2. As regards the knowledge of God:

(1) The knowledge of God, like all other knowledge, must come by way of life. It will be the knowledge of acquaintance, not the knowledge of information, knowing God and not merely knowing about God. Religion will therefore hold the primacy here, not theology or philosophy, not tradition or authority. Tradition will be needed to serve religion, theology to interpret it; but the source of knowledge will be man's living experience in fellowship with God.

(2) Religion has its own ways of knowledge and they are determined by the nature of its subject matter, God. There

[5]William Beebe, *Harper's Magazine,* April, 1933.

are underlying principles that will hold good here as in all knowing. Observation and experiment, reflection and criticism are as much needed here as elsewhere; but if religion is a matter of life, of active commerce with the object that is known, then the nature of that object will determine what the relations are through which it can be known. If men have found that faith and moral loyalty are conditions for the knowledge of God, then that fact is not altered by the other fact that these attitudes and ways are not required of the biologist.

III. REVELATION AND EXPERIENCE

To the question, how man can know God, the Christian Church has always answered, by revelation; we know God because he has revealed himself to men. That answer is widely questioned today and the idea of revelation itself is far from clear in the minds of men. At the right are those who hold tenaciously to the idea but assert it in a form which the modern man cannot accept. At the left are those who either eliminate it or practically ignore it in their emphasis on human experience and discovery. It is necessary then that we should ask what this idea of revelation really means, and we begin with the form it took in traditional theology.

1. In the main, traditional theology, Protestant and Catholic, was one in its idea of revelation. There is a certain knowledge of God, it held, which man can gain, not indeed without the help of God, but through reason and conscience and the study of nature. But such "natural" knowledge is insufficient for salvation. For this there is needed a supernatural revelation through which we learn of Incarnation, Atonement, and the Trinity. This revelation is given in the Bible. More commonly men simply said, the Bible *is* this revelation.[1] The conception of the way in which God revealed

[1] See Wilhelm and Scannell, *Manual of Catholic Theology,* I, 3–13; Charles Hodge, *Systematic Theology,* I, 22–26, 363–365. *Cf.* the same authors as to the difference between the Protestant and Roman Catholic positions, and on the latter point note especially W. P. Paterson, *The Rule of Faith.*

himself and the nature of his revelation were determined by the concept of God and his relation to the world. God had two ways of acting: (1) through the ordinary "natural" processes, (2) by direct action, that is (as these terms were understood), in strictly supernatural, or miraculous fashion. Whatever means God employed in this last case, the action was strictly his own. Thus in the case of the Bible, there was more than an illumining and inspiring of the minds of men; God himself determined the ideas, indeed, the very words that were set down. It followed then, since the Bible was the direct work of a perfect God, it must itself be perfect, an infallible book in every part.

We do not need to discuss this theory of revelation but only to indicate what has happened to it. (1) Historical study has disproved it. The study of the Bible shows that it is not such a book. These writings are immersed in the stream of history; they reflect historical situations and root in human experience. They take color from their age and surroundings and show a clear process of development. (2) This theory misconceives Christianity in thinking of it as a sum of doctrine. In this intellectualism which sees religion primarily as a matter of ideas, orthodoxism made the same mistake as rationalism, except that the one thought of doctrines communicated by God and the other of a system achieved by man. (3) More fundamental is the fact that we have gained (or regained) a truer conception of the relation of God to his world. The old idea was too dualistic and mechanical. Human discovery and divine revelation were set over against each other. It made inspiration a matter of absolute control, and that implied a mechanical instead of a moral-spiritual process.

As a result, the whole idea of revelation has been vigorously repudiated in certain quarters. There is only one way by which man can know, we are told, and that is by his own patient observation, study, experiment, and interpretation. The belief in revelation is not only untrue but harmful; it makes men satisfied where they should be pressing on toward increasing knowledge, and dogmatic where they should be humble and teachable. Hence religion should give up the idea of revelation. But this objection makes the same mistake as the old theory. Both conceive of revelation as the communication of ideas. Both set the divine and human over against each other, assuming that divine revelation and human discovery exclude each other. We need, therefore, a fresh study of the whole matter, inquiring what revelation really means and how divine and human are here related.

2. The idea of revelation is a vital element in all prophetic religion. The real issue is not that of belief in revelation but of faith in a living and personal God. For pantheism, for all abstract idealisms, and for that "pan-nomism" whose God is simply the cosmic order, there can be no talk of revelation. The universe in each case is simply the whole which man, the part, is trying to understand. Knowing God is much the same as knowing the atom or the galactic system or the Einsteinian, four-dimensional universe. But so soon as you believe in a personal and living God, the whole situation changes. The universe is no longer a system passively awaiting our study. There is a redemptive Good Will which is seeking to reveal itself to men. There is a double search, that of man for God and of God for man. Men sense a Spirit that is seeking them, a Voice that is calling, a Presence that has "beset them behind and before and laid its hand upon them."[2]

It is the service of Karl Barth and the dialectical theology once more to have emphasized this conviction that there is a living God speaking to man. Modern thought had reacted from the old dualistic supernaturalism. It discovered the human side of religion. By its historical, psychological, and

[2]So in Francis Thompson's, *Hound of Heaven:*

Still with unhurrying chase
And unperturbed pace,
Deliberate speed, majestic instancy,
Came on the following Feet,
And a Voice above their beat.

social studies, it showed that every aspect of religion—Scriptures, creeds, Church, sacraments, spiritual experience, could be traced as a human and historical process. The idea was vigorously applied by religious thinkers under the guidance of the concepts of immanence and evolution, the great words of modernism; and the practical conclusion was a doctrine of social progress, of social redemption with man as his own savior. Thus it seemed as though religion had found man only to lose God. Karl Barth came to his new vision when as a pastor he first stood up to preach and asked himself what Christian preaching meant. His answer was: The Church's reason for being is that it has a word from the living God. The heart of the Christian faith is the conviction that God has spoken to men in Christ; and the central event of human life is the judgment, the crisis, which occurs when through this Word man is confronted with God.

But Barth does not answer the question, how revelation takes place. So far from being of aid here, through his conception of God and the world he tends to make incredible the revelation which he asserts, and in no case shows how that revelation enters human life. In his fear of humanism and relativism, he makes revelation the sole and absolute action of God, coming in direct and unmediated fashion from without. He uses the figure of a vertical line transfixing a plane at one point, coming *senkrecht von oben*. A point as such has no dimensions; the action of God in an ongoing process is here excluded. There is no revelation of God through nature, history, or human experience. God is present in these but he is hidden—*deus absconditus*. Man, having lost utterly the image of God through the fall, has no capacity to know God and no desire for him. It is not simply that the initiative is with God; from beginning to end it is God's action. Here, as elsewhere, Barth's dualism gives an either-or theology, with a constant protest against any suggestion of both-and: grace and not nature, revelation and not experience, God and not man. Nominally Barth admits that we have in revelation a person-to-person relation in which there is knowledge and experience, but the admission is only verbal. Knowing becomes not knowledge but mere acknowledgment (*anerkennen,* not *erkennen*), a recognition and a submission of the subject to his Lord; experience is defined as the determination of man by God (*diese Bestimmung der Existenz des erkennenden Menschen nennen wir Erfahrung*); man must make the response of faith to God, but faith is defined as a vacuum (*Hohlraum*), the empty room into which the Word is dropped.[3] So everything finite and human is denied significance as a medium of revelation, including history itself, yes, including the life and character of the historical Jesus. Emil Brunner, not so extreme, yet declares that "Truth can become effective only as absolute negation of all that is purely temporal," and that "One cannot take both seriously, God and history." Man is simply an empty vessel for the divine content, a mirror that reflects, a membrane that gives back the sound.[4]

3. The Old Testament offers us interesting material on this problem of revelation and experience. In general it shows two levels of thought, moving slowly from the lower to the higher. For the lower level the transcendence of God implies a certain externality, and revelation appears as the action of God from without. Hence it is sought in the unusual and extraordinary. It may be in something physical: fire falling from heaven, words spoken by an ass, a fleece dry or covered with dew in miraculous contrast with its surroundings, or literal tablets inscribed by a divine finger. If the action be in the realm of the spirit, it is found in dreams and visions or states of ecstasy.[5] The higher conception appears with the prophets and follows from their conception of God. There is

[3]*Dogmatik,* I, 1, 2nd ed., pp. 214, 255, 256, and sec. 6 as a whole. Translated into English as *The Doctrine of the Word of God.* See sec. 6, divs. 3 and 4.

[4]See *Erlebnis, Erkenntnis, und Glaube,* pp. 112, 96.

[5]1 Ki. 18:38, 39; Num. 22:28–31; Ju. 6:36–40; Ex. 31–18; 1 Ki. 18:2; Ezek. 8:1–4.

no loss here of the idea of transcendence and no thought of man's reason as sufficient to discover God. They see the Lord high and lifted up. They know the majesty and holiness of God, the finiteness and sinfulness of man. What is new is the moral nature of this transcendence. God is not mere Power demanding submission and sacrifices; he is righteousness and mercy and truth. Hence his transcendence, or holiness, means not judgment but mercy. "I will not return to destroy Ephraim: for I am God, and not man; the Holy One in the midst of thee."[6]

This radical insight has profound consequences for the conception of revelation. As religion becomes a morally conditioned personal relation, revelation means increasingly person speaking to person, truth to reason, righteousness to conscience, mercy to sin and man's need. The Eternal says: "Come now and let us reason together"; "Son of man, stand upon thy feet." The holiness of this God is no aloof transcendence; it is a high purpose of justice and mercy. He is the living God, carrying out this purpose in the world. Men are summoned to see God, not in the isolated and unusual, but in human history, in human experience. Profound personal experiences enter, as indicated in Jer. 1, Isa. 6, and Hos. 3. Necessarily, an ethical God is known most clearly through moral experience and insight. The prophets dared to believe that in such experiences in individual and national life they discerned the spirit of the Eternal. The forgiving mercy that Hosea found in his own heart, the righteous anger that Amos and Micah and Isaiah felt against social oppression and international iniquity, these were to them not mere human ideals or achievements; they were God's Spirit speaking to them of his purpose and judgment. They cry out with Micah: "I am full of power by the Spirit of Jehovah, and of judgment, and of might, to declare unto Jacob his transgression, and to Israel his sin."[7]

Three significant elements bearing on the idea of revelation

[6]Isa. 1; 6; Hos. 11.

[7]Micah 3:8.

thus appear. (1) There is no separation of natural and supernatural, though there is the clearest recognition of the God who is more than man. (2) There is no mutual exclusion of divine and human; God is found in the insights and experiences of man, and man finds God not in passive submission but in the active response of the sensitive and sympathetic heart, the alert understanding, and the obedient will. Revelation and discovery are thus different aspects of one process. (3) The realm of the ethical, particularly as seen in historical events, is the special field of divine revelation and human discovery.

It may be argued that this account misses that immediate awareness of God, that sense of the holy, or numinous, which Rudolf Otto has rightly emphasized in his *Idea of the Holy* as basic to all religion and to that of the Old Testament. We may grant the importance of this mystical sense; but what it brings is primarily the realization *that* God is, not the knowledge of *what* God is. And the crucial question for religion is not just the existence of God but his character and purpose. The sense of the holy (that is, the sense of a higher, a more-than-human) we may call the common denominator of religion; but what is distinctive and meaningful in a given religion is its insight into the character of the Holy One. That formed the distinctive revelation of God to the prophets and constituted their message.

4. The New Testament carries to completion this idea of revelation as that which is at once divine gift and human insight and experience. It holds the same idea of a high and holy God. Revelation is his word just as life is his gift. Yet God is no mere voice speaking from above or arm reaching down in power; he is Love entering into humanity, Life giving itself to man, Spirit dwelling in man. The knowledge of God is in and through the life which God gives to men: revelation comes through redemption.

Jesus is our great witness to the way in which divine and human unite to give us revelation and life. Jesus knows that his message and his work are wholly the gift of God; but with this sense of utter dependence there is a wonderful freedom. He does not find God in some occasional word from on high, or some miracle in answer to prayer, or in a passing ecstatic state. He finds the word of God within, in his own sure insights; and his own spirit, the spirit of love and truth, is for him the guide to the understanding of God. That spirit is his own, and therefore he speaks and moves with freedom and quiet assurance; but it is God's gift, and therefore he is humble and dependent and utterly obedient.

The early Church, in its religion, and so in its idea of revelation, moves around two focal points, and these bring us to the heart of the Christian conception of revelation. The first of these is Jesus. "God was in Christ" is their common conviction. There are two significant sides to this. First, it was *God* who was in Christ. That was their supreme concern, to know God. Jesus was not for them first of all a great teacher or a good example. He was one in whom the living God had come to men to reveal his way and to give them life. The point of emphasis varies: for the fourth gospel, Jesus is the word God speaks to men, for Paul he is above all a deed of God for men. But always it was their conviction that in him the living God, the Holy One, had come to men. Equally important, however, was the second conviction, that God was in *Christ*—not in writings or doctrines or miracles or subjective experiences or sacramental forms, but in a historic person, in Christ's spirit, his word, his life, his death. Here again, as with the prophets, the historical, the human, the personal and ethical furnish the sphere in which the transcendent God becomes known; and God is here as deed not primarily as idea.

The second focal point for the New Testament idea of revelation is the idea of the indwelling, light-giving Spirit of God. A historic fact or figure taken by itself is not enough. In the end there is no revelation until the truth speaks to me, until I know God for myself. Apart from this the historical, however lofty, remains a mere tradition. And that is what has happened too often in the Christian Church; instead of a word of the living God bringing to men conviction and life, there has been offered to men a book or institution or doctrine to which they were to submit. It is not so in the New Testament. Its conception of revelation is knowing God, not knowledge about God. Following the Hebraic line, as contrasted with the Greek, such knowledge is no mere rational apprehension, whether by logic or by intuition; it is the knowledge of acquaintance, of personal relation; it is a sharing of life. The historic fact of Jesus, with all its meaning, is not enough. Men know God because they are led into that life of fellowship with God which Jesus lived. Men know God because they share that Spirit of God which was in Jesus. God ceases to be merely a transcendent Being made known by some word or deed; he is the life that is given, he is indwelling presence. This is the significance of the New Testament idea of the Holy Spirit. Through that Spirit the external becomes inner, the historic becomes present, the living God speaks through the words of the past and the men of the past. Through that Spirit men are not only led to apprehend as their own what the great tradition brings, but they are led into larger truth.

IV. TRADITION

Our consideration of revelation and experience thus far has been primarily from the individual viewpoint. But revelation and experience are not mere matters of the individual or the moment. Revelation is historical; there is a self-disclosure of God in the process of events. And individual experience always takes place in a social setting and in dependence upon the historic past. The results of this historical revelation and ongoing group life come to each new generation and to each individual in what we call tradition. It becomes necessary then to consider the meaning of tradition and its significance for our knowledge of God.

1. The Meaning of Tradition. Man's life is conditioned by

a twofold heritage, biological and social. The former he shares with other animals; at the latter point he is unique, first, in his capacity for learning, second, in his ability to conserve what he learns and to pass on from age to age an increasing store of knowledge, skills, and insights. It is this inheritance that has made possible human advance; without this we should never be far from the jungle. The material part of this inheritance is the lesser part—some buildings and roads, machines that will soon be scrapped, and a little store of food and clothing. The great heritage is that of the spirit: on the one hand the sciences and techniques which make us masters of our physical world; on the other the insights of faith, the vision of ideals and values, a wisdom as to ways of fruitful living, apprehensions of beauty, and their embodiment in works of art and literature. To this heritage, handed down from generation to generation, we may give the name tradition, using the term in the broad yet literal sense of that which is handed over. In the words of an eminent scholar, "Tradition is the spiritual bond which, despite remoteness in time, unites each present with the past, so that there are no isolated individuals, but each man attains to spiritual existence only because he stands in historical relations."[1]

What is true of man's general cultural life is pre-eminently true of religion. The religious life of individuals has no existence and no comprehensible meaning apart from the group and from the cultural past. Where men seek to separate themselves from these, their religion tends to become abstract theory, subjective vagary, or hopeless quest.[2] So for all men at the beginning, and for most men throughout life, the great source of religious knowledge is tradition. It comes through the home with its intimate personal contacts, with its ideals and ideas that are taken in almost with the air that we breathe. It is conveyed by the teaching of the Church, by its hymns

[1]Heinrich Holtzmann, art. "Tradition," in *Religion in Geschichte und Gegenwart,* 1. Aufl., Bd. V.

[2]See Christopher Dawson, *Progress and Religion,* pp. 244, 245.

and prayers, and by that literature, especially in the Bible, through which the great spirits of the past though dead yet speak. There is more here than passive conformity or acceptance of lifeless ideas; there is something warm and vital. Deep calls to deep; life kindles life. There is an objective embodiment, indeed, in ideas and customs and writings; but these come to us as expressed in the life of the group which, at its best, is instinct with reverence and faith, with idealism and devotion, and as such wakens in us the sense of God and the desire for this life.

The modern age has shown a marked revolt against tradition, evident especially in religion. The first reason was that tradition had come to mean an external authority demanding unquestioning obedience and an absolute truth discouraging the search for knowledge. Further, it tended to make the teachings of the past a substitute for the living knowledge of God. The reaction against this authoritarianism was supported not only by the new empirical temper, but also by a rather naïve confidence in "progress" and a new authoritarianism which spelled Science with a capital letter and made it in turn exclusive and final. The result was a "contemporaneousness," shallow and insecure because it neglected the great results of man's corporate and historic experience and insights. There are signs that religious thought is turning from this, though the renewed appreciation of historic values will not be without the attendant danger of the old authoritarianism.

2. The Appreciation and Use of Tradition. What we need then is a new appreciation of tradition while guarding against its misuse. To furnish a man with the ideas of the past does not give him a knowledge of God any more than it gives him an education. But to start in religion without the help of the past would be as great a folly as to scrap our past knowledge in the name of experimental science, or to throw overboard our ideals and moral insights in the name of ethics. Baldly to oppose tradition to experiment, dead past to living present,

is, to say the least, superficial. Whether we think biologically, socially, or individually, the life of the present is rich because it carries on the life of the past; and the past is not dead but lives on in the present. That is what makes advance in life possible: the past can live on, the present can inherit the past and at the same time advance beyond it. It is the peculiar capacity of mind that it can retain the past in the present. Tradition, function, and change go together, as Whitehead has pointed out, and the tradition is not a static affair.[3] We need to realize that experience is racial as well as individual, a historical affair and not merely that of the passing moment. This racial experience is "a dynamic and creative movement of the human spirit experimenting with life, gaining deeper insights into its meaning, searching for the factors of its control, reaching out toward, and in some degree realizing, the human, the moral, and the spiritual values that are still in process of creation."[4]

There has been an increasing appreciation of the significance of tradition as thus conceived, and that includes many who stand over toward the left. Thus Walter Lippmann speaks of ethical insights in terms that would apply equally to religion: "The virtues are grounded in experience. . . . The cardinal virtues correspond to an experience so long and so nearly universal among men of our civilization, that when they are understood they are seen to contain a deposited wisdom of the race."[5] So Aldous Huxley declares that among " 'free men' there has been substantial agreement for the last eighty or ninety generations as to the ideal individual."[6] John Haynes Holmes makes a specifically religious application and calls us to use the wisdom of the past, "what man has learned through millions of years, at a cost of pain and death too

[3]See *Science and the Modern World,* 261–264. *Cf.* W. P. Montague and his reference to Bergson's doctrine of *durée* in *The Chances of Surviving Death,* p. 69.

[4]W. C. Bower, *Character Through Creative Experience,* p. 143.

[5]*A Preface to Morals,* p. 226.

[6]*Ends and Means,* p. 4.

terrible to estimate, of the ultimate with which he has to deal." He mentions specific moral imperatives "which have become, through the course of time, a straight and narrow path beaten smooth by the feet of loyal men." He appeals, however, not just to the mass of experience, but to the testimony of certain transcendent geniuses of the spirit.[7] The principle used in these instances is obvious. You cannot settle what is right and true on a quantitative basis, whether you count heads or years; but mankind rightly gives weight to the results tested by the experience of the generations. What are our classics but the works whose beauty and insights have stood the test of the years? As Maxwell Anderson declared, in his 1937 Founders' Day address at Carnegie Institute in New York: "The test of a message is the continuing effect on the minds of men over a period of generations."

All this does not mean a return to religious authoritarianism, whether biblicistic, confessionalistic, or ecclesiastical. So Nicolas Berdyaev says, in words the more interesting because they come from the Orthodox Church: "The conception of tradition as the profoundest expression of historical and spiritual reality depends upon its acceptance as the inner life of the knowing spirit and not as external authority."[8] Tradition is not a substitute for first-hand thought and living experience, but rather occasion and stimulus for the latter. Man is thrust into a world where he must act before he can think things through; tradition offers him the lessons learned by action and reflection in the past. It is not a command to stand still but to march, a summons to further appropriation and exploration. And in such vital writings as those of the Bible, it is not simply ideas that come to us but the spirits of the past which live on in these deathless words. Somehow they are able to kindle our dull spirits, awaken longing, create faith, and lead us into the presence of the Eternal.

It is significant that it has been the creative spirits of

[7]*The Sensible Man's View of Religion,* pp. 52, 53.
[8]*The Meaning of History,* p. 26.

our race, the men whose courage and insight and adventure have led the race onward, who have at the same time felt themselves most deeply indebted to the past and have made largest use of it.

For Christianity history has a special significance; it is not merely the experience of man, but the self-revealing and redemptive deed of God. Hence there is in history something super-historical, the Eternal in time. The error of traditional theology has been twofold. It has sought this Eternal in the wrong place—the letter of Scripture, creeds, a sacrosanct organization, in each case something external, unchangeable, infallible. And it has demanded a wrong attitude toward it, that of unquestioning submission. But the great tradition for Christianity is not an institution or a doctrinal system; it is a person. It is the conviction that in Jesus Christ the Eternal has spoken, that here God has revealed his purpose and the way of life for men. It offers men a faith which, if it be true, gives infinite meaning and possibilities to life. It believes that its message will discover to men their sin and need, and work conviction within. It holds that the Eternal Spirit which has wrought this deed in the past will bring home this truth to the present. The great tradition, therefore, is not a dead past but a living present. Its summons is to an adventure of faith by which men are to move forward with God.

We may summarize by saying (1) that tradition represents that significant past which lives on in the present, the heritage of past achievement which makes possible future advance. It includes the great moral and religious insights which, once gained, remain an abiding possession, a possession that each generation needs to make its own but not to discover afresh, and the great spirits who, whether by special endowment, by clearer vision, or by purer devotion have through their achievement rightly become our teachers and guides. (2) Jesus Christ is "the great tradition," the supreme revelation of the character of God and the way of life for men. (3) No tradition is to be accepted unthinkingly. The past has authority only as it lives on in the present, winning inner conviction, meeting the criticism of the mind, and approving itself in the practice of life. (4) The tradition is an instrument and not an end; the end is not preserving the tradition but achieving life. It is ours to make the truth our own, to know God for ourselves, and to advance a little further this human life and its knowledge of the truth.

Chapter Nine

MYSTICISM AND INTUITION

THERE are many for whom the acceptance of the idea of revelation and the recognition of the meaning of the Christian tradition constitute the sufficient answer to the question of the knowledge of God. We have seen, however, that they represent but one side of the matter, that, rightly conceived, they imply another side, that of religious experience. Once recognize that the knowledge of God is not mechanical but a matter of conscious, personal life, and you must go on to ask: What are the experiences or ways of life in which men can know God for themselves? To this problem we now turn. Here, too, we do not start *de novo*. We call for help upon the great spirits, past and present. But we ask from them not so much the ideas of God at which they arrived through their experience, as the ways in which their experience moved, that we may profit from these to come to our own knowledge of God.

The emphasis upon religious experience has marked modern theology since Schleiermacher. Typical are the words of the editors of *The Library of Constructive Theology,* who "desire to lay stress upon the value and validity of religious experience and to develop their theology on the basis of the religious consciousness."[1] The new emphasis came from a

[1]See *God in Christian Experience,* by W. R. Matthews, p. 8. Dean Matthews and Doctor H. Wheeler Robinson are the editors of this series.

protest against identifying religion with doctrine and institution, and from dissatisfaction with the prevalent methods of theology which were either speculative or authoritarian or both combined. Positively, it revealed the influence of the new empirical temper and a realization of the wealth of concrete material which religion afforded.

The dangers in this appeal need to be recognized. There is the danger of assuming a specialized religious sixth sense by which, in some mysterious fashion, the soul may have direct knowledge concerning God and absolute certainty, and the tendency to narrow religious experience to an emotional-mystical-intuitive affair. As against this we must recognize, as already indicated, that there is no knowledge anywhere of immediate and irrefragable character, that the whole man is engaged in religious experience, and that mind and will are as vitally concerned as emotion. Experience is nothing less than the total conscious life of man. Religious experience is that conscious life viewed as involving possible relation to a world of a higher spiritual order. If it is wrong to suppose that this concern with experience reduces the knowledge of God to subjectivism as against an appeal to revelation, it is equally mistaken to imagine that immediate knowledge and certainty are thus gained without reflection, interpretation, and criticism, or without faith and moral action. And it is important to see that these last are elements in religious experience, and not merely something that we do with this experience.

Our task then is to survey the various forms or fields of experience through which men have come to the knowledge of God, and to inquire as to their validity and value. The organization of this material is not easy. A suggestion from Baron von Hügel may help us. He sees three elements in religion which represent in turn the approach made by childhood, youth, and manhood. For childhood religion is historical, traditional, institutional, presenting itself as something external and authoritative. For youth it is something to be grasped by reason and argument. For manhood it is primarily a matter of intuition, feeling, and volitional requirements and evidences. As a matter of fact, these elements belong together. Every man in his religious life has to deal with tradition, to use reason, and to find place for feeling and will, that is, for the intimately personal and practical. But there is value in the distinction, and it applies in a broad way to the successive stages of the race as of the individual. In primitive religions tradition is all-important, religion being a matter of ideas, sanctions, and customs to be taken over by the individual without question. The reflective and critical approach comes later, and in its extreme represents the confident attitude of youth. The manhood of the race tends, not so much to give up confidence in reason, as to realize that religion's highest knowledge comes by insight and that its deepest concern is with the practical issues of life.[2]

Following von Hügel's suggestion, we may distinguish broadly three ways by which men have sought to know God. (1) There is tradition, in which the experience of the past presents itself for our use. (2) There is the way of reason, reflective, interpretive, and critical. (3) The feeling-willing side constitutes a group of ways which differ markedly among themselves. Some take the way of mysticism and intuition. Some stress the way of insight, moral loyalty, and faith in connection with our experience of the world of values. Some emphasize the knowledge of God that comes through the experience of saving help or, in more modern terms, through the fulfillment of life gained by right adjustment. But all have in common the insistence that religion must be vital and personal, not a matter of mere institution and authority; all emphasize the willing-feeling side of life. Our order of discussion will vary, however, from von Hügel's. Religion, like all else, reaches us first as the tradition of our group, and this way we have already considered. It comes next in the feelings that it evokes, in its appeal to

[2]See *The Mystical Element of Religion,* Vol. I, pp. 50–65.

inner conviction, and in the practical needs that it meets; and, indeed, there is no real personal religion till this happens. Finally reason enters in with its task of reflection and criticism. Needless to say, these stages overlap each other, just as they interpenetrate each other as processes.

I. THE WAY OF MYSTICISM

1. Mysticism is as hard to define as religion itself and has almost as many meanings. J. B. Pratt makes a simple and helpful distinction between two general types, the mild and the extreme. The latter is the mysticism of ecstasy and visions and revelations, and is what we usually associate with the names of the great mystics of history. The former is simply "a sense of the Beyond, the feeling of the presence of the Divine," something so common that most people would simply identify it with religious experience as such.[1] The division made by Charles A. Bennett follows the same general lines, though his analysis goes deeper. He distinguishes speculative mysticism from the simpler "mysticism as a way of life."[2] The former is more metaphysical. Underlying it is a philosophy exemplified by the neo-Platonists and especially Plotinus. God is pure being, one, indivisible, unchangeable, and is utterly opposite to this finite and changing world. There is in man a divine spark, a bit of reason, an "apex" or "fund" or center of the soul opposed to this world in which it is immersed and belonging to God. The mystical experience is "the flight of the alone to the Alone," the soul leaving the world of sense, of time and change, of thought and effort, of human relations, to lose its individual being in

[1] J. B. Pratt, *The Religious Consciousness.* Chs. XVI–XX.

[2] Charles A. Bennett, *A Philosophical Study of Mysticism,* p. 7. *The Psychology of Religious Mysticism,* by James H. Leuba, gives the most thoroughgoing presentation of mysticism from the standpoint of one who sees in it a purely human if not wholly pathological phenomenon, and who assumes that to the degree in which we describe an experience psychologically we have eliminated any possible reference to a more than human source.

unity with God. This "negative way" is classically expressed in a passage from Pseudo-Dionysius of the fifth century, who profoundly influenced the mysticism of the western Church: "In thy intent practise of the mystical contemplation, leave behind both thy senses and thy intellectual operations, and all things known by sense and intellect, and all things which are not and which are, and set thyself as far as may be to unite thyself in unknowing with him who is above all being and knowledge."[3]

It is this type of mysticism that has received the principal criticism. Some have seen in these mystics only pathological cases whose experience could be equally well induced by drugs. Better founded is the criticism which points out that there is nothing distinctly Christian in its point of view; that it tends to a disregard or at least a depreciation of the historical, social, ethical, and rational aspects of religion; that it stakes the certainty of religion upon uncertain emotional states which are at best the attainment of but a few; and that it is grounded in an untenable conception of religion, of God, and of man.

If all this be granted, however, there remains for consideration the "milder" mysticism, or "mysticism as a way of life." Religion is concerned with the reality of an unseen world and the possibility that man may know this. Just this is the conviction of the mystic, who believes that he can know God for himself in direct and vital fashion. Hence some would say that mysticism "is nothing but the fundamental feeling of religion, the religious life at its very heart and center."[4] "It is religion in its most acute, intense, and living stage," writes Rufus M. Jones,[5] while R. R. Marett declares flatly: "No mysticism, no religion."[6]

[3]*E. R. E.*, IX, 93, article on "Mysticism, Christian, Roman Catholic," by John Chapman.

[4]Otto Pfleiderer, quoted by W. R. Inge, *Christian Mysticism*, p. 339.

[5]*Studies in Mystical Religion*, p. 15.

[6]*Faith, Hope, and Charity in Primitive Religion.*

2. What this milder mysticism means can be best indicated by a few concrete examples. Nicholas Herman, or Brother Lawrence, was a humble lay brother who entered the order of the barefoot Carmelites in Paris in 1666. We know him through a series of conversations and letters published under the title, *The Practice of the Presence of God.* In simple speech he tells how he practised the presence of God, not through special exercises or by ecstatic experience, but by recognizing God as always and intimately present, addressing himself constantly to God, and doing each common task with a conscious reference to him. A kindred spirit, yet markedly different, is John Woolman, a Quaker who lived in America in the middle of the eighteenth century and who has left to us his *Journal.* Unlike Brother Lawrence, he is concerned less with the furtherance of his individual spiritual life and more with the "misery of my Fellow-creatures separated from the divine Harmony." The institution of slavery weighs upon him, and beyond that the economic situation which means ease and selfishness to those who possess and want and suffering to others. What is distinctive, however, is his deep sense of the presence of God and his conviction that men who wait upon God, who yield themselves in single-hearted obedience, may have from God his truth, his spirit of love, and his guidance.

We may take as a third example Rufus M. Jones, well known through his many writings. He is an example of mysticism in the modern scene, one who shares the common mystic concern for the inner life and adds not only the social concern of John Woolman but the interests of the philosophical thinker. Mysticism for him is not ecstatic experience, nor a matter of visions and voices. He tells, indeed, of one experience of audition, when, completing an important address after long toil of preparation, he heard a voice, clear and startling, that said to him: "But thou wilt never give it." Sure enough, the night before he was to speak he had a severe attack of ptomaine poisoning. Only, he discredited the voice, made every effort, and gave the address![7] He illustrates how a modern man, alive to present-day currents of thought and life, can yet practise religion as "vital communion with God," as "immediate consciousness of personal relationship with the Divine."

It is mysticism of this type, Rufus Jones holds, that characterized Jesus. The central fact of early Christianity is the life of one who had personal experience of God and who was able to lead others into that experience. "It is Christ who is the true mystic," says Canon R. C. Moberly. The real truth of Christian mysticism is "the doctrine, or rather the experience, of the Holy Ghost."[8] And this, it would seem, is Pauline Christianity: the religious life, not as a conclusion of reason or an effort of will, but as a knowledge of God through a historic revelation and a sharing of the life of God through the indwelling Spirit.

There is another expression of mysticism which must not be passed by. It is not like the even tenor of the religious life which marks the mild mysticism which we have been considering. It deals with unusual experiences, occurring rarely or even but a single time, and yet those concerned cannot be classified with the extreme mystics. *With the Door Open* is a record of personal experience by J. Anker Larsen, a Dane, a prize-winning novelist, an actor and instructor at leading theatres in Copenhagen. The experience is given here in his own words but condensed. "I had been sitting in the garden. It was still and peaceful—around me and within me. Then it began to come, that infinite tenderness. It was in me, but it also came to me, as the air came to my lungs. It extended further and further—it became all-present. I saw it, and it developed into knowing, into knowing all; at the same time it became power, omnipotence, and drew me into the eternal Now. That was my first actual meeting with Reality. Existence is no Maya, no delusion, but we

[7]See *The Trail of Life in the Middle Years,* 238–241.
[8]*Atonement and Personality,* pp. 312, 314.

are deluded until we open our eyes in the Now, where the temporal and eternal are merged into a unity, where a workday becomes a holyday, and life a sacrament. The eternal sanctifies the temporal, the temporal realizes the eternal."[9]

A Wanderer's Way is a religious autobiography. Its author, Canon Charles E. Raven, has a marked interest in natural science as well as historical and philosophical studies. Two experiences are given here, again in the author's words but condensed. The first had a nature background, a wonderful sunset: "For a moment time had stopped, the visible world had become transparent, the eternal reality behind the things of sense had been unveiled and in an instant of rapture had enfolded me into union with itself. The effect was deep and characteristic: one came back to earth seeing it as if through the wrong end of a telescope small and bright: and yet with this sense of detachment an equally strong sense of oneness with all that is. For we were all sustained by a life infinite and unchanging, in which one's emotions were quickened, one's intellect clarified, and one's goodwill enormously increased." A second experience belonged to later years, and its background was not the nature beauty of the Cambridge scene but the common people with whom he worked in the great city. "On my walks in the mean streets, God, as I had learned to call him, met me in splendor. Always the sense of his presence was unexpected, even startling; always it had the same effect of exhilaration and enlargement. But now the meaning of it was more plain. Mankind was transfigured by it and made infinitely dear. Not only was the earth full of the glory of the Lord, but humanity, the crowded folk of the city, were his family, each and all in his keeping."[10]

In *Twenty Minutes of Reality,* Margaret Prescott Montague tells how there came to her one day, unexpectedly and

[9] *Op. cit.*, pp. 72–75.

[10] Pp. 62, 63, 109. Note also material in his volume, *The Creator Spirit.*

without preparation, the feeling that she was seeing for the first time what life really was. All the old things were seen in a new light in their rich beauty and meaning, and with this came the sense of the great Whole, the realization that she belonged to it, and the spirit of love for her neighbor. The account, first appearing as a magazine article, elicited hundreds of letters, many of them recording similar experiences.

In all three of these cases the experience came under "normal" conditions. J. Middleton Murry, on the contrary, was passing through a severe crisis at the time of his mystical experience. He had lost his wife, the brilliant Katherine Mansfield. Isolated in spirit, separated from men, he sensed the world in its immensities, and himself, alone, "as a little island against whose slender shores a cold, dark, boundless ocean lapped devouring." And then the darkness changed to light, the cold to warmth. The ocean swept in one great wave over the frontiers of himself, bathed him and renewed him. "The room was filled with a presence, and I knew I was not alone—that I never could be alone any more. I was part of it, I belonged, and because I belonged I was no longer I, but something different, which could never be afraid in the old ways or cowardly with the old cowardice."[11]

These experiences could be multiplied without number. They are not limited to a particular group; they come from all lands and ages and belong to people with widely varying viewpoints. They are not like the passing effects of drug hallucinations; they are organic to the man's life and represent abiding results of creative power and high value. It is hardly openminded to pronounce them without significance. Their agreement at certain main points is most striking. Three broad aspects constantly recur. (1) In relation to the world there is the experience of sensitive awareness or vision, the conviction that one has come face to face with reality, or with God, that the meaning of the world and life has been

[11]See *God,* by J. Middleton Murry, pp. 26–31.

opened, and that one has seen it in its unity, its goodness, and its beauty. (2) As regards the self, there is the sense of an immense enlargement, a feeling of peace and joy, above all of belonging to or being at one with one's world. (3) Very generally there is a sense of good will toward one's fellows and toward all living things.

3. Our concern is with the first of these aspects. What is the value of mysticism as a way of knowledge? Certain facts seem to gainsay the claim. Very commonly the mystic declares that though he has seen and known, his experience is ineffable; it cannot be put in rational concepts or propositions. Further, when the mystic does express his ideas, as on God, for example, he uses the forms of thought furnished by his social background. Thus St. Teresa writes: "The three Persons of the Holy Trinity then show themselves to the soul with a radiance as of fire. . . . Then she sees those three distinct Persons and she knows with a sovereign truth that these three are One in Substance, One in Power, One in Wisdom, One God."[12] Finally, mystics differ radically in their interpretation of the experience. For Middleton Murry, God is "a venerable but now empty word"; this "presence" to which he belongs he conceives as "Life," or "organism in evolution," a combination of mysticism and naturalism not unlike that of Julian Huxley in his *Religion without Revelation.* Canon Raven also uses the term life, and makes mysticism "the communion of life with life," but he adds: "The Being beyond and within the universe constrains me at such moments to recognize him as loving and good. To rank him as less than the highest that I know, as lower than the personal, would be to be false to the whole quality of my experience."[13]

Certain other considerations are important here, and they apply to all claims to a direct knowledge of God loosely made

[12]See Evelyn Underhill, *An Introduction to Mysticism,* p. 132, and note this entire chapter on "Mysticism and Theology."

[13]*The Wanderer's Way,* pp. 65, 66.

in behalf of "religious experience." (1) There is no separate faculty of knowledge; it is the whole man that knows, and he needs every resource of mind and moral insight and feeling-awareness. (2) There is no such thing as an immediate knowledge without activity on our part, whether it be knowledge of God or of the physical world. There is sensitivity and awareness, but there is no knowledge till we begin to interpret. The mystic's use of the word God for this object of his experience is itself an interpretation. (3) There is danger in tying up our knowledge of God and our certainty of God with any state of feeling, no mattter how deep and persuasive, for feeling is subjective and individual and changing. Some have been lured by the idea of the subconscious, of a life below the rational and reflective, by which man can make direct contact, as William James suggested, with that "More" of the same quality, the God of religion, the source of our help.[14] But that opens a wide door to the psychological attack which insists that religion is nothing more than such subjective feeling issuing in wish-projections. (4) There is the danger that the mystic, interested in this individual and immediate experience, shall depreciate other avenues for the knowing of God: the way of tradition in which race experience and historic revelation become available, the fellowship in which the fragmentary individual life finds completion, and the way of moral insight and moral obedience. (5) Finally, there is danger in the emphasis on the *via negativa.* So profoundly is the mystic convinced that what he has is given to him, is God's deed and not his own achievement, that there is danger that a needed emphasis on the purgation of evil on the one hand, and receptivity of spirit on the other, shall pass over into an idea of pure passivity and emptiness and inertness. Against this we must rather hold that the highest insight will come when man brings the fullest measure of appreciation, aspiration, mental alertness, and response of will. The moments of special insight are those "of greater mental integrity than usual, in which consciousness

[14]*The Varieties of Religious Experience,* pp. 498–519.

is more concrete, the associations and resources of the mind more instantly collected and fused into a total grasp of the meaning of its present object."[15] To which may be added the word of A. N. Whitehead: "Religious truth must be developed from knowledge acquired when our ordinary senses and intellectual operations are at their highest pitch of discipline."[16]

In his significant and widely influential volume, *The Idea of the Holy,* Rudolf Otto has emphasized the mystical aspect of religion. The basic element in religion, he declares, evident in its highest forms as in the lowest, is the sense of the holy. The term "holy" does not primarily involve the meaning of good and rational but rather the transcendent, the supernatural, the "numinous." It is that before which man falls in fear and awe. In the higher religions like Christianity this numinous is filled out with moral and rational content; the Holy One becomes the true and the good. But even on the highest level there remains something of this original idea of the transcendent, of a majesty and mystery that cannot be put into the clear ideas of reason. Thus even in the highest religion there will always be not only insight into the true and reverence for the good, but the attitude of awe and "fear," the feeling of the creature in the presence of the Eternal.

Otto has done a service in calling attention to this sense

[15]W. E. Hocking, *The Meaning of God,* p. 429; *cf.* p. 373.

[16]*Religion in the Making,* p. 123. Besides this practical aspect, the "negative way" has a theoretical or speculative meaning in this type of mysticism, namely the idea that we cannot know God in his essential nature but can only say of him what he is not. The two aspects belong logically together. If God be wholly other, then no experiences in this finite world and no activity of human mind and will can afford any point of contact with him or way of knowing. Then only the spirit that is purely passive, and wholly empty not merely of evil but of all conscious activity, can know God or possess him. It is interesting to note here the points of parallelism with Karl Barth's position, despite obvious differences and his repudiation of mystical errors. The extreme emphasis on the divine otherness, the effort to eliminate the human, and the resultant essential agnosticism belong to both.

of the holy and its fundamental place in religion. His discussion is in line with that of R. R. Marett in his *Threshold of Religion,* and N. Söderblom in his *Das Werden des Gottesglaubens* and his article on "Holiness" in the *Encyclopedia of Religion and Ethics.* The weakness of Otto's position is in giving too much significance to the more primitive forms of this experience. He is right in holding that religion is not an appendix to ethics nor exhausted in the concepts of reason, but he does not adequately realize that the moral world, with its solemn majesty and its absolute authority, as Wordsworth reveals in his "Ode to Duty," is itself a place for the experience of the holy. The deepest sense of the ethical is at the same time an awareness of something transcendent. And when reason recognizes a unity, an order, a meaning in the world of truth, which is something not made by man but only discovered, something that infinitely transcends this finite knower, then the world of the rational also becomes an occasion for the experience of the holy. Surely no one can read Plato or Spinoza appreciatively without realizing this. Nevertheless, Otto has served us by showing that the larger mysticism is at the heart of all religion, and we must repudiate religion as such or recognize in it something of an immediate awareness of the Higher.

4. Mysticism, however, is an aid to knowledge. The work of the mystics has a definite value because they have concerned themselves with discovering the favorable conditions for such an experience of God. In broad outline, as we have seen, all knowledge must follow the same way: observation, action, reflection, experiment; but in any given field the way of knowledge is determined by the nature of the object known. In no field is there such a demand upon the knower as in the spiritual realm. The reason is plain: in this realm we are asking about the highest values, the ultimate meaning, the supreme reality; and the cost of such knowledge is nothing less than the surrender of a man's whole self. We are not concerned here with "the mystic way" in the more specialized

sense, as this is discussed, for example, in Part II of Evelyn Underhill's *Mysticism.* Our interest is in those insights which are available for the common man seeking a knowledge of God.

(1) Mysticism emphasizes the receptive side of knowledge. Life has two sides: the active and outgoing, the passive and receptive. As Havelock Ellis says: "All the art of living lies in a fine mingling of letting go and holding on. . . . All life is a building up and a breaking down, a taking in and a giving out, a perpetually anabolic and katabolic rhythm."[17] There is a necessary activity in all knowledge: in sense perception, in the searching and questioning of reason, and in the practical conduct of life. In religious knowledge this necessary activity appears as moral obedience and the venture of faith: "He that willeth to do shall know." But the other word is also in point: *"Be still* and know." That does not imply quietism or pure passivity or day dreaming. In religion it is most clearly expressed in worship: the worship in which we call before us the highest that we know and open to it the doors of the spirit, somewhat as the soul of the artist waits in the presence of beauty; the worship in which we cease for the time to dissect and analyze, and try to see things whole; the worship in which the "heart at leisure from itself" is ready to see the meanings and values of this world that are higher than its individual concerns and interests. The essence lies in the inner mood quite apart from the form of worship. Maude Royden tells the story of a Quaker friend, greatly exercised and besieging God in the quiet of a Quaker meeting that he would manifest himself to her spirit, to whom at length the answer of the inner voice came: "Yes, I have something to say to you, when you stop your shouting."[18] What we have here in reality is not a way of knowing inde-

[17]*Affirmations,* p. 220. Quoted by C. A. Bennett, *A Philosophical Study of Mysticism,* p. 48. *Cf.* W. E. Hocking, *Meaning of God,* Ch. XXVIII, "The Principle of Alternation."

[18]Reported by Harold Begbie, *Painted Windows,* p. 110.

pendent of other experience and of reason, but rather a way by which the self is unified, its life deepened and intensified, and so the whole being made more sensitive to spiritual reality than in our ordinary dull, distracted, and divided condition. It is man offering his whole self at its highest pitch of perception to the eternal Spirit which is always seeking to reveal itself.

(2) Mysticism has a valid suggestion in its idea of purgation, or of the negative way. The soul which is freed from anxiety, from the unloving spirit, and from other evil, is the soul which is surest of that fellowship with God through which the real knowledge of God must come. So John Woolman in his *Journal* again and again brings out how selfish interests, as in the keeping of slaves, warp the judgment of men, how the understanding of truth is hampered when selfish passions enter in, and how in his own experience loyalty to the truth conditioned alike inner life and spiritual vision.

(3) And this brings naturally the third consideration. The results of mysticism in terms of character and life are evidence that here is a way by which men enter into transforming fellowship with the Eternal Spirit; and such a fellowship, in turn, implies knowledge in a real sense. Everywhere in the better examples of mysticism certain elements constantly appear: unification, or integration of life; a quietness and confidence and strength of spirit; a deep sense of at-oneness with God and men and life; a marked quality of good will which often issues in notable service; a heightening of moral and spiritual energy. Wide discrepancies among the mystics in their terms and ideas need not surprise us; we can but use the thought forms we have to interpret our experiences. But clearly there seems to be here such a knowledge of acquaintance, such an insight into spiritual reality, as would seem of highest value for that successful adjustment and consequent achievement of life which the mystics demonstrate.

(4) We must recognize both the dependence of mysticism upon other elements of experience and its own contribution. The soul's awareness of God does not come out of a void. It has its necessary background and occasion. That may be, as with Kant, the starry heavens at night and the majesty of the moral law within. It may be the silent worship of a Friends' meeting house with a group spirit unified in reverent expectation, or a deep sense of the brotherhood of the common life as with Canon Raven in the slums of Liverpool. It may be less than any one of these; for, as Browning suggests in "Bishop Blougram's Apology,"

> "Just when we are safest, there's a sunset touch,
> A fancy from a flower-bell, some one's death,
> A chorus-ending from Euripides—
> And that's enough for fifty hopes and fears."

But we must not confuse the occasion with the matter itself. Nature does not give us God, neither does the moral law; nor is God a mere deduction made by the mind from any one of these. These situations are but the occasion of this awareness of the Higher. There is a Presence that speaks and something in man that can discern and respond; and in this impact and response is the very essence of religion.

It is interesting to note in what widely varying quarters one meets the recognition of something comparable to mysticism as thus broadly conceived, that is, as awareness or apprehension of a higher world in an experience, not independent, indeed, of sense-perception and reason, but transcending them in a real though indefinable manner. "The fact of the religious vision," says A. N. Whitehead, "and its history of persistent expansion, is our one ground for optimism."[19] "True religion is a deeper thing," declares W. C. Dampier, "founded on the impregnable rock of direct experience. Some may have no religious sense, but others live and move and have their being in the transcendent glory of God."[20] "The

[19] *Science and the Modern World*, p. 238.

[20] *A History of Science*, p. 486.

desire for truth," Eddington inquires, "so prominent in the quest of science, a reaching out of the spirit from its isolation to something beyond, a response to beauty in nature and art, an inner light of conviction and guidance—are these not as much a part of our being as our sensitivity to sense-impressions? Consciousness is not wholly, nor even primarily, a device for receiving sense-impressions. . . . At the very beginning [of scientific study] there is something which might be described as an act of faith—a belief that what our eyes have to show us is significant. I think it can be maintained that it is by an analogous determination that the mystic recognizes another faculty of consciousness, and accepts as significant the vista of a world outside space and time that it reveals."[21]

In his *Four Stages of Greek Religion,*[22] Gilbert Murray writes: "Man must have some relation toward the uncharted, the mysterious tracts of life which surround him on every side. And for my own part I am content to say that his method must be to a large extent very much what St. Paul calls *pistis* or faith; that is, an attitude not of the conscious intellect but of the whole being, using all its powers of sensitiveness, all its feeblest and most inarticulate feelers and tentacles, in the effort somehow to touch by these that which cannot be grasped by the definite senses or analyzed by the conscious reason. What we gain thus is an insecure but precious possession. We gain no dogma, at least no safe dogma, but we gain much more. We gain something hard to define, which lies at the heart not only of religion, but of art and poetry and all the higher strivings of human emotion."

Not far removed from this is the suggestive word of Albert Einstein. "The most beautiful thing we can express is the mysterious. It is the source of all true art and science. He to whom this emotion is a stranger, who can no longer pause to wonder and stand rapt in awe, is as good as dead: his

[21]*Science and the Unseen World,* pp. 42, 74, 75. [22]P. 21.

eyes are closed. To know that what is impenetrable to us really exists, manifesting itself as the highest wisdom and the most radiant beauty which our dull faculties can comprehend only in their most primitive forms—this knowledge, this feeling, is the center of true religiousness. In this sense, and in this sense only, I belong in the ranks of the devoutly religious men."[23]

We may close our discussion with a summary of the discriminating statement made by Norman Kemp Smith in a paper on "Is Divine Existence Credible?" We cannot reach God by inference, he declares, by arguing from nature and history, or concluding, by analogy, from the nature and experience of the self. "We experience the divine in a direct and immediate manner." That does not mean that we experience the Divine "sheerly in and by itself"; rather it is in connection with what is other than the Divine. The experience is first aroused in connection with nature and it is especially the otherness of God, his non-creatureliness, his power, which we so apprehend. Yet our conviction is based, not on inference, but on fellowship, just as we have immediate experience of our fellow men though we do not know them in isolation from all else, certainly not from their bodies. What we immediately experience is always mysterious, and that is especially true of the experience of God. In its first stages it is ambiguous and vague. It needs moralization, but it continues to the end to be more than morals. Tradition and institution (the group life) are necessary to bring in modes of activity and to prescribe a way of life if the higher forms of experience are to be made possible and the Divine is to be known not only as more than man but as akin to man.[24]

[23]In *Has Science Discovered God?* E. H. Cotton, editor, pp. 96, 97.

[24]In *Proceedings of the British Academy,* Vol. XVII. Delton L. Scudder, in his *Tennant's Philosophical Theology,* gives a discriminating discussion of religious experience as a source of knowledge, opposing Tennant at this point.

II. THE WAY OF INTUITION

1. Insight and Whole-Knowing. One of the most familiar distinctions as to ways of knowing is that between knowledge of fact and knowledge of acquaintance, to which William James gave currency. In many languages this is marked by the use of different words. Thus we have in German the verbs *wissen* and *kennen, wissen* concerning the knowledge of fact and giving the noun *Wissenschaft, kennen* referring to the knowledge of acquaintance and giving the noun *Bekanntschaft.* The same general distinction appears in the French *savoir* and *connaître,* the Greek εἰδέναι and γνῶναι, and the Latin *scire* and *noscere.* We recognize the distinction in English though we have but the one word, *know.* The knowledge of our everyday life is that of acquaintance. We come to know the nature of people and objects and forces by observing their behavior, especially in our own dealings with them. We do not simply know facts about them; we say that we know them.

In this knowledge of acquaintance we deal with wholes. Science does not exclude whole-knowing, but its emphasis is upon part-knowing. Its great advance has been made by analysis. Its motto is *Divide et impera;* it divides in order that it may master, in order more accurately to describe and measure and classify and bring the great mass of facts into some manageable order. It is this kind of knowledge which has secured for science exactitude and its mastery of the forces of nature. But whole-knowing has an equally significant place. "In knowing any object," says Charles A. Bennett, "we not only begin with the whole but we work continually with that idea. Understanding is not only 'part-working' but 'total-working' as well. To sum up the characteristics of total-working: (1) In it the mind apprehends the whole. It is synoptic. It is intuitive, not analytic. (2) The knowledge it confers is inarticulate in the sense that it cannot readily be translated into conceptual terms. (3) Yet it is destined to become articulate, for total-working and part-working need each other. They are mutually supplementary and knowledge is the fruit of a harmonious alliance between them."[1] One may say, look at the parts that you may know the whole; look at the whole if you would know the parts.

The knowledge of wholes through acquaintance is important because the significant meanings and values of our world belong to wholes and escape us if we limit ourselves to the method of analysis and the search for mere facts. The real world is a world of organic wholes. We are increasingly sure of that, not only when we consider the personal self and the social group, but even when we regard the atom and the cell. The *Gestalt* psychology shows us human behavior as the response of a unitary being to a total situation. The scientist in his theory of emergent evolution deals with the obvious fact that the process of development is one in which ascending levels of life are reached through new forms of organization, through more inclusive and more significant wholes.

We must use this same idea of the whole in understanding history; it belongs to time equally with space. It is the merit of Bergson to have brought this out in his concept of duration, but the idea is common to all world views which recognize meaning in change and creativity in time. To try to understand history by mere analysis, by looking at the moment, is to destroy its life and lose its distinctive meaning. The real world of history we discern only as we look at wholes. Then we see, not mere change in a succession of events, but life moving out upon high adventure, creativity shaping something new and higher, ends being achieved and a meaning to it all. Not only does analytic naturalism fail here, but equally that religious and philosophical absolutism whose God has no real relation to the world of time.

Intuition in its general meaning is simply immediate perception. As such it may refer to the senses or to "the eye of

[1]Condensed from Chapter VII, *A Philosophical Study of Mysticism.*

the mind." Our concern with it is in the realm of the spirit and more especially in religion. It has often been discredited here by the assumption that it meant a mysterious short cut to knowledge that was independent of observation and reflection and that offered an irrefragable ground of certainty. It is used here with the much more modest meaning of insight added to awareness. To see things whole, to gain insight into realities and meanings that escape sense perception and analysis and are no mere matter of labored deduction, this is intuition as here considered. It is not limited to the few, though some will far excel others. It appears in our understanding of people, our penetration beneath the external to the motive, the intention, the real spirit of a man. Concrete facts are required, but a world of facts added together would not yield it. It is needed in the work of the scientist. It does not relieve him of the task of observation, criticism, and experiment, but it adds a necessary something to all these. A former pupil of Professors Millikan and Michelson writes of "the everlasting patience and courage of these men, who won Nobel prizes, not by flashes of genius, but by relentless, unceasing work, illuminated by godlike imagination and sustained by childlike faith."[2] Unceasing work; yes, but godlike imagination too. There are thousands of scientists who toil unceasingly; there are not many who, like Darwin, can illuminate the mass of gathered data with the needed insight that will discern order and meaning.

2. Insight and Values. But the chief importance of such insight is found in the realm of values, the world of ethics, æsthetics, and religion, and especially in the intuition of the personal self, of other selves, and of God. Here knowledge comes from insight as we look at the whole. No analysis will yield the beauty of a landscape, no deduction or demonstration can give it to another; it is seen directly or it is not gained at all. An act of unselfish devotion like that of Schweitzer in Africa, a heroic witness to the truth like that

[2]Donald Richberg, in the *Survey Graphic*, January, 1929.

of Luther at Worms, is grasped by an intuition which sees its essential rightness. So in religion. The prophet is not necessarily a mystic in the strict sense, but he has his own sure insight through which his message comes. The prophets saw that Jehovah was not autocratic will but the spirit of righteousness. Jesus saw that love was the heart of the Eternal, and that it was the one way for men to live and the one way by which humanity could be saved. Paul saw religion, not as a belief held, or a task imposed, but as a free creative life in men given them through the indwelling Spirit of God. These were not ideas externally communicated or laboriously deduced; they were direct and illuminating insights, and none the less such because they were viewed as the gift of God.

A consideration of the field of art will help to make plainer the meaning of intuition. Art deals with concrete materials. It does not use the abstract ideas of philosophy, or view nature under the generalizations of science. Whether its form be music or literature, painting, sculpture, or architecture, it uses the rich concrete stuff of the world of nature and man. In that sense art is always realistic. But it is not mere realism; it does not simply reproduce. A transcript of human action is not literature, not even history; it is simply chronicle. A reproduction of a bit of nature is not painting; it is photography. As Schopenhauer insisted in his *Laocoön,* art is the effort to set forth the idea which is struggling for expression in nature. Thus the first requisite of all higher art is insight. That does not mean paintings that tell a story, or literature that teaches a lesson or propagates a philosophy. It does mean that in art there is insight into meanings in the world about us, realization that the world is more than what appears on the surface, and an effort to make this evident to others by the same concrete media of sight and sound by which nature "half reveals and half conceals the soul within." "Meaning" must be taken here in the widest sense, including the idea of beauty. It does not connote simply the rational and good; but even in the literature of futility and despair the writer assumes that he has won a certain insight, and he makes use of that insight in his very act of judgment on his world. Great literature naturally makes this most clear, and poetry most of all. The poet, as the derivation of the term indicates, is a creator in the realm of beauty and truth. Browning's Abt Vogler is speaking for the poets when he says:

"But God has a few of us whom he whispers in the ear;
The rest may reason and welcome: 'tis we musicians know."

And it is the poets of whom Lowell declares in his "Columbus":

"It is they
Who utter wisdom from the central deep,
And listening to the inner flow of things
Speak to the age out of eternity."

"All significant art is ultimately a form of revelation," says Charles A. Bennett, who criticizes Santayana when the latter finds the likeness of poetry and religion in the purely imaginative character of both.[3]

So while theology is akin to philosophy, the great works of religion are closely related to poetry. The seer knows God as the creative Artist, and finds in nature and history and the strange ways of the human heart the ideals and ends that God is seeking to reveal and create. Not only with man but with God he finds

"Thoughts hardly to be packed
Into a narrow act,
Fancies that broke through language and escaped."

And then the seer, like the poet, having seen the beauty and glory and truth which mere ideas cannot express, turns to the concrete, to sign and symbol which God himself employs,

[3]C. A. Bennett, *The Dilemma of Religious Knowledge*, p. 68.

in order not so much to demonstrate and define as to suggest the divine meaning, and to evoke the sense of the Eternal. That is why the Hebrew-Christian Bible, religious literature of undying vitality, has so little theological interpretation and so much concrete expression. Nor should it surprise us that its greatest passages take the form of poetry, though not always by intention. Not merely the Psalms and large portions of the prophets are to be considered here, but such passages as the hymn on the Logos in John 1, Paul's great lyric on love in I Cor. 13, and such words of Jesus as the Lord's Prayer, the parable of the two houses, and the closing verses of Matt. 11. The misuse of the Bible in the name of theology, both lay and professional, is in no small part due to a failure to appreciate the form in which its insights are expressed.

3. How does this insight or intuition come? It is more easy to illustrate than to analyze, and in the end we find something that must be accepted without further explanation. Various efforts have been made to indicate its rationale. In religion it has been explained as inspiration, or as a supernatural communication of ideas. That there is a living God who through outer deed and inner Spirit seeks to make himself known, we have reason to believe; but there is the human side, and a study shows that the insight of the greatest of the prophets is akin to intuition in other fields. Appeal has been made to the unconscious: "The psychological fact for which the vision stands," says Canon B. H. Streeter, "is the sudden emergence into consciousness of an idea or resolve reached in the subconscious."[4] But it is well first to use for explanation what we can know before we appeal to what from its nature is unknowable, and Canon Streeter indeed makes such use. Still less convincing is the principle suggested by Professor Sanday, following William James, "that the proper seat or *locus* of all divine indwelling, or divine action upon the human soul, is the subliminal consciousness." The divine element in religion, he holds, makes itself felt in con-

[4]*Reality,* p. 331.

sciousness, "but it seems to come up as if from some lower and deeper sphere."[5]

Rudolf Otto gives another explanation of intuition in his already cited work, *The Idea of the Holy,* and in an earlier volume on *Die Kant-Fries'sche Religionsphilosophie.*[6] Otto's argument moves about two points. One is the idea that the unique element in religion is a feeling of awe, wonder, and fascination that comes with a sense of the "numinous," or holy, the sense of the divine as something transcendent and "wholly other." The second is the assertion that this awareness of the holy is an *a priori* matter, resting upon a special capacity or faculty of the self, though this may vary greatly and may be quite undeveloped in some. Intuition is this sensing of the numinous. It is the faculty "of genuinely cognizing and recognizing the holy in its appearance, the faculty of divination." It is the religious *a priori* as Kant posited the rational *a priori.*

Whatever may be said about the idea of a religious *a priori,* or a special capacity of divination, or discernment of the divine, Otto's treatment is not an adequate account of religious intuition. The object of such intuition is something more than a nonrational, a wholly-other numinous. Otto insists, it is true, that this numinous has been rationalized and moralized, and that this process is the mark of higher religions; but the consciousness of the numinous, the distinctive religious intuition, seems to be a matter apart from this. Rather we must say, the religious intuition which begins, it may be, with this primitive sense of the holy, is more than this feeling-awareness; it is insight, it is appreciation of the highest and richest meanings and values, into which the rational and ethical enter. In proportion as it is insight, it transcends mere feeling of whatever kind. And such intuition, psychologically considered, is analogous to the process

[5] *Ancient and Modern Christologies,* p. 159. See also Wm. James, *The Varieties of Religious Experience,* pp. 511–519.

[6] In the former, see pp. 148–152, 179; in the latter, pp. 111–122.

that takes place not only in the discernment of the beautiful, the sublime, and the good, but in the common man's understanding of his fellow man and the great scientist's insights of discovery.[7]

It is important to note definitely the relation of intuition in all its forms, religious included, to other ways of knowing, and its dependence upon them. We may take the striking example of scientific intuition reported by the distinguished French mathematician, Henri Poincaré. Dealing with a problem which he could not solve, discharging it from his mind and turning to other things, the idea comes to him with "conciseness, suddenness, and immediate certainty, that arithmetical transformations of indefinite ternary quadratic forms are identical with those of non-Euclidian geometry."[8] But Poincaré makes plain that his sudden discovery was preceded by long study and reflection and that he followed it with careful verification. Nor should we overlook the type of man to whom it came. J. H. Leuba gives a number of similar illustrations in an article on "Intuition" in the *Forum* magazine of May, 1928. Intuition here is not a substitute for careful observation, reflection, criticism, and experiment, but it does have a place. When all else is done, the whole man, with every resource of mind and imagination, sees the whole, and perceives meanings and relations which no study of parts and no summation of discrete facts could yield. Lord Kelvin is re-

[7]John Baillie's able criticism of Otto should be read, though he hardly does justice to the significance of mysticism and intuition as here discussed. See his *Interpretation of Religion,* pp. 246–255. In his more recent volume, *Our Knowledge of God,* he has modified his earlier position by doing more justice to the idea of a knowledge of God through immediate awareness as contrasted with that which is gained through inference. He speaks of "the continual invasion of our life by his holy Presence," and asserts that we must acknowledge him to be not only the most real of all realities, but "that by which we are most directly and intimately confronted." *Op. cit.,* pp. 174, 175.

[8]*Science and Method,* p. 53. See the report with comments in *Reality,* by B. H. Streeter, pp. 332–337.

ported as saying: "Newton was accustomed to let his thoughts become so filled with facts on which his attention was concentrated that the relation subsisting between the various phenomena dawned upon him and he saw it as if by some process of instinctive vision denied to others."[9] It is so with religious intuition. Writing of the mystical experience, Rufus Jones says: " 'Ideas' and 'communications' and 'information' . . . do not drop ready-made into the world from some other region. The mystical experience has undoubtedly a noetic value. But it consists of leaps of insight through heightened life, in an intensifying of vision through the fusing of all the deep-lying powers of intellect, emotions, and will, and in a corresponding surge of conviction through the dynamic integration of personality, rather than in the gift of new knowledge-facts."[10]

4. To understand intuition it is important likewise to see its relation to faith, especially in this realm of religion. Rufus Jones reports Josiah Royce as saying that faith is "the soul's insight or discovery of some reality that enables a man to stand anything that can happen to him in the universe," and himself declares that "Invincible surmise and practical adventure on the strength of the insight are our two essentials for our conquering faith."[11] Intuition is insight into the meaning of the whole. Faith affirms such insight, takes it as a revelation of the Eternal, and makes it the ground for the adventure of life. It is these two aspects, the surmise of the soul and the adventure of faith that Santayana unites in his well-known sonnet:

"O world, thou choosest not the better part!
It is not wisdom to be only wise,
And on the inward vision close the eyes,
But it is wisdom to believe the heart.

[9]Quoted by Rufus M. Jones, *The Trail of Life in the Middle Years*, p. 198. *Cf.* Alexis Carrel, *Man the Unknown*, pp. 122, 123, 137.

[10]*E. R. E.*, art., "Mysticism," p. 84.

[11]*Pathways to the Reality of God*, p. 18.

Columbus found a world, and had no chart,
Save one that faith deciphered in the skies;
To trust the soul's invincible surmise
Was all his science and his only art."

Faith requires this aspect of intuition that it may be open-eyed and not mere submission to authority; it is a confidence based on insight. But faith goes beyond intuition, for in faith the insight becomes the determination of will and life. Faith is confidence in our insight and surrender to it.

We may summarize by saying: Intuition is the apprehension of ultimate meanings, relations, and values which comes when we look at things whole. It is insight as over against sight. It brings us understanding as compared with the mere awareness of mysticism. It is not independent of the experiences that come through sense and reason, but it sees what these mean. It is Moses seeing God in a flaming bush, Hosea finding him in an experience of forgiving love, Isaiah discerning him in the claims of justice, Paul recognizing him in the spirit of Christ. Such intuition may remain sterile; it becomes vital knowledge when faith builds life upon it.

Chapter Ten

THE EXPERIENCE OF VALUES AND THE WAY OF FELLOWSHIP

THE WORLD of our experience comes to us in two ways. We know it, first, as a world of things and events joined in manifold relations and ceaseless change. This factual world is the province of the natural sciences. But we know it also as a world of personal beings and of values, of values that can be known only as they relate to personal beings and are apprehended by them. We are concerned here with one question: How does this sphere of experience contribute to our knowledge of God? We will consider three aspects of this general field as serving this end: the experience of values, the fellowship with men, and the fellowship with God.

I. THE EXPERIENCE OF VALUES

It is not necessary here to set forth a theory of value; two preliminary comments are required, however, to guard against common misconceptions.

The contrast of a world of values with a world of "fact" does not mean that the former is a matter of theory or imagination. When men look up at the glory of the heavens, or see the nobility of a life of unselfish devotion, or reach the sublime thought of a world of unitary order and high purpose, they do not feel that all this is less real than the material bulk of the hills or the physical force of the storm, or that the beauty and truth and goodness which they thus contemplate are mere evanescent idea or subjective imagining. They feel rather that they are discovering the reality that is behind appearance, that in which the true power and meaning of their world come to view.

These values and meanings are not individual and private. True, nowhere does difference of private opinion enter in so much as in relation to what is adjudged good and beautiful and true; and with respect to the idea of value, we are quite apt to ask first what is of value to us individually, or to think of what is of value to the little humanity of our globe. But that limitation is simply the kind which we must everywhere transcend in our thinking; it does not belong to the matter itself. Value is indeed always value for some one; there is no value in any ultimate sense apart from persons, apart from the understanding and appreciation of beings who have worth in themselves and for whom the world of things and events has significance. But that does not mean something merely individual. On the contrary, the conception of meanings and values leads from the individual to the group, then to humanity as a whole, then to the thought of personal beings aside from our race, and finally to God himself. For if these values are real, then they must be real in God and for God, and not simply for passing finite beings who may or may not discover and achieve them.

And now we are ready for our thesis: The world of values is our way to the surest and highest knowledge of God. It is our way to the highest knowledge of God because it is here rather than in some mystic sense of divine transcendence or in some vision of power in nature that the *character* of God is discerned. And it is our surest way because it is open to all men and it leads not simply to ideas about God but to that deeper apprehension in which we know God because we enter into his life and share it. For concrete consideration we select the three values to which human thought has always been led: beauty and truth and goodness.

1. The way of beauty. The western religious mind, following the Hebrew tradition, has stressed the good rather than the beautiful. But beauty is not a casual or accidental affair; it belongs to the basic order of the universe. In his Gifford Lectures, J. Arthur Thomson argues that beauty, thought of in the past as a quality of the exotic, is now seen as pervasive through nature. Apart from disease, almost unknown in nature, from unfinished organisms, and from some plants and animals which show man's hand, "all organisms are artistic harmonies, pleasing to the unprejudiced eye, evoking the æsthetic emotion, especially when seen in their natural setting." "Beauty crowds us all our life." The farthest reach of structure disclosed by the microscope reveals the same symmetry and beauty. Maude Royden tells of happening in upon an illustrated lecture by Professor Thomson and seeing upon the screen what looked like a beautiful rose window, only to learn that it was a magnified cross-section of a spine of the lowly sea urchin. Clearly beauty is no incidental or casual affair. It is, in fact, a mark of life which has attained and a condition of such attainment. In Croce's term, it is "successful expression." In the struggle for existence, the unharmonious, the impossible, have been weeded out. "Nature pronounces her verdict upon ugliness by eliminating it. Beauty is nature's stamp of approval on harmonious viable individuality." As Meredith put it: "The ugly is only half way to a thing." That does not mean, following Darwinian precedent, that beauty merely denotes a certain survival value in the struggle for existence, becoming effective by chance in some special instances. Rather it is a revelation of a "principle which pervades all reality with its living activity." "Æsthetic emotion" is thus "another right-of-way path towards reality."[1]

The meaning of beauty for the knowledge of the divine, traced thus in the realm of nature, becomes even more evi-

[1]J. Arthur Thomson, *The System of Animate Nature,* Vol. I, Lecture VIII and p. 62.

dent when we consider it in literature and art, where beauty of idea is fitly wedded to beauty of form, and in character and life. We must agree with those who insist that beauty stands in its own right and cannot be resolved into truth or goodness, or made their mere servant, even if we cannot say with Keats:

> "Beauty is truth, truth beauty, that is all
> Ye know on earth, and all ye need to know."

These three, beauty and truth and goodness, are inseparably joined, and no one of them is complete without the others. The highest truth has in it a certain quality of perfection which we can only call beautiful; in it the unity and meaning and harmony of the world come to expression. In goodness, too, there is something faulty if it be not beautiful; if it lack harmony and unity, if it does not speak to us as something fine and fair, then its goodness is not complete. Surely no work of art or scene in nature was ever so beautiful to look upon as the spirit that moved in Jesus. On the other hand, those whose cult is that of beauty consciously divorced from any regard for truth and goodness miss beauty at its highest, leave life a fragment when it should be a harmonious whole, or even drop at times to what is foul.

What all this points to is a deeper unity, a Being in whom these three are one. That is God, and beauty belongs to him equally with truth and goodness, and helps to reveal him. Him we are to worship in the beauty of holiness. To him we pray: "And let the beauty of the Lord our God be upon us." And we can understand Augustine's word when he laments: "Too late have I loved thee, Beauty so ancient and so new." Thus in beauty, though in widely varying degree, God is speaking to us. And because there is in beauty this quality of the divine, we are summoned in its presence not only to enjoyment but to wonder and awe. For the same reason it brings a certain imperative with it. There is something wrong in the ugly, morally wrong. Alike in our own life and character, and in the world as we touch and shape it, we are to make all things not only honest and useful but fair. Thus he who sees beauty gains some vision of God and he who creates beauty becomes a partner with God and knows him by sharing his life. So we may say with Edwin Arlington Robinson:

> "Oh, brother man, if you have eyes at all,
> Look at a branch, a bird, a child, a rose,
> Or anything God ever made that grows,—
> Nor let the smallest vision of it slip,
> Till you may read, as on Belshazzar's wall,
> The glory of eternal partnership."[2]

2. The way of truth. If beauty has place as a much neglected but important word in religion, that is even more the case with truth. Men have drawn back from it for fear of intellectualism in religion, but the word stands for something central in the religious spirit and in the quest for God. Jehovah is "the God of truth." In the coming kingdom, "Mercy and truth are met together." The word plays a special role in the fourth gospel. That gospel may be a bridge between Hellenism and Judaism at this point, but the author retains the vital, ethical quality which belongs to the Hebrew use of that term. Christ is the Word, "full of grace and truth." His followers are to receive the divine Spirit, which is the Spirit of truth, and it is the truth which is to make them free. But "the truth" which they are to know demands truth, or trueness, in themselves: "If ye abide in my word ye shall know the truth"; "If any man willeth to do his will, he shall know."[3]

The word truth has a double meaning for religion, as is indicated in these passages. In its first aspect it is more the rational. It is concerned not with facts, indeed, but with the meanings involved in these. It is the search of the mind for

[2]*Collected Poems,* 1924, p. 96.

[3]Ps. 31:5; 85:10; John 1:14; 16:13; 8:32; 7:17.

the One that lies back of the many, for the real universe. God is the final answer to this search; in him all things find their meaning. But if God be truth, then the patient search for truth is one of the roads that lead to God. Whatever helps us to see the relations and meanings and purpose of things helps us in the search for God.

But the distinctive religious emphasis appears in the other meaning of truth. Truth means here a certain quality of spirit and way of life. It is not only the open mind that willingly accepts, but the eager, searching spirit that cares more for the truth than for prejudice or partisan opinion or personal privilege which might be disturbed. It does not mean indifference to security or mere love of adventure and search, but rather the conviction that there can be no real life and no abiding security apart from the truth. The desire for truth, the faith in the truth, and the confidence that truth will triumph in a world of honest search and free discussion mark a high stage in human life. It is at bottom a spiritual faith, a faith in truth as something basic to our universe, and thus essentially a faith in God. And as inner truth, or trueness, it is not only a high quality of spirit which marks the presence of God, but it is the condition of knowing truth in the objective sense. "Thou desirest truth in the inward parts"; and upon that follows the second: "In the hidden part thou wilt make me to know wisdom."[4] But the truth that we find in this way is no mere abstraction; it is life, it is God. It is truth that makes free—free from narrowness and limitation, free from the slaveries of prejudice and fear, free from the evils of selfishness and bitterness and hate.

3. The way of moral insight and loyalty. Of even greater importance in the search for God is the way of moral insight and loyalty. Here is the distinctive contribution of prophetic religion: not the sublimity and power of nature, not the mystic emotions of the soul, but the moral insights of man are for the prophets the surest revelation of the nature of God. The

[4]Ps. 51:6.

logic of this position might be put thus: However much more God is than all that is finite, God cannot be less than the highest that we know; the highest that we know in man is our surest clue to God. It is the *via eminentiæ*. But the prophets did not reach their goal by logic. They were men who loved righteousness and hated iniquity, whose hearts were stirred with pity for an oppressed and needy people and filled with a spirit of good will. They did not argue from this to God; they found God in this. It was not a conclusion from ethics but an experience of religion.[5] Hosea had the experience of a strange and limitless mercy. Amos was stirred with pity and indignant revolt at the cruelties of war and oppression. Micah knew the meaning of political corruption and economic exploitation, seizing natural resources, making a slave of the common man; and it quickened in him a nobly passionate devotion to justice. Now, other men have felt like this, but these men went farther. They said, this is the Lord speaking, this is the word of the Eternal. Moral vision and social passion were for them an experience of the Holy, bringing a sense of God and a vision of his nature. It was the channel for the self-revealing God. We find the same attitude with Jesus. He, too, had a deep and reverent sense of "the Lord high and lifted up"; but it was the *moral* transcendence of God that stirred him most deeply, the divine mercy that not merely forgave when men repented, but went out at infinite cost to seek the sinner. His appeal was definitely to the moral insights and experiences of men: the father going forth to meet his son, the shepherd looking for his lost sheep, the gift to the eleventh-hour laborer of a wage determined not by desert but by need, the spirit of parents in the treatment of their children, and above all his use of the word father for God.[6] This is not merely illustra-

[5]The moral argument for the being of God has sometimes exposed itself to criticism at this point by making God a mere inference from moral experience and failing to see that moral experience is an experience of God and so itself religious.

[6]Luke 15; Matt. 20:10–16; 7:7–11. On the prophets, note Hosea 3; Amos 1 to 2:8; Micah 2:2; 3:9–11; 6:6–8.

tive material employed by Jesus; it reveals the way by which he himself saw into the heart of God.

A suggestive illustration is furnished by a story of old Japan told by Lafcadio Hearn and reported by Joseph Fort Newton.[7] A peasant working his farm on a high hillside saw a great tidal wave which was following on the heels of an earthquake shock, and which threatened with imminent death his neighbors in the valley below. There was no time to run down and warn them. Sacrificing his summer's harvest, he set his rice ricks ablaze and then rang the temple bell. His neighbors hurried up from the valley to his aid only to discover how his sacrifice had saved their lives. In after years, these men worshipped in their village temple the spirit of this man, their neighbor, and that, too, while he lived. Perhaps it would be more true to say, these men saw in his spirit something divine, and it was this divine, in their neighbor and more than their neighbor, which they worshipped.

But moral insight is not enough. At each step it has been made plain that the values of life, the beautiful, the true, and the good, call not simply for insight and appreciation, but for achievement. They all come with a certain authority, demanding expression in our life. Indeed, they cannot really be known except as they are obeyed and become regulative for life. Insight and feeling must be completed in the will. The knowledge of God is a knowledge of acquaintance, and the acquaintance means the sharing of life. It is fellowship, participation, *koinonia.* "The character of God is known only as it is shared."[8] If then God be righteousness, he can be really known only through moral loyalty.

Religion is first of all a challenge to the will. It offers not so much a theory of the universe as a way of life. That does not mean blind obedience. It asks men to be loyal to their highest insights. It does not promise the truth to men except

[7]*Things I Know in Religion,* pp. 30, 31.

[8]H. W. Robinson in *The Future of Christianity,* edited by Jas. Marchant, p. 43.

at the cost of obedience. The whole man must be given in order to secure this knowledge, not the mind alone, but the heart and will. "If ye abide in my word, ye shall know the truth." "If any man willeth to do his will, he shall know." "If thine eye be single, thy whole body shall be full of light."[9] The problems of life are solved not in cloistered retreats but on the highways of life. It is to the obedient will that God is known. "Let him, therefore, who would arrive at knowledge, train his moral sense; let him act and conceive in accordance with the noble essence of his soul; and, as of itself, nature will become open to him. Moral action is the great and only experiment in which all the riddles of the most manifold appearances explain themselves."[10] "It becomes more and more clear that cognition cannot be separated from action, or tendency to action, in which it is expressed." The concept of God "is known in a response of man to that which makes the highest of all demands upon him. In that response we know that we have met that which gives meaning and significance to all the rest of our experience. There is a certain level of existence which attests itself as sacred. The idea of God takes shape in our response, of whatever kind, to those occasions in which that significance, that character of sacredness, reveals itself."[11]

4. The way of good will. Moral loyalty, however, involves a further step, that of good will. "God is love; and he that abideth in love abideth in God, and God abideth in him."[12] The love which the New Testament exalts as the spirit of God and the way of man is no sentimental affection and no mere attitude of general benevolence; it is creative good will, seeking to give its own life to the world, building up here on earth an order of beauty and truth, of justice and love—the kingdom of God. For the highest knowledge of God man must

[9]John 8:31, 32; 7:17; Matt. 6:22.

[10]Novalis, quoted by Henry Jones in *Browning as a Philosophical and Religious Teacher,* p. 210.

[11]L. W. Grensted, *The Person of Christ,* pp. 201, 205, 206.

[12]1 John 4:16.

share this life. That is strikingly expressed by Kagawa of Japan: "By divine revelation is meant the entrance of truth into the depth of living. As long as the truth does not hold sway over the whole of life, cognition and life are two separate entities, God and man are living apart from each other. . . . Therefore he who seeks for the divine revelation will not find God through the theory of cognition. First of all let him endeavor to create values. Let him liberate those who are oppressed, feed those who are in want, give sight to the blind, find a way to enrich the poor. Then will he be able to see divine revelations every day."[13]

The same truth is voiced by Tagore in his volume, *Gitanjali.*

"Leave this chanting and singing and telling of beads! Whom dost thou worship in this lonely dark corner of a temple with doors all shut? Open thine eyes and see: thy God is not before thee!

"He is there where the tiller is tilling the hard ground and where the pathmaker is breaking stones. He is with them in sun and in shower, and his garment is covered with dust. Put on thy holy mantle and even like him come down on the dusty soil!

"Deliverance? Where is this deliverance to be found? Our master has joyfully taken upon him the bonds of creation; he is bound with us all forever.

"Come out of thy meditations and leave aside thy flowers and incense! What harm is there if thy clothes become tattered and stained? Meet him and stand by him in toil and in sweat of thy brow."

What this creative good will is, Jesus has suggested by such a simple illustration as giving a cup of cold water. The essential idea is that of love in action, action motivated by

[13] *Kagawa,* by William Axling, p. 125.

love. It is not a matter of occasional and incidental service; it involves a man's whole life and its underlying motive. The social order should give every man an opportunity to contribute creatively to the common good, and should demand this of all. Religion reveals this task, ideally conceived, as a sharing in the creative work of God, an expression of love. It is a means of fellowship with God and a means to the knowledge of God through the bond of a common task taken up in common spirit and purpose. This is the real "glory of eternal partnership."[14]

II. THE WAY OF FELLOWSHIP WITH GOD

The idea of fellowship, or communion, with Deity belongs to all religions, for everywhere religion has this common concern, to bring man into right relation with the divine so that he may attain life. But for Christianity the word fellowship has a special significance, first because of its character as ethical and personal, second (and this follows from the first) because it moves on two planes, man and God, man and man, with each involving the other. Fellowship on both these planes gives us the simplest and surest way to the knowledge of God.

[14]A great human document that belongs in this general discussion is Mahatma Gandhi's autobiography, with its emphasis on the words truth and love. It is entitled significantly *My Experiments with Truth. Mahatma Gandhi: His Own Story* is the title of the first of the three volumes in which this work appeared in the Occident; in it the introduction and the conclusion especially should be noted. For Gandhi, God is above all else truth. "I worship God as truth only. He alone is real, all else is unreal." But the way to the knowledge of this truth which is God is mercy, love to men. "To see the universal and all-pervading Spirit of Truth face to face one must be able to love the meanest of creation as oneself." The knowledge of God is morally conditioned; truth and love are the way to the knowledge of God. This is surely not far from the Christian declaration. To this may be added the word of a great surgeon, Doctor William Mayo, of Rochester, Minnesota, who said to a friend: "A selfish man does not see straight. I have always tried to see the other man's interest."

1. The knowledge of God through prayer and worship. Religion is life with God; prayer is this fellowship coming to conscious expression. Simple though its expression may be, it has varied aspects: awe and adoration in the presence of the Holy, reverence for that which is worthy (worship implies worth-ship, the quality of worth), aspiration toward the highest, pure devotion, and a faith that lies back of it all. It is man's soul meeting the Most High and making answer with mind and heart and will. Here is religion on its receptive side as quiet and meditation, and so as receptivity and renewal. But here, too, is the active aspect, demanding every spiritual energy: the mind rising to its highest vision, the soul in its loftiest aspiration, the will affirming its supreme devotion. Paul Sabatier has well put this side of it in his *St. Francis of Assisi.*

"To pray is to talk with God, to lift ourselves up to him, to converse with him that he may come down to us. It is an act of meditation, of reflection, which presupposes the effort of all that is most personal in us. . . . With St. Francis, as with Jesus, prayer has this character of effort which makes of it the greatest moral act. . . . For him, as for his Master, the end of prayer is communion with the heavenly Father, the accord of the divine with the human; or, rather, it is man who puts forth his strength to do the will of God, not saying to him a mere passive, resigned, powerless, 'Thy will be done,' but courageously raising his head: 'Behold me, Lord, I delight to do thy will.' "[1]

Now if there be a God who is above us in holiness, akin to us as person, and near us as love and life, then fellowship like this, though it may not mean miraculous illumination or mystical rapture, will be the way alike of life and of knowledge.

We must look once more at these words, life and knowledge, in their mutual relations. "Life" for religion is not mere existence; it is not quantity of duration but quality of

[1]Pp. 187, 188.

being; it is vision of truth, love and service, mastery and freedom, deliverance from evil, and devotion to highest good. In all this it is oneness with God, but a oneness that is personal-ethical, not mystical-metaphysical. Because it is the supreme fellowship it demands the highest that is in us: meditation, a renewed vision of what the divine life is, a clear recognition of sin and failure, the reaffirmation of ideals and devotion, and with it all the replenishing of confidence and courage and strength. And that is the way of knowledge, for in religion knowledge is inseparable from life. It comes not in facts that can be easily communicated, or ideas that can be inculcated, but as the knowledge of acquaintance reaching its highest point in conscious communion with God. Fellowship with a God that is personal and ethical is only possible through the sharing of his spirit and his ways, that is, in character and conduct; for fellowship means just this, a having in common. In prayer this fellowship with the divine is at once consciously expressed and definitely furthered. The testimony to this has been universal. Worship and the conscious practice of fellowship have brought not only help for life and a deepened sense of the reality of the unseen, but a clearer perception of its values, its morally commanding ideals, and its nature as at once transcendent holiness and immanent good will and help.

2. The knowledge of God through saving help. There is a second aspect of this fellowship with God which is significant for man's religious knowledge, and that is the experience of saving help. Man is burdened with a sense of danger without and conflict within. He knows the wide disparity between his actual self and his ideals, the gulf that separates him from the holy God, and the constant tension between himself and his world. The awareness of evil to be overcome and good to be attained is at the very center of his being as man.

To this universal problem religion addresses itself. It claims that there is a higher world which is not simply ideal and demand, but which means saving help. As William James put it: "There are resources in us that naturalism with its literal and legal virtues never recks of, possibilities that take our breath away, of another kind of happiness and power, based on giving up our own will and letting something higher work for us. . . . In a word, the believer is continuous, to his own consciousness, at any rate, with a wider self from which saving experiences flow in."[2] The literature of religion is full of the witness of men to such an experience. It is set forth with a wealth of illustration in such works as James' *Varieties of Religious Experience* and A. C. Underwood's *Conversion: Christian and Non-Christian,* where they discuss the "twice-born" man; but it appears equally in those "once-born" individuals who have taken a deliberate life-attitude of faith in God, have lived in fellowship with him, and have found through the years an ever-growing measure of insight and strength and peace. It is not a matter of passing emotions but of abiding results in threefold form: a life of fellowship with God, integration and enrichment of individual life, and the creation of human fellowship on a higher level.

But here the objection is interposed: The facts as to this richer life are one thing, their interpretation is another. Underwood's book shows that conversion is found in many religions and even apart from any religion. Paul in his ascription of saving help to Christ was paralleled by others of that day who pointed to Isis or Osiris or Mithra. Is it not then a purely intra-human affair, requiring only psychological description? The reply requires discrimination. We accept the distinction between experience and its interpretation, but that applies equally to all knowledge. We realize that the interpretation must be compared with that of others, criticized, verified by further experiment, and brought into relation with other knowledge; but that is just what Christian thought has been doing for centuries, submitting to a test which the mystery religions of that day were not able to

[2] *A Pluralistic Universe,* pp. 305, 407.

endure. Clearly we must exercise the greatest care in deducing from experience a system of doctrine. Paul's doctrines of Christ and the atonement may not follow from the spiritual results wrought in his own life. But all this is beside the main issue. The point is that these men are all convinced that their new and larger life has come from a power not their own. That is rather hard to dispute. If life everywhere is thus dependent and conditioned, why should it not be so in the world of the spirit?

Our conclusion then is this: Men through the ages have found themselves in the presence of forces spiritual as well as physical. Their response to these spiritual forces has secured certain results. Through this experience they have come to a knowledge of this spiritual world, a working acquaintance it might be called. The Christian faith is an interpretation of this experience. Its ideas may not be perfect; they may demand refinement, enlargement, correction. But at least there is here a way of knowledge, and the challenge of the Christian faith is this: Take these convictions as a guide. Test them for yourself and find in them both life and knowledge.

The issue of such experiment and interpretation will, of course, vary, for the back-lying philosophies of men will have their influence. For one it may yield no more than the cautious conclusion that there are forces in the universe which are productive of these values which we observe, that there is a definite "process" which is "supremely significant for human living." The Christian conviction is that the life which has come to men through Jesus Christ has brought a living relation with God and a knowledge of God.

III. THE WAY OF FELLOWSHIP WITH MAN

"Nothing, and least of all God the deepest of realities, is known to us at all except in and by means of its relation to our own self and our fellow creatures. . . . God is not to be found in some dehumanized void of the soul's wilful making."[1] If it be true that the knowledge of God can come to us only through the concrete experiences of life, then man's life in relation to his fellows has unique importance. We have been considering the personal life in relation to God from the individual standpoint; we know, however, that personal life never exists in merely individual form. Alike in its origin, its development, and its highest expression, it is dependent upon social relations and is expressed most fully in these. If it is human experience that we are considering, then we must study it in its social forms if we are to find it at its richest and highest.

The discovery of God through human relations has been characteristic of the Hebrew-Christian tradition, which stands here in sharp contrast with other tendencies in religion. Buddha finds his way through the negation of life instead of its affirmation and harmonization, and so the social life is excluded; his return from the individual search for salvation in order that he may help men is a noble inconsistency. Hinduism rests upon an impersonal principle; it is an impersonal cosmos in relation to which both these religions take their stand. Confucianism is built upon social relations, but there is no way leading from these to God. In the religion of the prophets and Jesus, the world is at once affirmed and transcended. The transcendent God is found in history and human fellowship. God is more than the world and man, but these are not meaningless; for that which is highest in man points to the nature of God and the life with man is a sphere for fellowship with God and the knowledge of God.

We note first the insights that come through social experience. As already noted, the prophets saw in the passion for justice and the spirit of love, however imperfectly apprehended and expressed, a sign of God's working and a revelation of his character. Especially significant are the Servant of the Lord passages of Second Isaiah. It makes little difference here whether the reference be to an individual, a group,

[1] A. L. Lilley, *Prayer in Christian Theology,* p. 125.

or the nation as a whole ideally conceived: the prophet saw in the human scene vicarious suffering serving for the redemption of others and concluded daringly that this was the deed of God and so a revelation of God.[2] The Christian Church saw in Jesus the fulfillment of these Isaianic words, and voiced its faith in this conviction, that the eternal God was himself present as love and truth and saving help in the shame and agony of the death of Christ, and that this human life was the supreme revelation of God.

Human fellowship leads us to the knowledge of God not only by the insights it gives, but by becoming for us a sacrament of God; we know God through sharing his spirit and life and it is in the group that these are most richly, continuously, and creatively present. The dangers of institutionalism in religion are only too obvious, but the corporate nature of the Christian life and the value, nay, the necessity, of fellowship for faith and love should be equally apparent. The young John Wesley entered one day into conversation with a casual fellow traveller. One word from this acquaintance left its impress on all his later work: "Young man, the Bible knows nothing of solitary religion. You must find companions or make them." Rightly A. H. Gray suggests: "If a man wants to find God, let him first find some group of people to whom God is real and join himself to them."[3]

A study of the apostolic Church as reflected in Paul's letters and the book of Acts is illuminating. Religion for these first Christians was a fellowship into which men entered. Becoming a Christian was not a mere matter of individual opinion and conduct; it meant entering upon a life which was social of its very nature. The great word was fellowship, *koinonia.* The fellowship was not a divine form of organization, with prescribed constitution and by-laws and officials; but neither was it a merely human association. It had two

[2]Isa. 42:1–4; 49:1–7; 50:4–9; 52:13 to 53:12. *Cf.* 63:9, 16; 57:15; 40:11.

[3]*Finding God,* p. 116.

sides. There was the human aspect: the group with its common life, the spirit of love, the mutual care in material as in spiritual matters, the common faith and worship and devotion. But there was a divine aspect also, and this was fundamental. *Koinonia* meant the fellowship, or communion, both in terms of its members, and in terms of that which they had in common (*koinos*). It meant the sharers and that which was shared. But that which was thus shared, that which bound them together, was something more than human; it was something from God, it was God's deed, it was God himself in their midst. Sometimes this divine and creative element which was their common life was conceived as the Spirit of God—so in the benediction of II Cor. 13:14. Here *koinonia* is perhaps best translated fellowship instead of communion, the reference not being to fellowship with the Spirit but to the fellowship that is in the Spirit and of the Spirit. Sometimes they thought of the living, indwelling Christ as the creative life of the fellowship, which thus formed the body of Christ. The right understanding of this *koinonia* is thus of vital importance for our conception of the Church. This *koinonia* is the Church; this fellowship is at once the divine presence which unites the group and the group which is united, both that which is shared and those who share it. Only, since that which is shared is personal and ethical, a third element must come in: the active life of sharing, the fellowship as something practised in human relations of love and mutual help. We need here to avoid the transcendental mysticism of the Greek Orthodox Church, whose Platonic idealism conceives the Church as something that was eternal in God and so exists essentially apart from humanity, and whose realism tends to make the divine something substance-like, almost thing-like, shared in the sacraments, while human relations are relatively negligible.[4] But we must realize the equal danger that appears when the stress is laid on the shar-

[4]See N. Arseniev, *We Beheld His Glory,* and S. Bulgakov, *The Wisdom of God,* VII.

ing and the sharers, not on that which is shared, and the Church is often little more than a voluntary human association.

What then is the meaning of such a fellowship for our knowledge of God? (1) It is the channel through which the wealth of the past and the living message of Christ are mediated to the men of today. (2) It is itself an incarnation of God, the embodiment ("the body") of the spirit of Christ. That is the only way we can know God, that he shall come to us in some apprehensible form, in some incarnation of himself; and with all its limitations, the fellowship of men of faith in whom the spirit of Christ lives on is the highest form in which God can express himself. (3) The life of the group kindles life in the individual; it brings heightened sensitivity, clearer intuition, stronger faith, and furnishes an atmosphere in which spiritual life is more easily possible.

Other forms of human fellowship must by no means be excluded, occurring within or without the visible Church, or cutting across all lines. There is the fellowship with the high spirits of the past, who reveal their secrets through the printed page. Poetry and drama, history and autobiography, hymn and meditation and prayer, all may serve to bring God to us through some noble spirit who has found God and the way of life. There is the fellowship of friendship, intimate and personal, and that within the home. There is a fellowship of devotion in some common task of serving humanity or some real creative effort. Whatever leads us into fuller life brings us to the knowledge of God, even though it be at times by men who do not speak his name.

The individual by himself is a helpless creature. The law of life everywhere, as our study of organicism and emergent evolution indicated, is that the way to higher levels and richer quality of being is through the association of the individual with a larger whole. And nowhere is that more true than in religion. How shall the life of the spirit be lived in the miasmic atmosphere of our day, with its stifling and destroying greed and lust, materialism and selfishness? In *Invasion,* a novel of the first World War, Maxence van der Meersch portrays movingly how the prosperous Decraemer finds faith and love and joy and peace for the first time in his life under the terrible conditions of confinement in a war-time prison. Then the heights that he gained through his fellowship with the noble Abbe Sennevilliers he loses in the selfish scramble for pleasure and prosperity that makes the inescapable atmosphere of his post-war world. There is no instrument for the mediation of good and ill alike that is as powerful as the human fellowship of which we are a part.

Chapter Eleven

FAITH AND REASON

I. FAITH

GOD CANNOT be known apart from faith: that statement voices the conviction of Christian thinkers through the centuries. Today religion's emphasis on faith is met with vigorous opposition. The way to truth, we are told, is through fact and reason; to believe without evidence is foolish, to go contrary to reason is wrong. "Which is the higher ideal," we are asked, "loyal belief or impartial investigation?" But the dilemma is a false one, and back of these objections lies a misconception of faith, not the less wrong because religious thinkers have often set it forth. Our discussion so far has led us to two conclusions: (1) The knowledge of God, in the significant religious sense, is a knowledge of acquaintance, the apprehension of something with which we are in relation, of something that comes to us in the sense of the holy, in commanding values, especially of the moral life, and in the response of saving help when we give ourselves in trust and in loyalty. (2) The knowledge of God, like other knowledge, demands a response of the mind, an understanding and interpretation of experience. There is no knowledge of heart and will that is not at the same time the mind's knowledge of God. To this we now add (3): this knowledge is always a knowledge of faith and must remain so even when the mind has done its best. No reason can prove it with compulsion, no vision of the eye can demonstrate it. The final word always rests with faith. What, then, is religious faith?

1. Faith is not acceptance upon authority in default of knowledge. We cannot agree with the Roman Catholic position, that faith is "assent on authority, that is to say, the acceptance of a proposition, not because we ourselves perceive its truth, but because another person tells us that it is true."[1] Traditional Protestant theology often fell into the same error, except that it made the Bible instead of the Church the seat of this authority. Now it is true that the appeal to reason is by no means excluded from this position. Catholic and Protestant both appealed to reason to prove that revelation was necessary and was contained in the Bible. The Roman Catholic further appealed to reason to prove the authority of the Church. It was agreed, too, that faith involved inner conviction. But the crucial fact remains: whatever the appeal to reason or inner conviction, faith involved acceptance of a given authority; and once the authority was accepted, it was not a matter of reflection or personal judgment or inner conviction, but of an obedient submission. Corresponding to this is the distinction made between objective faith, "the sum of truths revealed by God in Scripture and tradition, and which the Church presents to us in a brief form in her creeds," and subjective (personal) faith, "the habit or virtue by which we assent to those truths."[2] Here religion becomes intellectualistic without becoming rational. The free reason and inner conviction are a preliminary stage, to be left behind when the act of faith takes place. Faith is passive submission and the function of reason is not to explore or decide, but to defend.

Cardinal Newman exemplifies this position in his *Apologia pro Vita Sua*. The body of the volume is taken up with "The History of My Religious Opinions," his account of the reasons for accepting the claims of the Roman Church. Here

[1]Wilhelm and Scannell, *Manual of Catholic Theology,* I, pp. 114–116. *Cf.* art., "Faith," in *The Catholic Encyclopedia.*

[2]*Catholic Encyclopedia,* art. "Faith."

he appeals to "reflection" and "logical value." With his conversion the whole situation alters. "From the time I became a Catholic, of course, I have no further history of my opinions to narrate. . . . And now, having thus described it ["the infallibility lodged in the Roman Catholic Church"], I profess my absolute submission to its claim. I believe the whole revealed dogma as taught by the apostles, as committed by the apostles to the Church, and as declared by the Church to me. I receive it as it is infallibly interpreted by the authority to whom it is thus committed, and (implicitly) as it shall be further interpreted by that authority to the end of time."[3] This is not faith as Jesus exemplified it and demanded it, or as it appears in Paul. This is submission to an institution; theirs is confidence in a Person. This is a sacrifice of intellect; theirs is a devotion of life. The closed mind of such authoritarianism cannot be reconciled with the open mind of science.

Equally mistaken are those opinions which take faith to be an unsatisfactory substitute for knowledge. Some conceive it as necessary in a field where we must go by probabilities or make a decision when there are no real grounds for or against. For others it is mere "wishful thinking."

2. Consider now the nature of faith as this functions in human experience. The world with which faith has to do is the world of the unseen, the world of the realities and values of the spirit. That does not mean something in the distant heavens; it is near to every one of us. It is the world of truth and love and righteousness, of meanings and values. It is only as man knows this world, and lives in it and by it, that he becomes really human. Apart from this he is a machine, impelled by physical force or blind impulse; in this his real life is lived. Through this he becomes free; he discerns what life means, he senses goals worthy of his effort and follows them as a rational being. For the religious man its significance is summed up in the one word, God. "He asks the meaning of it all, and he names the name of God."[4]

[3]Everyman's Library edition, pp. 121, 215, 225.

[4]A. S. Pringle-Pattison, *The Idea of God*, p. 237.

What such a world calls for is insight that discerns its reality and meaning, a trust that is willing to surrender to its claims, and a loyalty that is expressed in life. And just this is what the Christian religion means by faith.

3. Faith thus conceived has a double significance for our knowledge of God. First, it is itself a form of knowledge. It is the affirmation that in its insights this world of the unseen is known to us and that this knowledge of insight and trust has its place by the side of the knowledge of sense-perception and logical demonstration. Faith is the confident affirmation of the reality and the goodness of the object of its trust and the belief that it is in real relation with that object. In the second place, it is the condition of further experience. If there be a God who is love and righteousness and truth, then this God can only be known in a fellowship of trust and obedience. Life and faith stand in continuous mutual relation: the experiences of life summon us to faith, and faith in turn becomes the way to larger life and knowledge. Knowledge and life are inseparable and both wait upon the venture of faith.

> "Are there not, Festus, . . .
> Two points in the adventure of the diver:
> One—when, a beggar, he prepares to plunge;
> One—when, a prince, he rises with his pearl?"
>
> (Browning, *Paracelsus,* I.)

The world of the unseen offers us life's highest goods and deepest meanings. It comes to us, however, not with a demonstration but with a challenge. It does not call for credulity, yet it offers proof of its reality and a share in its life only to those who will trust and venture. All life demands confidence and courage, and the life of religion most of all. There is a real tension between faith and knowledge: faith must outrun knowledge, knowledge can come only with faith. That tension, never wholly resolved, is as fruitful for knowledge as it is essential to life.

II. REASON

The ways to the knowledge of God so far considered might be grouped in three classes: the way of tradition, or that which is given us by others; the way of personal experience in such varied forms as mysticism, intuition, the moral life, human fellowship, and saving help; the way of faith interpreted as trust and moral obedience. We consider now a fourth way, that of reason.

We must distinguish here first between rationalism and the use of reason. Rationalism is the term used "both in philosophy and theology for any system which sets up human reason as the final criterion and chief source of knowledge."[1] The whole trend of thought today, alike in religion and philosophy, is opposed to such a position, and its criticism need not detain us. The source of knowledge in religion as elsewhere is not in abstract principles but in concrete experience, the varied forms of which we have been considering. Rationalism does not do justice to the rich realities of religion; under it religion becomes a meager, arid, and impotent affair of the intellect. The historical loses its significance; if reason can win unaided the necessary truth, why concern oneself with the traditions of the past? Jesus would thus become the contingent expression of a general principle, an expression which could be left aside when once the principle was grasped. With its intellectualistic bias, rationalism fails to appreciate the meaning of values and faith in religion. Finally, under its hands God tends to become an abstract idea or general order to be discerned and accepted, rather than that holy and living God of vital religion who reveals himself in history and in the experiences of life, with whom man may be joined in fellowship, and whom he may know as saving help. One cannot mount to God, the living God of religion, by the steps of logic. He speaks, and man responds with insight and faith; he gives himself, and man knows him in

[1] *Encyc. Brit.*, 11th ed., Art., "Rationalism."

the life that he bestows. He is more than the first principle of philosophy, even if that philosophy be a strict theism asserting a personal God.

But to reject rationalism does not mean to reject the use of reason as necessary to the knowledge of God. The word reason has been used in two broadly distinguishable senses: first, as pure reason (the *νοῦς* or *νόησις* of Plato, the German *Vernunft*), the power of insight or intuition, which sees the whole of things and perceives their meaning; second, as understanding (the *διάνοια* of Plato, the German *Verstand*), which compares, relates, deduces, judges, criticizes, verifies. We have already seen that in one or both of these forms the human reason necessarily enters into every one of the ways to the knowledge of God which we have discussed. The former has been noted in the discussion of intuition, and the need of reason and reflective understanding is apparent at every other point. We may note now in summary the principal ways in which reason, or mind, is used in the knowledge of God—taking reason here broadly as the aspect of intelligence and understanding contrasted with the feeling-willing side of man's nature.

Reason has a threefold task here, and first that of interpretation. Whether we speak of revelation or experience, no ready-made knowledge is offered to us. Barth says that God himself authenticates his message. Yes, but he does so not by mechanical means but in a person-to-person word, and that means an appeal to thinking man. Man must understand a given experience as a manifestation of God and interpret its meaning. The ignorance of man through the ages is not accounted for by the silence of God but by our failure to understand what we hear and see. Second, there is the need of criticism, comparison, relation, and continuous experimentation. We must criticize, asking whether we have rightly understood what has come to us. We must compare our ideas, relating them to each other, and testing them with other insights. We must ask what these insights mean for life, and then enlarge and verify or correct in the light of the on-going experiment of living. We must treat in the same manner the insights of the past which come to us in the great tradition. We must understand the faith of the fellowship to which we belong, revise the forms of its expression when needed, enlarge its apprehension, and make the historic faith a creative source rather than a limitation. Finally, it is the mind's task to gather all impressions and experiences and insights together, and then to look at the whole and seek to understand.

There are four considerations which we may note here by way of summary. (1) Truth is no mere matter of facts but primarily of relations and meanings, and all relations find their ground in God and point to him. He who knows truth, in so far knows God. To enlarge the apprehension of truth means to win a wider and truer and nobler conception of God. Faith in the God of truth means an open mind and a confident trust in truth as a way to God. (2) Reason is not our source of the knowledge of God, nor can it speak the final word. Even when appearances contradict and when the ideas in which we interpret those experiences do not seem to agree, there are convictions of faith, deep-grounded in experience, to which we hold; and that is true in other fields besides religion. (3) It is the whole man who knows and he must take his whole world into account. The mind is helpless without the materials of experience, and these must include not only the data of the natural sciences but of the spiritual life as well. (4) Faith can never content itself with untested tradition or uninterpreted emotion. At every step the mind must enter in "that mind and soul, according well, may make one music as before, but vaster." Strictly, then, our term, ways to the knowledge of God, is open to criticism. There is only one way, and we have been considering different aspects of it or elements in it.

III. THE TESTS OF TRUTH

How can we test the beliefs thus reached to make sure that they are true? Let us note two facts. First, the question is not one that belongs to religion alone; in science, in history, in everyday experience, we raise the same query. In all knowing there is a continual testing. Second, there is no absolute test for truth. There is no superior method by which we can "jump out of our skin" and, standing outside as it were, look first at our ideas, then at our world, and decide if the ideas correspond with the reality and so are true. Nor is there any superior power of mind by which we can look down at these common ways of knowing and pass a final judgment on their conclusions. The ways of knowing are the common ways that are open to common people, the ways of everyday living and thinking. We can, however, submit our experience to more careful reflection and our ideas to closer criticism and more persistent experimentation, in the effort to test the conclusions at which we arrive. It remains then for us to consider some of these ways of testing our conclusions which have been found of special value.

1. The test of coherence in one form or another is used by every one. It is the test of consistency or agreement. We constantly apply it to new ideas that propose themselves for acceptance. Such an idea is tested by the way in which it fits in with the results of previous experience. We believe that truth is one and that contradiction indicates error. Such a test is, however, not easy to apply. Our tendency is to reject at once ideas at variance with the body of our former belief. But what may be called for is the modification of the old rather than the denial of the new. Further, because our knowing at best is fragmentary and imperfect, we may for the time have to hold opinions or working hypotheses which we have not yet been able to bring into harmony. Thus we are told as to present-day physics: "Its classical setting, in the dynamics of Newton and the electromagnetism of Clerk

Maxwell, is still used and is still yielding results of great value. Yet in the most striking discoveries of today, the classical laws have broken down and we are forced to accept the ideas of relativity and quanta. As Sir William Bragg says, we use the classical theories on Mondays, Wednesdays, and Fridays, and the quantum theory on Tuesdays, Thursdays, and Saturdays."[1] It is important also that we keep in mind that duality of process which seems to characterize our world and which often leads to paradox in thought. Thus we may use the mechanistic ideal of explanation as a heuristic principle in scientific investigation, and yet in individual life and social relations proceed on the supposition that man is free and responsible. So the religious man faces the facts of evil and yet holds that God is good, and finds grounds in experience for both.

The traditional application of the principle of coherence in philosophy has been somewhat different. The common assumption has been, not simply that a given world view should be consistent within itself, but that such systematic consistency was conclusive evidence of its truth. But here we need to be on our guard. It is possible for systems to be consistent within themselves and yet in disagreement with each other; and you may gain consistency in a system of theology or philosophy by using only a part of the available facts. The limitations of the finite mind, the rich complexity of life which defies our logical formulæ, and that duality of process which we considered in our study of polarity, all should keep us from overvaluation of formal consistency. It remains true, however, that a fundamental contradiction would mean an irrational world, that our goal must be to bring all our knowledge into a unitary view, and that to common man and philosopher alike a conclusion that fits in with other knowledge and furthers such unity has met an important test.

2. Is our view inclusive? This test is especially important for religion and philosophy. A world view should be synoptic

[1]W. C. Dampier, *A History of Science*, p. 485.

It may not explain everything—it will not; but it should take in all the fields of experience, bringing our total experience into unity and affording an interpretation that will light up the whole.

3. Is this truth accessible to all and verifiable by all, or is it simply a private opinion? It has been stated that this is where religion differs from science, that in science any man can perform an experiment or observe the facts in question, while in religion we deal with private feelings and ideas. Now it is obvious that there can be no such purely objective attitude and impersonal methods in dealing with spiritual values and realities as obtain in natural science; knowledge in religion comes by way of life and that involves personal and positive attitudes. Further, there are clearly great differences in the capacity for spiritual apprehension and insight. Nevertheless the test is valid and Christianity has recognized it. Its preaching, especially its mission work, is predicated upon the belief that every man can know and respond, and it constantly challenges men to put its message to the test of action.

4. Verification in experience is the fourth test. Knowledge comes from the experience of life, individual and racial; the test of validity is further experience. In the natural sciences it is often possible to set a question to nature in testing a theory and to control the conditions; this is experiment in the strict sense as distinguished from the broader term experience. But the most important truths cannot be tested in so simple and exact a fashion. When ethics asks as to the goals at which man should aim, and religion seeks to know the Power in which man may trust, their answers clearly cannot be demonstrated in simple and summary fashion. And yet they are subject to this test. The test, however, must be applied not just individually and for the moment but in respect of the social group and with regard to the longer periods of history. It should inquire whether a particular faith or philosophy makes for the largest and richest life,

whether it satisfies human needs most fully, whether it leads to further insights and to permanent enrichment as well as momentary help. Taken with other tests, we may safely regard experience as a help to the verification of our beliefs, especially of the central conviction of religion, that there is a world of the spirit, that power and goodness in some real and ultimate sense are one, and that by trust and loyalty a man may come into living fellowship and life-giving relation with God.

Chapter Twelve

THE GROUNDS FOR BELIEF IN GOD

I. AS TO ARGUMENTS FOR THE BEING OF GOD

It has been a common conviction of traditional theology that the being of God could be rationally proved. The statement of Thomas Aquinas is classical, as his position has been influential and for Roman Catholicism authoritative. "The way of truth is twofold. For there are things true of God which surpass every faculty of human reason—that he is three and one, for example. But there are others which are in the scope of natural reason, such as, that he exists, that he is one, and others of that kind; these have been demonstratively proved by philosophers."[1]

Protestant thought today has very largely left this position. Some, like Barth, hold that natural theology has no place, and that finite man can know the Infinite only by revelation. Others simply say: Such considerations are not, indeed, without value, but God cannot be demonstratively proven. To demonstrate (so in its original sense) may mean to point out, that is, to the senses; but God belongs to the realm of spirit which must be otherwise apprehended. Or it may refer to deductive logic; but this can only give us what is already contained in the ideas or principles with which it starts. Or the demonstration may be inductive and experi-

[1]*Summa contra Gentiles,* Bk. I, Ch. III. For complete passage and comments, see Caldecott and Mackintosh, *Selections from the Literature of Theism,* pp. 12, 13.

mental, drawing conclusions from empirical data and testing them in experience. The importance of this is obvious but its limits must be recognized. No finite data can fully include the Infinite; no conclusion so drawn can be more than probable and tentative.

But to say that God is not logically demonstrable does not mean that belief in God is illogical or irrational, or that the traditional "proofs" for belief in God are without value. These arguments were all related to one or another of the three fields of man's experience: the physical universe, the moral and religious life, and his life as a thinking being. We too must consider this threefold world of experience, must observe and relate and interpret, and, looking at the whole, inquire what it means as to faith in God. That, of course, is just what religion has been doing to the degree in which it has been reflective and experimental.

H. N. Wieman has made an interesting proposal which, if it could be accepted, would eliminate all need of such discussion. He points out that religion is concerned with the achievement of the highest good, that such good within measure is actually being achieved, that obviously, therefore, there are conditions and forces in the universe which generate and sustain such goods. But that is what religion means by God, he declares. Our concern, then, is not with the question of the existence of God, which is obvious, but with so relating ourselves to these forces and processes that we may achieve abundance of life.

There are elements involved in Wieman's position that call for approval and emphasis: the concern of religion with life and with the gaining of life and knowledge through right relations actively maintained, the distinction between the basic certainty of religion concerning God and specific theological formulations, the need that these latter shall be held tentatively. But the crucial question remains: Just what is this God whose certainty is so easily achieved that all atheism is banished at a stroke? Is this the dominant force in the universe? No, this is the creator and sustainer of such good as there is, but not the creator and sustainer of the universe. Can we be sure of the ultimate triumph of the good? No, because this is but one force among others. Is this a unitary being? Not necessarily. Doctor Wieman thinks that this can be shown, but clearly that is something that must be proven—which means, in effect, a return to arguments for God. Only by a quite uncritical outrunning of his premises can Doctor Wieman use a singular personal pronoun, He, for those impersonal and undetermined and possibly plural cosmic conditions and trends and modes of behavior which together make possible the achievement of good. Whatever Doctor Wieman may be able to develop further in his philosophical system, so far as the initial assumption which is supposed to make unnecessary the discussion of the belief in God, one may fairly apply Montague's phrase about "the faintly devout naturalism of those who would reduce Divinity to whatever factors of the environment are conducive to the good life."[2]

From the somewhat different standpoint indicated later in this chapter, Édouard Le Roy argues that strictly there are no atheists. For him belief in God is primarily a moral attitude in life, the recognition of something higher toward which man should strive, and the devotion to it. Belief in the existence of God means "to recognize a definite orientation toward cosmic becoming, an ascending realization, a supernatural labor." But since there is no one who is absolutely content with what he is, "who does not admit at least practically as a motive principle of his life an ideal and a beyond of the spiritual order whose appeals acts upon him," there are no real atheists. "The only pure atheist then would be the man who did not seek for anything, who did not desire

[2]W. P. Montague, *Belief Unbound,* p. 2. *Cf.* the criticism of John Dewey, in *The Christian Century,* Feb. 8, 1933. For Wieman's position see *Religious Experience and Scientific Method, The Wrestle of Religion with Truth,* and *Growth of Religion,* especially Ch. I.

any increase, who in fact did not live."[3] Le Roy points out the implication of a moral attitude, Wieman that of an idea, that is, as to the presence and increase of goods or values. Both writers, however, illustrate the need, not only in their case but with all arguments for the being of God, of making the distinction between the "that" and the "what." One may find an easy road to prove *that* God is by reducing the connotation of the term. But the vital concern of religious faith is with *what* this God is.

II. THE WORLD OF NATURE AND THE BELIEF IN GOD

1. The world of nature cannot of itself give the God of our faith, for nature is the world of things and forces and God is the God of spirit and of values. Natural science cannot yield proof of God, nor disproof; it can only describe how this world of things behaves. But the God of religion is the God of all things, and what natural science brings may, when we interpret it, point toward God or away from him; certainly it will affect our conception of how God works and of his relation to his world. In our study of the setting for religion, we considered the modern world picture which science presents us and some of the interpretations offered. Let us summarize the significant points that bear upon our problem.

(1) Ours is a world of unitary and universal order. "Under the great celestial firmament there is order, interdependence, and unity," reads the inscription on a tablet at the Adler Planetarium in Chicago. Our world is cosmos, not chaos, universe, not multiverse. Without this, science, our mastery of nature, and civilization itself would be impossible.

(2) It is a world of a double order, an order that is and one that is becoming. The order that is is something universal, cosmic, basic, something within which all process takes place, without which no being would be possible. But there is also an order in the making; things are being brought

[3] *Le Problème de Dieu,* pp. 122, 123.

constantly into more and more inclusive and significant relations.

(3) The growing order means ascending levels of being and the achievement of values. According to the first law of thermodynamics, there can be no quantitative increase in energy but only a change in its forms. But there is a process of emergence, of qualitative increase; evolution is epigenetic. The energy that is working in the universe is creative. Strictly, the same thing never happens twice as in a machine, which simply repeats again and again. *Die Natur ist nur einmal da.* It is a living and growing universe, marked by unimaginable possibilities.

(4) The universe shows a certain purposiveness. The movement seems to have direction, not in detail but in the large. In this process of change there seems to be a principle, or power, or trend at work which is continually bringing things into relations. It is not a blind urge or nisus; it is one that orders and organizes, and the advance takes place through this creative synthesis, or coordination, or integration.

(5) Whatever the ultimate nature of things may be, our world is intelligible. It has a rational quality because mind can know it and can set forth its nature in rational terms. This rational quality is not something which the superior mind of man imposes on a merely lumpish reality. For man's mind was itself developed through active intercourse with this world, and our equations or formulæ are constantly put to the test, for example, in the processes of manufacture and engineering. Man, the thinker, is not an alien in a nonrational world of things.

(6) Not only is there an apparently purposive movement in biological evolution, but in the shaping of an environment in which life could appear and develop. The inorganic world, through an age-long series of events, reached here on earth a remarkable complex of conditions in terms of the presence of carbon, oxygen, and hydrogen in just the right propor-

tions, with the peculiar properties of their compounds, especially water, and the abundance of the latter; and through this alone, so far as we can see, life became possible.

(7) Finally, it must be noted that there are elements which point in another direction. There is contingency in nature as well as order, evil as well as good, dysteleology as well as teleology, blind alleys in the evolutionary process, and an element of drag or resistance which seems to contradict or oppose the movement to achieve order and advance to higher levels.

2. What conclusions, then, may be reasonably drawn in relation to belief in God?

(1) We cannot say that this "proves" God; we can say that the idea of an ultimate Power, unitary, intelligent, purposive, good, seems best to account for these data and most reasonably to interpret them. True, it is still possible for men to assert that blind experimentation and chance collocations brought about all the order of the universe. As to which Sir James Jeans writes, with approving reference: "It was, I think, Huxley who said that six monkeys, set to strum unintelligently on typewriters for millions of millions of years, would be bound in time to write all the books in the British museum."[1] Of course, chance would not only have to produce through these monkeys all the books in the British museum, but to account for the paper and presses, for composition and proofreading and printing, and for all the other bipeds, tailless and wise, who would read the books, not to mention the machines on which the monkeys would write. All of which suggests "the universe of perpetual miracle, on which the atheist sets his heart."[2]

(2) The God here indicated differs definitely in his method of creativity and control from that of traditional theology. We no longer have the idea of a Power standing over against the Universe and working with irresistible might by direct

[1]*The Mysterious Universe,* pp. 4, 5.

[2]W. P. Montague, *Belief Unbound,* pp. 72, 73.

action. We have to revert here to the previously considered principle of polarity. There is a tension here which seems to be a condition of progress and a duality which belongs to the creative process. But the conclusion is not a metaphysical dualism or pluralism. What we have is, on the one hand, a process that can be described scientifically in terms of immanent forces and continuous change, with elements of spontaneity, "freedom," and continuity, and of inertia as well as *élan vital;* and, on the other, a something more than finite, that gives unitary order and direction and works in genuinely creative fashion. As Whitehead has pointed out, we must unite the ideas of flux and permanence, instead of separating them and conceiving a God of absolute but static perfection and a world that showed nothing but meaningless change. What our world points to is order in change, and change within this order.[3] And it is this newer conception (which is as old as Plato) that affords a real possibility of meeting the problem of evil.

III. THE FACT OF KNOWLEDGE AND BELIEF IN GOD

In the matter of man's life as a knowing being, there are three considerations that challenge attention. (1) There is a body of accumulated and tested knowledge that we call science. We may recognize, with the most critical among the scientists themselves, that it does not disclose the ultimate mysteries of our world; but we do accept it as giving us some trustworthy account. (2) This knowledge, and man's total rational life, is social; men assume a common rational quality which makes possible rational intercourse with each other and cooperation in scientific research. These two considerations imply a rational character or basis for our world, the world of which human society is an integral and important part. It is such a world since it is intelligible to man, and this rational quality is not eliminated because in nature as in man there are brute facts that seem to defy order and

[3]A. N. Whitehead, *Process and Reality,* pp. 525, 526.

go against reason. (3) The conclusion is further supported by the fact that this world is amenable to rational human action, action based on the assumption that the world is intelligible and orderly and that our knowledge of it, by and large, is trustworthy. Man's whole life and all social progress have been a matter of adjustment to this world based upon this knowledge.

It is this extraordinary fact of man's knowing and its significance that Alfred Noyes dwells upon in his *Watchers of the Sky*.

> "Yet we, who are borne on one dark grain of dust
> Around one indistinguishable spark
> Of star-mist, lost in one lost feather of light,
> Can, by the strength of our own thought, ascend
> Through universe after universe; trace their growth
> Through boundless time, their glory, their decay;
> And, on the invisible road of law, more firm
> Than granite, range through all their length and breadth,
> Their height and depth, past, present, and to come."[1]

Our conclusion must be, like Noyes', that the ultimate nature of this universe, and of the creative power which has shaped alike the world and man, is unitary and rational. Only with such a common basis can there be knowing man, an intelligible world, and fruitful human action based upon such knowledge.

There is another line of thought which, starting with the fact of knowledge and its assumptions, points to a similar conclusion. Science recognizes a dual aspect to the world which it studies. On the one hand is the aspect of brute fact, not simply as that which is given to it for study, its *data,* but that which resists its efforts to explore and order: the fact of specificity, of the individual and particular in being and behavior; and the fact of becoming, of change that is unpredictable and inexplicable. On the other hand, science is

[1]Pp. 241, 242.

always seeking unity and relatedness and meaningful order. It brings individuals together into classes and subsumes particular happenings under laws, not simply because it would otherwise stand helpless before a chaos of facts, but because it is convinced that unity and rationality are actually existent in the world. It is seeking an order that is there, not trying to impose one from without. So it recognizes recalcitrant data, the contingent and inexplicable, yet assumes unity and order as well as intelligibility. To give this up would be to give up the possibility of carrying on its work.

All this brings us to our ultimate problem. These "explanations" in part which science brings demand that we push forward to that explanation of the whole which lies outside of science's province; for what right have we to assume explanation of the parts and refuse its consideration for the whole? Or insist on unity and relatedness in the fragment and deny it to the whole? Or seek for finite wholes and deny that there can be an ultimate whole which gives relatedness and meaning to the parts? We may give up the quest in confession of agnosticism, but that is to deny for the whole what science assumes for the part. And to deny unity and rationality and meaning for the whole is to make these inexplicable if not impossible for the part. Brute fact no more describes the whole than the part, and the parts which have relative meaning point to a whole of transcendent meaning and power. Thus, pressing on, we move toward the idea of unity and rationality in God. Such is the line that a whole succession of thinkers has followed from Aristotle to our day.[2]

IV. THE MORAL ARGUMENT FOR THE BEING OF GOD

In studying nature we ask how things appear and how they behave. But besides the question of fact, we are even more deeply concerned with that of value. We are not setting

[2]See the brief formulation by A. E. Taylor, in *Essays Catholic and Critical,* E. G. Selwyn, ed.

fact over against value here, as though fact was real and value was a matter of subjective opinion. On the contrary, we are convinced that when we get into the world of values we are getting at the very heart of things, at their real meaning and nature.

Ever since the great days of Greek philosophy, men have thought of three forms of value: the beautiful, the true, and the good. We should add one more at least, that which we gain in the religious experience of the Holy, that aspect of the Divine in its majesty and sublimity which includes these three and goes beyond them. For the sake of brevity, we shall deal only with moral values in the stricter sense, that is, with the idea of the morally good. Our question is this: If this experience is real, what does it indicate as to the nature of the universe?

What is the nature of moral experience? Strictly, we cannot define it. Definition means describing in terms of something else, but here we have something ultimate. It is like my experience of beauty, or my intuition of what the personal self is, whether in myself or in my friend. To analyze is not to explain but to miss its distinctive nature. So I cannot describe moral goodness in terms of anything else. And as I cannot tell just how and why I perceive beauty or selfhood, so I cannot tell why, when I look at this world about me, I discover not only things and forces that I can measure, but quality that I must simply recognize and appreciate as having value. I can, however, point out what this distinctive meaning of the moral value is. (1) I experience it as something objective: I do not invent it, I discover it as something that is there and that is not made by my opinion or that of society. (2) It is absolute in value. Here is a good that I must achieve if I would gain the life that is life indeed. It is desirable that I should be physically well, that I should escape pain, that I should prolong my years, that I should have material goods for my needs. None of these things, however, is absolute; I may miss these and yet find the supreme good of life. But if I fail of truth and love and righteousness, then indeed I have failed. (3) Involved in this absolute aspect is the note of the imperative expressed by the word "ought." It is not conditional; it does not say, *if* you want that, then you must do this; it says, Thou shalt. It may even summon me to sacrifice all else that is dear. To lose here is to lose my "soul," to lose what is more than material possession or physical existence.

What, then, does this moral experience mean? I may, of course, repudiate all this. I may say it is untrustworthy or purely subjective, and insist that the only real world is the "solid" world of things. But for critical thought, the world of things is anything but "solid," anything but what it seems; and there is no reason why we should discredit moral experience any more than our experience of the physical world. It is more rational to recognize that man belongs to his world on the moral side as well as on the physical. These insights and convictions have come from the action of this world upon him as truly as have his organs of sight and hearing, and point as truly to something real in the environing cosmos. What is it then to which this experience points?

The crucial fact about the moral, as we have seen, is its quality as absolute and imperative. If we accept it, we must give it first place. It cannot be the dependent or the incidental, or simply one among others. It claims the right to direct and command. But such an absolute right can rest only in what is ultimate and absolute in our universe. To recognize the full meaning of this "ought" is to declare that the moral universe has priority over the physical. It is to put goodness, not power, in the supreme category; it is to believe in God. Further, if the World Ground is moral then it must be personal. Love, truth, righteousness exist, if at all, only in personal life; that is their meaning. There is no love in the abstract; there are only personal beings who love. There is no righteousness except in personal will that holds to what is true and just and turns from wrong and oppression.

In all this, we are not simply making God a postulate, something that we have to assume in order to validate the moral order or to assure us of the final triumph of the good in the universe, as with Kant. The moral life is a sphere in which we experience God. It is not the only sphere, but surely there is none higher, none in which the reality of the Eternal and its right over our life make themselves known with more of majesty or of convincing power. What comes at first as stern duty, or as the summons of a high ideal, reveals itself at last as the presence of the Eternal and "the Godhead's most benignant grace."

The moral argument will appeal much more to some than to others. It belongs to the ethically minded Western type of religion rather than the mystically minded East. It is directed to the modern idealism of the type reflected by Lippmann's *Preface to Morals,* which clings to the ethical after it has lost religious certainty. It makes a double appeal to such. First of all, it summons to action and makes moral insight and obedience a way of life by which the spiritual becomes real. It was this way that Frederick Robertson set forth in a notable passage in which he described his own anguish in the loss of religious faith and his way out. "I know but one way," he wrote, "in which a man may come forth from his agony scathless; it is by holding fast to those things which are certain still—the grand, simple landmarks of morality. In the darkest hour through which a human soul can pass, whatever else is doubtful, this at least is certain. If there be no God and no future state, yet even then it is better to be generous than selfish, better to be chaste than licentious, better to be true than false, better to be brave than to be a coward."[1]

The other way of serving the age at this point is to summon men to see what their moral faith involves. F. W. H. Myers writes of George Eliot: "I remember how at Cambridge I walked with her once in the Fellows' Garden of

[1]*Life and Letters of F. W. Robertson,* p. 86.

Trinity, on an evening of a rainy May, and she, stirred somewhat beyond her wont, and taking as her text the three words which have been used so often as the inspiring trumpet calls of men—the words God, Immortality, Duty—pronounced with terrible earnestness, how inconceivable was the first, how unbelievable was the second, and how peremptory and absolute the third. Never, perhaps, had sterner accents affirmed the sovereignty of impersonal and unrecompensing law."[2] To such moral idealists, we must reply: First, your moral faith involves a faith in God; you must accept the latter if you would retain the former; you will reach the latter if you will think through the former. Second, your very experience of the moral, of this peremptory and absolute Duty, is itself an experience of God. For only the ultimate has the right to such absolute command, only God can speak thus to man.

V. THE ARGUMENT FROM RELIGION

The arguments for the being of God in the past, as we have seen, have been an effort to find something outside of religion that would support the central conviction of religion, the belief in God. We have seen the force of some of these considerations, but the fact remains: their value is chiefly for those who have already found God. That is not an element of weakness in the religious situation but of strength. Religion does not depend upon independent rational demonstration. Its roots are in the religious experience itself. We turn then to the fact of religion and ask whether, rationally considered, this supports the belief in God.

The historical fact comes first. Quite apart from considerations of value and validity, religion is one of the most extraordinary facts of human history. In every land and in every age to which our knowledge reaches, mankind shows a belief in a world of the spirit to which it gives reverence

[2]Quoted by H. E. Fosdick, *The Meaning of Faith,* p. 41.

and worship, whose authority over conduct it recognizes, and from which it expects help. The beginnings are crude. The forms of belief and practice vary widely with different peoples, and change from age to age. Experience and reflection prove fatal to particular beliefs. There are places and periods and individuals marked by pronounced scepticism. But the basic belief in this higher and unseen world remains, and today, following an age of naturalism and secularism which had claimed the prestige of science, this conviction not only remains but seems to be moving toward a definite resurgence. This persistence, as seen in history, is not irrational and blind. Rather religion shows steady advance on the ethical and rational side and increasing significance for human life.

Now the simplest and most reasonable explanation of all this is the existence of such a higher world or, to use the common term, of God. That conclusion is further supported when we recall the nature of the religious experience and the elements entering into it: an awareness of this higher world, a sense of incompleteness and need, a response which establishes an active and working relation, with a resulting satisfaction and completion of life, and the constantly accompanying effort to understand and interpret. All this is best understood as representing a real relation with a spiritual world in terms of stimulus, response, and interpretation, in just the same fashion as with our common knowledge of men and things. And first as to stimulus. Religion does not begin with the idea of God, says Professor Alexander. "When we ask how we come to the cognition of God we must answer that, as with love and hate and appetite and aversion, it is because the world itself provokes in us a specific response which makes us aware, no matter in how primitive a form, of God."[1] Man's sense of a hunger that is not stilled with food, the appeal of the ideal that calls out aspiration, devotion, and effort, the awareness of the higher, of the numinous or holy, these point to a spiritual world whose

[1] S. Alexander, *Space, Time, and Deity,* pp. 374, 375.

stimulus we feel, which impinges upon us as surely as does the light upon the eye. Without this, the persistent and universal phenomenon of religion is as inexplicable as would be the development of the sensitive epithelial cells into the eye without the stimulus of light. Religion is response. The comment in Pascal's *Pensées* is in point: "Thou wouldst not be seeking me if thou didst not possess me." What is man's hunger for God but the mark of God's presence with man?

There are two voices coming to us from our universe. One is the voice of the finite, speaking of imperfection and change, decay and death. The other is the voice of the Eternal, abiding in all this change, challenging our imperfectness with its perfection, our weakness and evil with its goodness and power. Surely the one is as authentic as the other. We may well ask with Tennyson in "The Two Voices":

"Who forged that other influence,
That heat of inward evidence,
By which he doubts against his sense?

"Here sits he shaping wings to fly:
His heart forebodes a mystery:
He names the name Eternity.

"That type of Perfect in his mind
In Nature can he nowhere find.
He sows himself on every wind.

"He seems to hear a Heavenly Friend,
And thro' thick veils to apprehend
A labor working to an end."

VI. SOME CONCLUSIONS

Aside from the question of the validity of the particular arguments considered in this chapter, certain significant conclusions may be drawn.

1. We must ask of every argument: Where do you start? Every argument involves some assumption. We begin with

some postulate, such as the order of nature and its intelligibility, the dependability of perception and reason, the validity of the moral sense. The basic assumption common to all these considerations is the trustworthiness of human experience and of the mind's reflection upon it, under conditions of constant criticism and correction. There is, then, no strict "proof" of the being of God.

2. We must inquire as to every argument: How far do you get? It is clear that none of the traditional "proofs" brings us to the Christian conception of God. The cosmological proof indicates a World Artisan, the teleological proof suggests a World Planner; neither reveals to us a God of righteousness and mercy. Even the ontological argument, professing to prove the existence of the most perfect being, leaves us with an abstraction, which may or may not be the personal God of saving love.

3. All such discussions reveal a remnant of brute fact, of concrete actuality which seems to contradict all theories of a rational and good World Ground. At most we can say: the belief in God gives us the best interpretation of the greatest number of facts, including not only the physical, but the rational, ethical, æsthetic, and religious. Religion has its own roots and its own sources of certainty.

4. The chief value of these arguments is not to compel belief but to show the relation of faith to concrete experience and rational reflection, and to reveal the inadequacy if not falsity of other positions.

5. All this points to the fact that rational considerations, by themselves, are never adequate to the ultimate problems of life. These questions can never be settled without faith and action, which are demanded, indeed, in every sphere of man's life. This chapter, then, is incomplete without the preceding discussion of the ways of knowing God and the consideration of the nature of faith and the right to believe to which we now turn.

Chapter Thirteen

THE RIGHT TO BELIEVE AND THE CERTAINTY OF FAITH

I. THE RIGHT TO BELIEVE

OUR ARGUMENT thus far may be summarized as follows: Man's experience in the various fields of life gives him reasonable grounds for belief in God, but no compelling demonstration of the existence of God is possible. But if that be so, what right have we to believe?

1. To answer that question we must first consider the place of faith in man's total life. Negatively, in its broader meaning, faith is the refusal to be limited to the evidence of the senses and the demonstration of deductive logic. Positively, it is a confidence in our world as meaningful and in our experience as trustworthy. Now, whether we speak of faith or postulates or necessary presuppositions, some such life attitude underlies all human thought and conduct. Apart from this you have mechanical causation, or behavior conceived as stimulus and response; but as soon as you get distinctively human behavior, conduct that involves reflection, values, and purpose, then you find confidence in a meaningful and trustworthy world, and that is faith.

The empirical method of science is often pointed to as in flat opposition to faith. On the contrary, faith is the prerequisite of science. (1) The scientist believes in a unitary and orderly world. He does not undertake to prove this, for it is the presupposition of his method; and it is involved in his goal, which is to describe this assumed order in nature. He could not prove this if he would; for he knows at best only the tiniest fragment of the cosmos and what he knows is already past event. That the past is the key to the future and that he can infer what the great world is from the little corner that he perceives, this is a matter of confidence, or of faith. (2) The scientist believes in the trustworthiness of his senses, of his own rational processes, and of those of his fellows. So he confidently observes, classifies, and interprets. (3) He assumes that the universe is intelligible, that it has a basically rational nature. He therefore is constantly endeavoring to set it forth in rational propositions. Obviously the philosopher is in the same situation. If the world did not have a rational quality, he could not reason about it. If it had no meaning, philosophizing as such would be futile. Even the sceptic who seeks to discredit reason does so by what are presumably processes of reason. The "complete sceptic" would not philosophize at all, and refutes himself when he appeals to reason in an argument for scepticism. "Faith," says F. R. Tennant, "is not confined to the realms of moral values and religious ideas, but infects all existential and theoretical knowledge. The objective situation alone determines neither the probabilities of science nor the creed of religion; at most it suggests. . . . Science postulates what is requisite to make the world amenable to the kind of thought that conceives the structure of the universe and its orderliness according to quantitative law; theology, and sciences of valuation, postulate what is requisite to make the world amenable to the kind of thought that conceives of the why and wherefore, the meaning or purpose of the universe, and its orderedness according to teleological principles. Both are necessarily interpretative, anthropic, interested, selective. . . . All reason involved in the acquisition of 'knowledge' is leavened with faith."[1]

[1]*Philosophical Theology,* Vol. I, p. 299.

Faith is equally basic when it comes to the life of action. Human action is distinguished from the blind impulse and mechanical routine of lower levels of being by the observing, testing, questioning, critical attitude, but equally and at the same time by the attitude of faith. When the farmer sows his grain, when the engineer flings his bridge across a river, both attitudes are involved. There is a conclusion from observation and experiment, but there is likewise a confidence in an orderly and trustworthy world. This is pre-eminently true in human relations. Faith does not mean here, any more than elsewhere, credulity or stupidity or a disregard of facts; nor is it a poor substitute for knowledge. It stands in its own right as that without which life would be a poor and sterile affair.

The supreme expression of faith, however, is found in religion. Of course, religion includes more than faith; there is the empirical with its concern for concrete reality, and the rational with its reflection, interpretation, and criticism. But the heart of it is faith. It gathers together all other insights and surmises and confidences into one central conviction: this world "means intensely and means good." There is a world of spirit and meaning and value, an unseen world which is yet the supremely real world; and I can trust that world and build my life upon it. No man can point out that world to touch or sight. No one can prove it by rigor of logic. Religion challenges men to "trust the soul's invincible surmise," to believe where it cannot see, to act though it cannot prove.

2. And now we turn to our question: What of the right thus to believe? The answer is: The right to believe is the right to live. Knowledge is important for life, certainty is desirable, but action is imperative. In his *Will to Believe* James quotes Helmholtz as saying to the scientist: *"Hier gilt nur der eine Rat, vertraue und handle."* "Trust and act": if that counsel is requisite for science, it is even more demanded in the wider ranges of life. Faith is confidence giving courage for the deed: confidence in the insights of the

soul, in the unproved convictions of reason, in a world that has meaning, in life that has possibilities, confidence that the final Power is good—in a word, faith in God. Faith is not obscurantism opposed to enlightenment; it is courage as against timidity. Our real peril lies not in credulity but fear. "Fear is the great inhibitor of creative activity. Faith is its opposite. It is heroic and adventurous."[2] The failure of faith means the paralysis of life.

Our own day gives eloquent witness to this in literature and life. "It is not possible to be wholly at peace," writes Walter Lippmann of the modern man; "for serenity of soul requires some better organization of life than a man can attain by pursuing his casual ambitions, satisfying his hungers, and for the rest accepting destiny as an idiot's tale in which one dumb sensation succeeds another to no known end. And it is not possible for him to be wholly alive. For that depends upon his sense of being completely engaged with the world, with all his passions and all the faculties in rich harmony with one another, and in deep rhythm with the nature of things. These are the gifts of a vital religion. Our forefathers had such a religion. They had no doubt that there was an order in the universe which justified their lives because they were a part of it."[3] In similar fashion Joseph Wood Krutch in *The Modern Temper* shows us how the loss of religious faith is followed by loss of faith in all ideals, and how the issue of all this is not the discovery of some higher way of knowledge but only illusion and despair. And we know only too well how in our present-day social order, or social chaos, the loss of religious faith has carried with it the loss of faith in ideals and their authority, in such high goods as freedom and justice and peace, and in the possibility of their achievement, leaving instead the lust for goods and power, selfishness as the sole guide, and force as the final arbitrament. Contrast the liberating and inspiring

[2]John Macmurray, in the *Hibbert Journal,* April, 1926.
[3]*A Preface to Morals,* pp. 7, 8.

creed of Socrates as he approached death: "My only fear was the fear of doing an unrighteous or unholy thing. . . . Know this of a truth–that no evil can happen to a good man, either in life or after death"[4]; or hear Paul: "If God is for us, who is against us? . . . Who shall separate us from the love of Christ? . . . In all these things we are more than conquerors."[5]

Credulity has its obvious penalties. "Stop, Look, Listen" is a good sign elsewhere as well as at railway crossings. But the pause is only in order that we may proceed. There are highways of life upon which we can adventure only as we are ready to trust. Alike in human fellowship and in the life with God, the highest reaches are possible only to faith.

3. It is important, however, to make clear what the right to believe involves. To many it has seemed simply an assertion of the individual and arbitrary or the right to wishful thinking. On the contrary, faith rightly conceived is the recognition of an order and reason in the universe to which the individual will must bend, and this is particularly the significance of religious faith.

There are two meanings involved in the idea of a rational world. There is first the rationality which scientist and philosopher assume. There is a world of order and so science is possible; this world has something of unity and intelligibility and meaning, therefore serious and comprehensive human thinking (philosophy) is possible. The general acceptance of such a working faith is only made more obvious by so rare a voice of protest as Bertrand Russell, who declares that all this is rubbish and insists that "the universe is all spots and jumps, without unity, without continuity, without coherence and orderliness. . . . Indeed, there is little but prejudice or habit to be said for the view that there is a world at all."[6] This rationality does not mean a rigid mechanistic system any more than it does a perfect idealistic order; there is room

[4]*The Apology:* 32, 41. [5]Romans 8:28–39.
[6]*The Scientific Outlook,* p. 95.

for contingency, for indeterminateness. But not only science and philosophy, all man's mastery of his world and all his culture rest upon the essentially rational and dependable character of his universe. Just what this order is and how far it reaches can be determined only by empirical study. Speculative philosophy in the past has tended to make this order absolute, deciding theoretically what the world must be like, just as scientists from Aristotle onward long held that the planets must move in circular orbits because the circle was the perfect figure. For us, this order in its specific character is a matter of discovery.

But there is a second kind of order without which we could not call our world rational; that is the order of ends and values. The first order explains in terms of what comes before, the second in terms of what lies ahead. The first is "causal," the second is telic. The second kind of order is as inescapable for our thought as the first. The thought of a universe that comes into being blindly, that moves on without goal, that will some time reach a state of immobility, meaningless and endless, this is for us as irrational as the idea of a world of pure chance and discontinuity. "In cognition the rational impulse is to appreciate a connected system. In practice the rational impulse is to establish a harmonious system. . . . The ethical order then is rational just in the same sense as the cognitive order."[7] The double danger is the old one of supposing that to point out the purpose is to make unnecessary the search for "causal" explanation, and the modern one of thinking that the causal explanation rules out any possible reference to meanings and ends.

It is not necessary once more to review the grounds for such a belief in the order of purpose in nature and human life; preparation in the inorganic world, as Henderson has pointed out, purposiveness in evolution, the organicistic conception of the world with its implication of ends, the actual presence of values as brought forth in the world process,

[7] L. T. Hobhouse, in *Development and Purpose.*

all suggest this. These do not compel us to believe, but they point to such a faith and confront us with the alternative. On the one hand is the conviction that the world has meaning, that its meaning is good, and that we have the right to trust and to live on the level of high purpose and hope; on the other is the conception of a world basically irrational, where

"earth is darkness at the core
And dust and ashes all that is,"

while human life sinks to "a tale told by an idiot, full of sound and fury, signifying nothing." The grounds for considering the universe rational in the moral sense correspond closely with those on which we claim objectivity for reason. In neither case is there a demonstration, in both cases a postulate that justifies itself by its working.[8] Science postulates a basic order in the physical world, and holds that by understanding that order and by acting according to it we can maintain and advance our physical well-being. Religion postulates a fundamental meaning and goodness in the cosmos, and asserts that as man discerns this and responds in confidence and loyalty, he will attain the highest personal well-being. "We are as much entitled to assume that the universe is not bad, as to assume that it is not mad."[9] The latter is the postulate of science, the former of religion. As a matter of fact, if the universe is basically bad, then it is really mad; that is, it is irrational in the deepest sense. Both are needed assumptions for life; both must have their ultimate justification in action which corresponds with the conviction.

4. It is important to note that it is not the wish to believe that we are considering, but the right to believe. The theory that religion is the wish to believe, vigorously asserted by Feuerbach, we consider elsewhere. It is a sort of religious infantilism which argues: I want this, therefore it must be

[8]*Cf.* George Galloway, *Philosophy of Religion,* p. 359.
[9]Kenneth Edward, *Religious Experience,* p. 202.

so; I need this and so I will believe in it. Misleading, too, is the phrase of William James, "the will to believe," in his essay in the book bearing that title. The essay has been vigorously criticized.[10] Some of the criticisms are due to misunderstanding. "The Right to Believe" James later felt was a more accurate phrase, since he was not commending dogmatic and wishful thinking, but aimed "to criticize belief in order to determine the precise conditions under which a scrupulous man may give his credence to beliefs for which the evidence is imperfect."[11] He does not say that a man may decide by mere act of will what to believe in religion or ethics. First, he is opposing bald intellectualism, "the queerest idol ever manufactured in the philosophic cave," which would exclude the part which "heart, instincts, and courage" play rightfully in human decisions. Second, and principally, he would insist upon the right of faith without waiting "till intellect and senses have raked in evidence enough." For the refusal to believe cuts us off alike from treasures of life and from a possible gaining of truth which can come only by faith and the intercourse which faith makes possible. For James three conditions limit this right to believe. There must be a live option; the will does not decide where no appeal is felt. It must be a momentous option, one in which the real issues of life are concerned. It must be a forced option, one where some choice is inevitable, where refusal is itself a choice. Clearly these three conditions are met in the case of a religious faith.

We may summarize our general position as follows:

(1) The right to believe does not mean indifference to facts. It does mean that there may be the right to trust and act when evidence is not theoretically compelling.

(2) To claim the right to believe is not to oppose wilful speculation to empiricism; it is, indeed, more congruous with

[10]See the discussions by D. M. Baillie, *Faith in God,* IV, and John Baillie, *The Interpretation of Religion.*

[11]See *In the Spirit of William James,* by R. B. Perry, p. 170, and the whole chapter on "The Right to Believe." *Cf.* also *The Right to Believe,* by Eleanor Harris Rowland.

a sane empiricism than it is with rationalism. For it extends the scope of the empirical to include the moral-spiritual, and it insists that faith and action are prerequisite to the largest experience.[12]

(3) To claim the right to believe in God is simply to claim on the highest plane that which we take as a necessity on all other levels of life.

(4) The right to believe is the right to live. The ultimate question, as Perry has pointed out, is a moral one. Is the supreme obligation the intellectual one, never to go beyond the full warrant of evidence? Or is it the obligation to face high demands and commit ourselves in life and action? Obviously the farther-reaching beliefs are least capable of securing theoretical proof or compelling evidence; religion, asking about the ultimate, the highest, and the whole, puts the final questions of life. Its convictions are not without rational grounds, and they must not go contrary to evidence; but if life be the supreme demand they may outrun evidence.

II. THE CERTAINTY OF FAITH

Nowhere should man be more concerned about certainty than in religion, for here the supreme interests of life are at stake. If the existence of God cannot be demonstrated, is there any certainty in religion and, if so, what is its character?

1. Religion's quest for certainty and her assumption of certainty have been vigorously criticized. The very essence of the scientific attitude, we are told, is to keep the open mind, to hold all ideas tentatively, to find the triumph of the spirit not in confirmation of past beliefs but in the attainment of larger knowledge, no matter what change may be involved. Beliefs we must have, writes the English biologist, J. B. S. Haldane, "but the intellectually honest man must recognize the utterly provisional nature of his beliefs."[1]

The most vigorous attack has been made by John Dewey

[12]See R. B. Perry, *op. cit.*, 170, 171, 190, 202.

[1]Article, "What I Believe," *The Nation*, N. Y., July 23, 1930.

in his volumes, *The Quest for Certainty* and *A Common Faith.* The quest for certainty, he insists, commits religion to a false philosophy and a mistaken goal. The philosophy is that idealism which assumes that above this world of change there is a world of immutable reality and absolute worth, and that there is an absolute and certain knowledge by which man can possess this world. It holds that "certainty, security, can be found only in the fixed and unchanging; that knowledge is the only road to that which is intrinsically stable and certain; that practical activity is an inferior sort of thing." Thus religion is turned aside from its true goal. Let religion "surrender once for all commitment to beliefs about matters of fact, whether physical, social, or metaphysical." He has in mind especially belief in God, which he rightly sees to mean "the fixed union of the actual and ideal in ultimate being." He wants "an idealism of action that is devoted to creation of a future." The field of religion is to be action. The only security to be sought is that gained "by means of active control of the changing course of events." This is instrumentalism applied to religion. Religion itself is "a sense of the possibilities of existence and devotion to the cause of these possibilities."[2]

As a matter of fact, there is no such absolute opposition between Dewey's instrumentalism and the position which he attacks. On the one hand, neither religious faith nor the old idealism excludes action as a way of knowledge. On the other hand, Dewey leaves a place for the ideal and he has his own certainties underlying his program of action. Nature for him is something more than a flow of change. It is dependable and orderly, or the control which he seeks would not be possible. He recognizes that it is the source of ideals, of possibilities, of aspiration. He believes in values and realizes that values differ in quality.[3]

[2]*The Quest for Certainty,* pp. 51, 204, 303, 304.

[3]Cf. *The Quest for Certainty,* Ch. XI; *Human Nature and Conduct,* pp. 329–332.

Dewey's idealism is not simply one of goals. It is Bertrand Russell who illustrates what a thoroughgoing instrumentalism means which really surrenders all certainties. In science, he declares, we give up the effort to understand the world. "In the Instrumental Theory (which Russell here approves), there is not a single state of mind which consists of knowing a truth—there is a way of acting, a manner of handling the environment. . . . To know something is to be able to change it as we wish." As it gives up the thought of truth to be known, so this instrumentalism gives up the idea of a good to be revered. There is a new attitude toward the universe. The idea of reverence toward the universe "is hardly compatible with the modern belief of man's omnipotence through the machine. We do not contemplate a flea; we catch it. The modern point of view is in its infancy, but we foresee a time when it will lead men to regard the non-human world in general with as little reverence as we now feel towards the poor flea." This instrumentalism "constitutes the philosophy appropriate to industrialism, which is science in the sphere of practise."[4] One may well ask, if the universe has nothing in it to be reverenced outside of man, why should man reverence himself, not to say his brother? Why not take the last step, treat men also like the poor flea, and make life the occasion for that successful behavior which, giving up any God and truth and right, treats all else as means to serve our individual advantage? Obviously it is quite a different viewpoint which Russell's own social programs and attitudes involve—witness his opposition to fascist ideology and Nazi methods which represent the logic of this viewpoint, as well as his longer opposition to capitalism and economic imperialism. But his statement at least makes clear by contrast the degree of idealistic conviction to which Dewey holds, not only in his social ethics but in his conception of the cosmos, and what a thoroughgoing instrumentalism would involve.

[4]In *Whither Mankind,* edited by C. A. Beard, pp. 72, 66.

2. The traditional grounds for religious certainty call for criticism. Three forms have been most common. (1) There was certainty based on authority, sometimes claimed for the Church, sometimes for the Bible, in each case assuming a supernaturally communicated body of truth available to men in some absolute and perfect form. But authority must always first approve itself to us, and so it comes back to human judgment, and when the tests of history and criticism are applied, the doctrine fails. There is no such seat of infallible truth. (2) The way of logical demonstration, as we have seen, is also closed. We may have what is probable and rational, not what is certain in any absolute sense. And any such certainty, as Dewey and Russell would be among the first to point out, is denied to science also. (3) The appeal sometimes made to religious experience, as usually understood, that is, to the mystical and emotional, has no more valid basis. For the experience has to be interpreted and thus we are left in the end with human opinion based on fluctuating feeling.

Dewey is right in much of his criticism of the first two theories of certainty, which have been dominant in traditional theology. There has been a backlying dualism in both cases: above, an absolute and unchanging spiritual world in which alone were truth and goodness and reality; below, the world of the finite and changing, without meaning or value. And there has been an intellectualism here, viewing truth as a doctrine that could be apprehended apart from life. Both failed to see that the primary concern of religion is not with a command to which we are simply to submit, nor with a body of truth in whose possession we are to rest, but with a living Spirit with whom we are to have fellowship in a life of truth and love.

In a well-known passage in *The Brothers Karamazov,* Dostoyevsky pictures Christ returning to earth, unknown, as of old, yet drawing men by his love and deeds of mercy. The cardinal, the Grand Inquisitor, has him thrown into prison and there visits him. He knows the Christ but challenges him. Why do you come to interfere with the Church? he says. We know what men are and want, and we have settled their problem accordingly. Men do not want freedom and responsibility; they prefer peace, even death. "There are three powers, three powers alone, able to conquer and hold captive forever the conscience of these impotent rebels for their happiness—these forces are miracle, mystery, and authority. Thou hast rejected all three."[5] Dostoyevsky's picture is correct. Men have been most concerned about security, and they have been willing to bow to the authority that would assure this through miracle and mystery, or through creed or Scripture; and the Church has too often substituted this for what Jesus offered.

3. But though the traditional ways are not open to us, there is in religion a certainty of another kind; it is moral certainty, or the certainty of faith. It is that quality in our convictions which makes them for us the basis of thought and action. It is the assurance, rooting more deeply than sense evidence or logical proof, that here is something which we can trust, trust so confidently that life can be built upon it. How it arises we have seen in our consideration of the ways of knowing God and of the nature and place of faith. As in other fields, so in religion, it "comes out of life, and issues in life."[6] In them all there is a sense of the breaking through of a world of meanings and values, of a Reality which "eye hath not seen nor ear heard," which is in our world and yet transcends it. This higher world reveals itself through our sense of need and dependence, through the experience of higher values which at once appeal and command, and through an awareness of an Other and Higher which may be called mystical. It calls for reverence, confidence, and devotion. It does not compel us logically or overwhelm us by force; it is rather a challenge to us. But it works

[5]Pp. 305–319, Modern Library edition.
[6]F. J. McConnell, *Religious Certainty,* pp. 7, 8.

in us a certainty, a conviction. We have met the Highest, not only as a good to be achieved but as a power to be trusted.

Édouard Le Roy has well described this experience and the nature of this certitude, "One believes in God rather than proves him. To speak rightly, one does not demonstrate him, one experiences him, one lives him. . . . In other words, it is a question of moral certitude, a name which indicates . . . not a degree but a kind of certitude. It is called moral first because its object is a moral reality, then and primarily because it demands moral conditions. . . . In the moral order one cannot perceive the truth of a doctrine, that is, its living, creative power, if one will not allow himself to be given life by it. . . . One who refuses the experience has no right to form a negative conclusion; and he refuses the experience who holds himself to a critique that is purely intellectual and rational, who argues and discourses instead of acting."[7]

Does this deserve the name certainty? Is it not rather a hypothesis, a theory which we are testing, or a postulate, an assumption made by us as necessary to further action? No, these certainties of life lie back of our changing hypotheses. They are rather like the postulates which science, for example, finds necessary. But they are more than necessary suppositions; they are convictions, convictions wrought in experience, held by an act of confidence, and made the basis of life.

4. Now we are in position to meet the double objection raised against the conception of religious certainty. Religious certainty, we are told, means a closed mind, assured of the truth, intolerant of opposition, and seeking no further. And it means inertia of life where there should be ceaseless effort, since men feel that with this truth they possess security and salvation.

However valid these objections may be against the old static certainty, they do not apply to the idea of moral certainty, or the certainty of faith. What men like John Dewey and Julian Huxley do not see is that, in their measure, a

[7] *Le Problème de Dieu,* pp. 127, 130.

certainty of this kind lies back of their own philosophy of life. Huxley summons religion to make sacrifice "of her old certitude, to be offered up on the altar of humility." Yet he has just expressed a very positive certainty of his own in saying that "any religion which is not an affirmation of the ultimate value of truth and knowledge, beauty and its expression, and goodness and moral action, is in that respect a false, low, and incomplete religion."[8] When J. B. S. Haldane, in the article quoted above, insists on "the utterly provisional nature" of the modern man's belief, that does not prevent him from flatly declaring "that the meaning of the visible world is to be found in the invisible," or from adding: "I have not very much use for people who are not in touch with the invisible world. At best they are good animals, and too often not even that." Back of Dewey's whole pragmatic program with its idealistic ends lies his belief in a world "not inherently vacillating or unstable," in religion as "a sense of the whole," "an enduring and comprehending whole" which gives meaning to the individual.[9]

Now, though it is more definite and farther reaching, the certainty which religion offers is of this kind, especially in the case of the Christian religion. True, as Dostoyevsky points out in the passage cited above, too often "man seeks not so much God as the miraculous, and an easy happiness and security through this"; but it is not this kind of certainty that Jesus proposed. He offered certainty with adventure, inner rest with unresting activity; and the former was the preparation for the latter. His own undaunted quest, which shrank from no hardship or peril, was made possible by this very certainty of faith. Men can fare forth because

[8]*Religion without Revelation,* pp. 373, 374, 379.

[9]*Human Nature and Conduct,* pp. 329–331. It is unfortunate that Dewey and many other critics of religion evidence so limited a knowledge of current Christian thinking outside the authoritarian, dogmatic, static type with its dualistic supernaturalism. *Cf.* his sweeping statement: "The association of religion with the *supernatural* tends by its own nature to breed the dogmatic and the divisive spirit." (In *The Philosophy of John Dewey,* edited by Paul A. Schilpp, p. 595.)

there is a God who goes with them and a Spirit that guides their search. Jesus offered men a double certainty: faith in a God that was good and life in fellowship with this God. But the God of this faith is no abstract order, no Aristotelean unmoved Mover. He is the living, saving, creating God. And the fellowship that belongs to such a faith means not quiescent security, but unceasing adventure.

But if the certainty summons to effort, the effort is one that requires some such certainty. Bertrand Russell points out rightly that a pure instrumentalism, such as he champions, is fatal to the adventure of scientific thought. Ruling out all causal order, and every other order, it brings a scepticism which is "a canker at the heart of science, . . . capable in time of paralyzing the whole army of scientific workers." Science deals with induction, and induction rests upon "animal faith." What this loss of certainty means for human life and values, that Mr. Krutch and many others have illustrated. They leave us a world in which there are no longer either assured values or certainty of attainment.

In a suggestive article on "Christianity—Pagan or Scientific?" in *The Hibbert Journal* for April, 1926, John Macmurray has made some interesting comparisons and criticisms, with a clear discrimination between formal security and Christian certainty. Science, he declares, has been more Christian at this point than has organized Christianity. To trust in the truth and fear not is Christian faith in a God of truth; to follow truth wherever it may lead is loyalty to the God of truth. Greece and Rome, he says, "agree that the ideal at which social organization aims is security and stability." For the Greek mind (reflected in traditional theology), this depends upon an absolute and unchanging system of truth; and belief on authority is the attitude required. "The Roman paganism seeks to attain the same ideal of stability by external organization. Its requirement is simply obedience." Clearly the Roman Church is its successor. Christian teaching, on the contrary, "sets a creative dynamic in opposition to formal security." From this standpoint, faith is not so much the secure harbor at which one arrives as the confident quest on which one sets forth.

Our conclusion then may be briefly put. There is a pseudo-certainty often asserted in the name of religion, coming by the easy way of dogmatic authority or logical demonstration. That certainty is neither possible nor desirable. The only certainty open to us is the certainty of faith. It is not arbitrary, for it comes as an inner conviction wrought in us by contact with a higher world which demonstrates its reality and demands our trust. It is not easy, for it comes only through life and to those who will give themselves to the high demands of life. So far from stopping thought and action, it is itself incomplete without these and is the necessary condition to these. It gives no detailed conclusions; it does not supply a set of doctrines for belief or of techniques for successful behavior. What it does is to give a basic faith that both inspires and guides. Our way then is neither a certainty that claims full knowledge and achievement, nor an instrumentalism that disclaims certitude, but a combination of both. We may apply to religion what Hocking says concerning philosophy: "Philosophy aims at certainty and can be content with nothing else. . . . Some such certainty is necessary to give structure to our system of knowledge, as well as to the experimental business of daily life. The life of knowledge as well as the life of action swings, I believe, in irregular rhythm or alternation, between this pole of certainty and the region of exploration, tentativeness, probability, hypothesis."[10]

5. Certainty in religion grows clearer and stronger with the ongoing experiences of the religious life. True, to the very end it must remain moral certainty, the certainty of faith which trusts and ventures despite contradiction of appearance. Yet it is empirical at the same time. It is conscious of being in constant and living relation with the spiritual

[10]*Types of Philosophy,* p. 443.

world and its forces. Life, knowledge, and certainty go together. Is not our certainty of the physical world based upon such intercourse, and all our certainties as regards our fellows? When we try to segregate knowing and treat it as some separate function of the mind, we land in impotent intellectualism, empty abstraction, or insoluble doubt. Knowing is living, living become conscious, reflective, critical; but criticism, useful in destroying false certainties, can neither supply the final certainties of life nor overturn them. These come out of life and grow with life. The way to certainty, as to knowledge, is to live life at its fullest, with every aspect of our being responsive and active, with mind open, alert, and critical, with a spirit sensitive to spiritual realities and moral values, with a will that is instant in loyalty and courageous in adventure. It is through the active intercourse of a life like this that spiritual certainty grows ever deeper and stronger.

6. The distinctive character of Christian certainty appears first of all in that which calls it forth, the historic personality of Jesus Christ. As with those who first knew him and to whom the Christian message was first brought, so with us the word about his life and message, his death and resurrection, works the inner conviction that here, in the highest which earth can show, the Most High speaks to men. Certainty here has this same moral character: inner conviction, willingness to trust, courage to adventure. Christian certainty is further marked by the character of that religious life and experience in which certainty grows deeper and stronger with the passing years. Personal communion with God, the experience of spiritual presence and power working in the transformation of life, the gaining and the sharing of all this in the Christian fellowship, and the expression of it in the wider human relations, this is the sphere of living in which the certainty of faith is clarified and confirmed. And in all this the Christian experience is marked by a distinctive intimacy, moral quality, and power.

Part Four

SOME PROBLEMS FOR FAITH

Chapter Fourteen

ETHICS AND FAITH

I. CONCERNING APOLOGETICS

THE CHRISTIAN faith is not a philosophy, but it does involve a view of God and man, of the world and life, and because it brings such a world-view it must meet the questions and objections which any such view will call forth. This is the division of theology which has been called apologetics. Partly through misunderstanding of the term, partly because of the way it has been carried on, it has fallen into disrepute. It has been taken to mean something negative and defensive, the mere effort to preserve a system previously determined. So far as this is true, apologetics is at fault. For the concern of religion should be the truth, not the defense of particular opinions; and the best defense of any position is a constructive statement, one that commends itself because it is the most adequate interpretation of the total range of experience and gives the most significant meaning to life.

But there is a new apologetic of a different kind. (1) It is not concerned with a system of doctrines which must be defended at every point; neither does it proceed by concession, yielding this position or that under compulsion of criticism or new knowledge. It sees the significance of a central insight, a simple but crucial faith, the faith in the God and Father of the Lord Jesus Christ and in his meaning for life. (2) It realizes that apparent opposition is often the occasion for new and deeper insights. Beliefs must be restated, purged of error, made larger and truer. The seeming foes are often friends. (3) At the same time it realizes that the central issue remains. There is a final and irreconcilable opposition involved, a decision for faith and life with which Christianity challenges men. It is her faith that the final power in this universe is Spirit, not matter or blind force or impersonal trend; that this Spirit is good in character and purpose, good with the righteousness and mercy revealed in Jesus Christ; and that there is a way of life for men which is according to this Spirit and by which alone man's highest good can be achieved.

It becomes necessary then that we shall face some of the major challenges which are brought against this Christian view. For our purpose these have been selected from the fields of ethics, science, psychology, and history, a final chapter being given to the crucial problem of evil. At certain points, especially in relation to natural science, the discussion can be made relatively brief because of materials already presented.

II. THE ATTACK AND THE ISSUE

Though a richly living religion is always much more than a rule of conduct, it is never less than this, writes A. E. Taylor. "The infinitely serious issue for the whole future of European civilization is that of the soundness of the Christian ideal of human character and the Christian rule of life." If these can be maintained as authoritative for our day, then Christianity will survive. If not, then our successful rebuttals of this or that "historical" or "scientific" criticism cannot "alter the fact that the Christian faith, as a religion, is under sentence of death."[1]

It is this moral leadership of Christianity which is being repudiated today. A generation or two ago men were saying:

[1]A. E. Taylor, *The Faith of a Moralist,* Vol. I, pp. 10, 11.

The moral ideals of Christianity are to be commended but its doctrines are obsolete; today its moral authority is rejected alike in individual life and social relations. The attack is directed at three points.[2] (1) The ethics of Christianity, we are told, is that of external authority, absolute and static; ours must be free, autonomous, experimental, progressive. The only authority we recognize is that of our experience and insights as we seek the largest satisfactions of life through right relations with our world. (2) The Christian ethic, coming from the first century, is wholly inadequate to our new world, the world of modern science with its mastery over nature, of the industrial revolution and the machine age, and of all the complex political and international relations. There are large and important areas of life, such as economics, politics, art, recreation, and marriage, which Jesus either did not know or simply ignored. His concern was with the relation of the individual to God and with the other world. Particularly do we need guidance in the social problems of our day; and in these complicated and desperate situations, abstractions like the golden rule will not suffice. (3) At specific points the teachings of Jesus must be definitely rejected. Some of his maxims, literally followed, would make impossible all organized society. In general, the Christian ethic has been God-centered and other-worldly; ours is centered in humanity and in this world. In the Christian ethic human nature is evil and repression is indicated; for modern ethics human nature is good, repression, as we have learned from Freud, is dangerous, and self-expression

[2]An extreme and rather superficial illustration of this attack may be found in H. E. Barnes, *The Twilight of Christianity,* Ch. VIII, "The Jesus Stereotype." More thoughtful and discriminating is J. H. Randall, Jr., in *Religion and the Modern Age,* pp. 77–86, 208–228, whose argument is stated below. Most significant is not the literature which discusses Christianity's position, but that which ignores it. An excellent treatment from the Christian standpoint is *Christianity and the New World,* by F. R. Barry. *Cf.* also A. E. Taylor, *The Faith of a Moralist.*

is the indicated rule. Such are the more common objections.

Our first need is to see clearly what the ethical meaning of Christianity is and where the conflict really lies.

1. Christianity is not a supernatural, authoritative, and unchanging set of rules. Undoubtedly it has often been so treated. Mistaken theories of revelation pointed that way. As the idea of a supernaturally communicated doctrine promoted dogmatism and intellectualism, so this idea of a supernatural code made of Christianity a legalism. The gospel is not a new law; this is not Jesus' conception nor that of the primitive Church. Nor are the gospels an effort to present us an example for meticulous imitation. The earlier "social gospel" was mistaken in its effort to find directions in the Bible for a new economic order, and the liberalism which sought to solve modern intellectual difficulties in religion by reducing it to an ethical emphasis misconceived the New Testament. God is the supreme concern of Jesus, God and the life which man can have from him alone.

2. Jesus' gospel is religious but the religion is through and through ethical. The ethical is not something added on; it is given with his idea of God. His God is not the lawgiver of Jewish legalism and Mohammedanism, nor the metaphysical essence of the ancient creeds, nor the world ground of philosophy; he is transcendent power, indeed, but first of all he is character and moral will, more specifically redemptive good will. And men are to be like that. Here is the supreme demand of his religion: men are absolutely to trust this Good Will, utterly to surrender their life to him, and so in fellowship with God to be dominated by this spirit. "Love," he says, "that ye may be sons of your Father." F. R. Barry remarks rightly: "Our Lord's task was not to provide mankind with an improved system of ethics. It was to reveal new depths of meaning in moral and spiritual attitudes, to disclose the ultimate quality of spirit in communion with the Holy and Eternal." But Barry is at least misleading when he goes on to say that Jesus' concern "was not primarily with conduct at all"; that it was not so much

"to affect the relations of men and women to one another" as to "redeem the relationship of all men and women to God. His was essentially a religious vocation. His whole life moves in the sphere of the Supernatural."[3] In these last words there is too much of the religion-ethics dualism which Jesus overcame in principle. No one could believe in such a God without being primarily concerned with conduct and without desiring to transform the relations of men and women to one another in the spirit of that God. Of course conduct was not for him an external thing that could be divided into separated relations, to God and man. Conduct is spirit in action; spirit and conduct represent the man, and the whole man was to be made over in the new spirit.

III. WHAT CHRISTIAN ETHICS OFFERS

It is from this standpoint that we must understand the ethics of Jesus, meet objections, and inquire what he has to offer to our day.

1. Jesus presents us an ethics of the spirit, inner and free. The essential matter is the spirit and attitude of a man, a spirit of good will, of sincerity or trueness, of absolute loyalty. It is the antithesis of legalism, externalism, and authoritarianism. His teaching, indeed, is concrete, but his parables, his maxims, and even specific demands like his "Sell that thou hast and follow me," are not efforts to supply mankind with a set of rules, but rather to show in concrete and apprehensible fashion what this right inner spirit means. "The morality of the Gospel," writes Bergson, "is essentially that of the open soul." The intent of such maxims as that of giving all to the poor and turning the other cheek "is to create a certain disposition of the soul."[1] Hence the teaching is occasional. Important areas of life are not considered and there are no blueprints for a social order.

2. Jesus presents an ethics of authority and an absolute

[3] *Christianity and the New World*, p. 88.

[1] H. Bergson, *The Two Sources of Morality and Religion*, pp. 50, 51.

ethics. That follows, like all else, from his faith in God. There is a world of the true and good and right, existent in God, unchanging and eternal, waiting to be apprehended by man and to be achieved here in the world of time where God himself is working and where we are to work with God. The absolute is not in our knowledge—that is growing and must grow. It is not in the teachings of Jesus—it was not his task to communicate complete knowledge but to show men God and to bring men into right and living relation with God. But the absolute is there waiting to be recognized and demanding obedience. "There is that in human nature," as Randall agrees, "that demands unquestioned allegiance to some final end."[2] So, as he adds, the scientist must follow the truth. So in life man must follow the right. The scientist's growing knowledge and changing theory do not preclude the idea of an abiding order in the universe. His knowledge is relative; that order is not. The contrasted position of naturalism is plain. There are only nature and man. Man need have no rule but his desires, no goal but their largest satisfaction. There is no double world of "is" and "ought," only the world that is.

3. The Christian ethic, though not expressed in code or rules, is not abstract or indefinite. It is expressed concretely in the spirit of Jesus, as indicated in his life in relation with men, in his teachings, and not least in his death. In his contrast of a closed and static morality on the one hand and the higher, open, and dynamic morality on the other, Bergson declares that, "Whereas the former is all the more unalloyed and perfect precisely in proportion as it is the more readily reduced to impersonal formulæ, the second, in order to be fully itself, must be incarnate in a privileged person who becomes an example."[3] Here is the tremendous advantage of an historical religion like Christianity in its possession of Jesus. It is not merely that such ethics, as Bergson indicates, is more human and less institutional, that it is vastly more

[2] *Op. cit.*, p. 84. [3] *Op. cit.*, p. 26.

impelling, and that it looks toward the dynamic and the free; but it is more concrete and definite, and less abstract. An open-minded and sympathetic reading of the gospels will give the quality of this spirit, under whose creative influence so many of the noblest spirits of our race have come. Its central quality is love, a reverent good will for all men as men and as children of one Father, a good will that is positive and creative, that is realistic in its understanding of what men actually are, that has faith in what they may through God become. It is not self-negating, for each man is himself a moral personality, sacred and meaningful in God's sight, and he is to love his neighbor *as himself*. It is not repressive, for it is concerned with the fullest realization of the self. It is not individualistic, for its basic principle is social. It is solidaristic, not atomistic, for it roots in the God of good will in whom all men are one as children and brothers. Bergson declares flatly: "It is only through God, in God, that religion bids man love mankind. Humanity had to wait till Christianity for the idea of universal brotherhood, with its implication of equality of rights and sanctity of the person, to become operative."[4] "To become operative," for with Christianity these were no longer mere ideas, casually expressed and ineffective, but active forces rooted in its faith and at the heart of its life.

4. Obviously such an ethic does not offer programs for social reconstruction or detailed directions for individual conduct. If Christianity had begun thus it would have been obsolete in a few generations, and, indeed, impotent from the beginning. Yet the principles and attitudes above indicated have a decisive meaning for our day. That appears especially if we turn to the social scene. Some years ago the steel industry in certain lines ran on a twelve-hour, seven-day schedule. Certain representatives of the Church pointed out what this meant for workmen and insisted that men stood above steel and counted for more than output and dividends.

[4] *Op. cit.*, pp. 25, 69.

They did not assume to solve the problem involved in an industry, like steel, which requires a continuous process in production. The technique of industry and the plans of finance belonged to others, but this human demand belonged to religion. The industry, long opposing, at last yielded, and technicians and financiers found the way out. Today, speaking again in the name of ethical convictions, many Christian leaders insist that a competitive economy, flagrantly unequal in distribution, condemning large numbers to unemployment and more to insecurity and the lack of a fair chance at life for themselves and their children, is in opposition to the Christian principle which puts men above things, cooperation above conflict, and justice and good will above selfish exploitation. Positively it calls for an order which will work by cooperation. Christian ethics thus passes definite judgment upon our social institutions and processes and holds up definite ideals without attempting to indicate the exact means of their achievement. This same ethic cuts in decisively at other points. It condemns such powerful present-day tendencies as nationalism, militarism, and autocracy as directly contradicting its spirit and principles: nationalism as the apotheosis of collective selfishness and the denial of authority to any rule of right as against the will and interest of a given people; militarism as the trust in the supremacy of brute force, the degradation of men into fighting machines, and the killing of men in organized murder; autocracy, whether fascistic, communistic, or capitalistic, as the denial in the realm of the spirit of the sacredness of human personality and of the right of men to truth, free self-expression, and self-determination, reducing men to the status of property and tools.

5. The Christian religion bears decisively upon our desperate social need at another point: its ethics is not simply that of an ideal goal and a personal standard, it is that of a dynamic. The mark of this ethics is that it is never merely ethics; it lifts man into a new and creative relationship, transforming his spirit and giving him the power of a new life.

Here is our deepest need today, whether considered individually or socially: a new spirit in our motivation, a new faith and courage for our efforts. The world needs a new heart. It is true that scientific-technological progress has produced enormously complicated social conditions, economic, political, and international. It is true that we have only begun to develop the organization and technique needed to meet these swift changes. But it is also true, to take the most pressing situation, that the greatest danger to international peace and cooperation has not come so much from lack of knowledge and imperfection of machinery as from the defect in the spirit and attitudes of men. Our selfishness and narrowness, our indifference and inertia, our prejudices and fears have blocked the way. At the close of the first World War the democratic powers were given an opportunity unparalleled in history. They faced the choice between the old nationalist-imperialist-militarist method and the new method represented, however imperfectly, by the ideas of a world court and a league of nations. Nominally the latter course was chosen; actually there was lacking the spirit, the unselfishness, the courage to break away from the old method and follow wholeheartedly the new. The imperialistic tradition, enforced by the fears and hatreds that the war itself had engendered, was too strong. The basic failure was moral.

It may be insisted now that this was too much to expect in that day, and too much in our own day. Human nature cannot be changed, it is said. We remain in a world of evil, of necessary compromise, of rival quests for power, in which at best we can only hope that the weapons of the world will be wielded by those who are a little amenable to the appeals of the spirit. In any case, we are told, the weapons of the world, that is of force, must decide. Such a position can be understood when set forth by those who do not believe in the world of the spirit and its supremacy, but the Christian faith is different. True, it recognizes realistically the world of evil and the element of evil in the best of us. It knows that in such a world any course of conduct that assumes responsibility of action, whether of individual or of social group, will bring inevitable attendant evils. But it believes in another kind of power. It holds that the crucial point of attack must be upon the spirit and attitude of men and nations, that action and organization which do not rest upon this can offer no enduring help, that compulsion, no matter in whose hands, is at best a temporary makeshift and at worst an increase of tragedy, that the transformation of the human spirit is a long and hard way, but the only way. It seems idealistic and remote in this day to talk of the spirit of good will, the desire for truth, devotion to justice, willingness to serve, and cooperation for the common good. But by this road humanity has struggled upward, and apart from this we fall back into the pit from which we were digged. And the Christian religion claims just this power for the remaking of men. Its ethics is not remote and impotent ideal but transforming power.

6. In all this there is a definite and large place for the work of scientist, engineer, sociologist, psychologist, statesman, economist, inventor, artisan, and man of business. The open mind, the courageous and adventuring spirit, constant experiment, endless toil and patience are demanded. The emphasis on the spirit does not exclude attention to the instrument or the summons to patient labor. The Christian ethic has place for all these. It demands them indeed as the expression in life of its spirit of good will and devotion to humanity. It sees here man's task as he works co-creatively with God, and it realizes that it has failed unless it puts in men the spirit for such deeds. Here is, not a truce between science and religion, or a "reconciliation," but a vital union, the answer to the question raised by J. H. Randall, Jr.: "Can the religious life learn experimental flexibility from the spirit of science, without sacrificing the basic faith in terms of which it organizes man's feelings and action?"[5]

[5]*Religion and the Modern World,* p. 85.

Chapter Fifteen

PSYCHOLOGY AND FAITH

THERE are many who think that the battle between religion and its opponents now lies in the realm of psychology. "The conflict between religion and science, which broke out first in the field of cosmology, then of biology and the historical sciences, is now carried into the field of psychology."[1]

The modern psychological approach to the understanding of religion and to the exposition of religious belief may be said to have begun with Schleiermacher (1768–1834). It has profoundly influenced all religious thinking and practice. It rests upon the realization that religion is bipolar, that it includes God and man. The movement was a necessary corrective of the one-sided supernaturalism which interpreted religion solely from the God side, seeing religious knowledge as truth miraculously communicated and salvation wrought by an equally mysterious divine action from without. Further, both doctrine and salvation had been institutionalized by the Church, one in its dogmas, the other in its sacraments. The psychological students did not debate the reality of God, or the nature of religion as life from God. They stressed the obvious fact that religion was first of all human experience, individual and social, and that it must be understood from within. Religion has reference to a "Beyond," but it certainly

[1] J. H. Leuba, in a much-discussed chapter on "Theology and Psychology," in *A Psychological Study of Religion*.

involves a "within." Valuable results followed from this approach. It was more than a matter of light thrown by special studies upon particular matters like conversion and the mystical experience, or of practical applications in the field of religious education. It meant a deeper appreciation of religion itself in its personal and spiritual aspects. It influenced theology and made it more empirical and vital and less speculative and dogmatic. Historically it aided in the understanding and criticizing of religious beliefs by showing how they developed, and in this union of the psychological and genetical two of the most powerful factors in the modern viewpoint were focalized.

I. SOME PSYCHOLOGICAL CRITICISM OF FAITH

But all this does not touch the crucial issue of today. That issue can be put in terms of three conclusions which some have drawn from this psychological study: (1) Psychology by itself offers a complete account of religion and is our only way of studying it. (2) Religion as a purely psychological affair is subjective; so far as it claims an objective reference, as in the belief in God, it is illusion. To this some would add: (3) This illusion, psychologically explicable in the childhood of the race, should now be put aside as harmful by the adult mind. Some who hold the first two points would let religion stand as a purely humanistic affair. Those who assert all three propositions would rule out all religion. Admitting the value and validity of the psychological approach, we have now to consider whether these conclusions follow.

1. J. H. Leuba and E. S. Ames may be taken as representatives of those who have asserted that psychology is the one and sufficient approach to religion, and that theology with its discussion of God is ruled out. Leuba claims that psychology has the right to pass upon the objective reality of God. "Belief in the gods . . . rests upon inductions from the inner life. . . . Religious experience belongs entirely to psy-

chology," just as all other experience belongs entirely to science. "Since the gods of religion are empirical gods, they belong to science." Theology, limited to the empirical as found in this inner experience, must thus become a branch of psychology.[2] Ames is blunter and clearer. "If reality is given in experience (and where else could it be given?), then the science of that experience furnishes the reasonable and fruitful method of dealing with reality, including the reality of religion." Thus we have psychology, not as preparation for or adjunct to later studies, but as "already dealing with the essentials of theology and the philosophy of religion." "The idea of God, which is the central conception of theology, is subject to the same laws of mental life as are all other ideas, and there is but one science of psychology applicable to it."[3]

The error involved in these conclusions concerns the task and field of psychology. Psychology as science is descriptive; it has nothing to say as to possible objective reality that may correspond to these ideas and experiences. That is the task of theology and philosophy of religion. If all "reality is given in experience," why not use psychology as "the fruitful method of dealing with" atoms and chemical elements and galactic systems also? Then, by the same logic, physics and chemistry and astronomy would also resign in favor of the inclusive science of psychology. The more scientific position is that taken by J. B. Pratt: "The psychology of religion . . . must content itself with a description of human experience, while recognizing that there may well be spheres of reality to which these experiences refer and with which they are possibly connected which yet cannot be investigated by science."[4]

Professor Ames himself has apparently moved beyond his earlier position. In his later volume, *Religion,* he says: "No

[2]*A Psychological Study of Religion,* pp. viii, 213, 277.
[3]*Psychology of Religious Experience,* pp. 26, 27.
[4]*The Religious Consciousness,* p. 43.

doubt the ideals arise in human experience, but they are not on that account to be discredited by saying that they are merely human." He protests against the humanism which accepts the lower half of the old dualism, leaving "their humanistic realm suspended between the void of matter on the one side and the vacancy left on the other by the removal of the old supernaturalistic deity." The idea of God is "more than the mere projection of human ideals." Rightly he insists that "so long as man has a genuine, organic place in the order of reality, that order is marked by at least so much personality as man attains."[5] He does not move on to a theistic position—God is "the reality of a social process"; but the significant point is that religious experience ceases to be purely subjective and becomes valid for understanding objective reality.

It is necessary, however, to consider more closely the specific objections to faith in God which are raised today in the name of psychology.

2. The first objection concerns the claim to knowledge: religion has no knowledge of God because it moves purely within human interests and human ideas, that is, it is anthropocentric, anthropomorphic, and subjective. As far back as the sixth century B.C., the Greek Xenophanes pointed out the tendency of man to make God in his own image. "The gods of the Ethiopians are swarthy and flat-nosed, the gods of the Thracians are fair-haired and blue-eyed. . . . Oxen, lions, and horses, if they had hands wherewith to grave images, would fashion gods after their own shape." It might be replied that if horses and oxen could form the idea of God they would no longer be mere oxen and horses. But from the few surviving fragments of this philosopher we know that it was not to belief in God but to crude anthropomorphism that he was objecting.

It was Ludwig Feuerbach, in *The Essence of Christianity* (1841), who first elaborated this position, and all the argu-

[5] Pp. 170–174, 216.

ments in use today may here be found. Religion, he declares, is not an illusion; it is as real as man himself. But that is all that it is; it is purely human, anthropology, not theology. It "is the dream of the human mind." The God that man posits is simply his own nature, but in a purified and unconditioned form. "The other world is nothing but this world freed from all that appears as hindrance and evil." Running through half the book is a discussion which points out doctrine by doctrine how each idea of religion originates in man's own self, his own nature, his own desires, which he objectifies and sets over against himself. "Man is the beginning of religion, the center of religion, the end of religion." At the same time Feuerbach anticipates the idea indicated below, that is, the determination of religious thinking by man's needs and desires. Religion is essentially practical; its supreme concern is the salvation of man. "God is the love which satisfies our wishes, the needs of our heart. He is himself the realized wish of the heart."[6]

The element of truth in this argument has already been noted in our discussion of the nature of knowledge. All our perceiving and thinking, all our interpretation of the world outside of us, must be after the analogy of something that we find within us. "We derive our conception of unity from the unity of the self; our conception of function, which is so important in psychology and biology, from the experience of purpose; our conception of cause from the effort of the will to achieve its ends; our conception of law from our own reason."[7]

Now this situation, frankly recognized, places certain alternatives before us. (1) We may discredit human thinking because it is incurably subjective. In that case, however, we must be consistent and apply this to all knowledge; there is no ground for limiting this to religion. (2) We may use the

[6]*Das Wesen des Christentums,* pp. xv, 20, 269, 274, 275, 179. The references are to the second German edition.

[7]E. S. Brightman, *Is God a Person?,* p. 13.

suggestion quoted above from Pringle-Pattison and A. Wolf; in Professor Wolf's phrase: "Man is also a part of nature." He is organic to his world and this kinship makes knowledge possible. We assume two worlds and a gulf between, and then wonder how we can cross the gulf. We ask about the relations between ideas here and the world out there. How can human ideas, finite and subjective, have any relation to divine reality, infinite and wholly other? How can ideas which are inner and mental have any relation to things out there which are material? But this unnatural dualism, this diremption of our world, is of our own making. We do not deny differences in our world, including the fundamental difference of finite and Eternal, or that of mind and matter; but our world is one world and there is nothing surer in our experience than its interrelatedness in a unitary working order. There is no pure atomism, no isolationism in this world. All life is a unity, and every being has come to be what he is in a constant and mutual relation in which the world has acted upon him and he upon his world. The eye and the light are not separate affairs, they are parts of one process. Mind likewise is not an alien thing in the world. But there is no reason why we should stop here and not include man's moral and religious nature and the ideas in which these are expressed. They, too, represent man's response to his environment and adjustment to it through long development, and his apprehension, however imperfect, of the world about him. Naturally this does not mean that all religious ideas are valid. On the contrary, while it asserts that religious experience is as valid as that of any other realm, there is here the summons to just such reflection and criticism and purification of thought as is needed elsewhere.

3. The next psychological criticism takes a genetic-pragmatic approach. Man and all that concerns him must be understood biologically; he is a creature seeking life through right adjustment. That explains alike the origin of religious belief and why it must be rejected today. Primitive man,

ignorant, helpless, indolent, and afraid, created the gods as those who would reassure and help him. The position is stated most baldly by T. V. Smith in his *The Democratic Way of Life.* Religion "is the easy road. . . . The way is in essence a short cut to satisfaction. . . . There remains over and above science and art and philosophy the way of faith, the will to depend upon a short cut to success in the venture of life. This is religion. Scratch the skin of the most liberal person in the world; and if he call himself religious, some germ of this attitude will be found. It is this germ that makes him religious." To this the author adds a touch of Freud: "Our long infancy set this first discovery into a veritable law of nature for us. When in difficulty hunt a person to help: this the summarized moral of human experiences in infancy and childhood. Little wonder, then, that when the colossal discrepancy that adolescence reveals between the needs arising from glandular pressure and satisfactions reserved for adults drives us to dreams, we create a world of people who understand our needs and who would help us to their satisfaction. . . . Thus gods are made and angels that attend them."[8] Thus Smith finds in laziness and libido the explanation of religion. John Dewey, who has elsewhere more adequate words to say concerning religion, suggests somewhat the same point of view: "As a drowning man is said to grasp at a straw, so men who lacked the instruments and skills developed in later days, snatched at whatever by any stretch of the imagination could be regarded as a source of help in time of trouble. . . . In such an atmosphere primitive religion was born and fostered. Rather this atmosphere was the religious disposition."[9] Hence belief in God is to be repudiated today. For now we know there are no such powers on which to rely, but only man and his control of the forces of nature through science. Reliance upon God, writes M. C. Otto, following Dewey, leads men to regard themselves as spectators of a course of events which

[8]Pp. 4, 7, 12. [9]*The Quest for Certainty,* p. 10.

they in reality help to determine; it makes the highest human excellence consist in aquiescence in the supposed will of God. "Theism is in essence repressive, prohibitory, ascetic."[10]

We need not stop to discuss whether this account of the psychological origin of religion is correct. Conclusions as to the origin of religion are long-range guesses, usually based on the assumption that primitive people of today have preserved unchanged through the long ages the ideas and practices of the beginnings or reaching conclusions by a kind of psychological divination. And it is constantly overlooked that the nature of religion is not determined by its origin and that religion as such is not to be identified with its lower forms. It is more to the point to ask whether this is an adequate account psychologically of the nature of religion as we know it, either today or in such classic expressions as Christian Scriptures and Christian history afford. Let us take outstanding representatives of the Hebrew-Christian tradition such as Amos, Jeremiah, Jesus, Paul, Augustine, Francis of Assisi, Luther, and Wesley, to whom moderns like Schweitzer and Kagawa could be added. In these men religion appears not as ignorance but as insight, not as indolence but as ceaseless effort, not as an easy way but as the path of toil and sacrifice. The question is not whether religion in its beginnings may have stood on a lower level, or whether many religious people are not on that level today—religious leaders have been the first to recognize this. The question is whether religion as such is to be identified with this, and its God viewed as simply the creation of ignorance, fear, and laziness. Non-theistic humanists do not consider the radical difference made at this point by the different conceptions of God and his relation to the world, or recognize that the great believ-

[10]In *Is There a God,* by Wieman, Macintosh, and Otto, Eighth Cycle. Interesting is Otto's avowed refusal to take account of the difference made by the widely varying conceptions of God and his relation the the world. Such writers rarely deal with theism in any of its modern formulations.

ers in God cited above, and unnumbered successors, have found in God the courage to face the hard facts of life and the inspiration for ceaseless effort.

4. The criticisms of Sigmund Freud and his followers call for separate consideration since psychological objections to religious belief today are put mainly in Freudian terms, though the acceptance of the general Freudian position by no means involves the antireligious conclusions.

Religion, for Freud, is an illusion whose origin is psychologically explicable and apparently inevitable, but which belongs to racial infancy and should now be discarded as harmful. Religious ideas, we read, "are not the residue of experience or the final result of reflection; they are illusions, fulfillments of the oldest, strongest, and most insistent wishes of mankind." The supreme concern of these wishes seems to be security. The mother becomes the first love object, as she is "the first protection against all the undefined and threatening dangers of the outer world." The stronger father soon replaces her. "But the relation to the father is affected by a peculiar ambivalence. He was himself a danger, perhaps just because of that earlier relation to the mother; so he is feared no less than he is longed for and admired." In the dual attitude toward God of fear and trust (or desire), this ambivalence remains in all religions. "Now when the child grows up and finds that he is destined to remain a child forever, and that he can never do without protection against unknown and mighty powers, he invests these with the traits of the father-figure; he creates for himself the gods, of whom he is afraid, whom he seeks to propitiate, and to whom he nevertheless entrusts the task of protecting him." This religion was of real social value for primitive man; it assured that repression of instincts that was necessary for the communal existence. "Thus religion would be the universal obsessional neurosis of humanity. It, like the child's, originated in the Œdipus complex, the relation to the father." Religious beliefs are thus "neurotic survivals" and, however useful in the past, the time has come "to replace the consequences of repression by the results of rational mental effort, as in the analytic treatment of neurotics."[11] Religion thus is not a lasting acquisition of human evolution, but rather "a parallel to the neurosis which the civilized individual must pass through on his way from childhood to maturity."[12]

A somewhat more appreciative and constructive attitude toward religion has been taken by C. J. Jung, especially in his recent more popular works on *Modern Man in Search of a Soul* and *Psychology and Religion.* But closer scrutiny shows that his position has not changed from that taken in his earlier work, *Psychology of the Unconscious* (*Wandlungen und Symbole der Libido*), and that he does not differ essentially from Freud on the point under consideration. Religion is a purely subjective matter. It belongs to the realm of dream or phantasy thinking. God is a "representation complex which is grouped around a strong feeling (the sum of libido)." Such reality as this idea or symbol has comes from this feeling. God, in fact, is this libido, our own vital force. "In the Deity man honors his own libido."[13] The religious myth, that is, religious beliefs, though misleading when considered from the standpoint of actual truth, is, however, "psychologically true." It "gives man assurance and strength so that he may not be overwhelmed by the monsters of the universe." "It is the bridge to all the greatest achievements of humanity." But while the religious way is good, there is a better, that of moral autonomy. A creed represents a delusion; it "keeps us infantile and, therefore, ethically inferior." "Belief should be replaced by understanding; then we would keep the beauty of the symbol, but still remain free from the depressing results of submission to belief."[14]

[11]*The Future of an Illusion,* pp. 52, 41, 42, 76, 77.

[12]*New Introductory Lectures in Psychoanalysis,* p. 230.

[13]*Psychology of the Unconscious,* 1st ed., pp. 95–99.

[14]*Op. cit.,* pp. 262, 263.

In the popular mind, the psychological objections to the validity of religious beliefs are associated with the terms rationalization and projection. A. C. Tansley's *The New Psychology,* though an older work, is still representative at this point, and through its many editions has been widely influential. Tansley declares that projection and rationalization are two inevitable tendencies of our nature. There is in man an overmastering desire for some kind of unification, for some consistent scheme of things. Therefore, first in terms of himself and then in terms of the tribe, he projects his ideals and relates them to the forces of nature. "Thus he creates gods in his own image." "God is essentially a social God, a concentrated projection of all the qualities useful to the herd in a supreme supernatural personality—the supreme herd leader of humanity." Such ideals are valuable, indeed necessary to human progress. "It cannot be doubted that God has been a necessity to the human race, that he is still a necessity, and will long continue to be." Because religion is thus necessary and inevitable, because it is a "universal and self-consistent expression of the activity of the human spirit," it has a claim to the name of "truth." But "religious truth is incommensurate with scientific truth." The idealization present in all projection is "a common frailty of the human mind." It "confuses the ideal and the real." "The mind, like the Indian juggler, can climb up a rope the end of which it has thrown into the heavens." Religion then is an illusion, necessary for a time, but ultimately dispensable.[15]

Rationalization is "the production of a 'reason' for, as distinct from the true cause or motive of, an act or conation." Man is basically a creature of impulse and desire. This part of his nature is so strong that it bends the reason to its ends. He acts and believes according to his desires and then finds reasons for these. Here is expressed that same human need of securing unity in one's self and one's world. Religion illustrates this, as do morality and politics. Religious creeds thus

[15]*The New Psychology,* pp. 155–162.

draw their power not from any real basis of truth, but because they satisfy human needs and are the teaching of the herd, that is, of the Church.[16]

II. THE CRITICISMS CONSIDERED

The value of psychology to religion has already been indicated. The practical value of the psychoanalytic movement initiated by Freud is today widely recognized and its influence is being felt in the most diverse fields: in education, medicine, the dealing with delinquents, the treatment of all kinds of mental disorder, the administration of relief, pastoral work, and religious education. As against behaviorism it recognizes the significance of man's conscious life; it has helped in its own way to restore the meaning of the self, or soul. As against intellectualism it has stressed the instinct-impulse side of man's nature, while at the same time it sees the need of reason and will in order that man may understand what has been hidden, face issues, work out adjustments, and so secure unity and integration.

But the insights that are contained in this movement and the value of its techniques as they are still being developed make it all the more necessary that it shall be critically studied. That is especially important because of the tendency of some of its leaders, including Freud, to bring in philosophy in the name of science and to let critical thought be displaced by mythology and speculation. The psychoanalytic movement is primarily a technique for the diagnosis and treatment of mental disorder; it is secondarily, though some would dispute this, a distinct psychology. Both must be differentiated from the philosophical conclusions which have attached themselves as they usually do with popular movements of thought.

1. We note first the tendency to uncritical and unscientific speculation and mythologizing. These writers afford constant illustration of their own theory of wishful thinking in their treatment of the historical data of religion, including

[16] *Op. cit.*, p. 185.

Christianity. Freud says quite frankly in his *Moses and Monotheism,* "I use biblical tradition in such an autocratic and arbitrary way, draw on it for confirmation when it is convenient, and dismiss its evidence without scruple when it contradicts my conclusions."[1] Jung dismisses the whole matter of the historical foundations of Christianity with a casual comment on "the religious emptiness of an historical Jesus, of whose person we know nothing."[2] His pages abound with interpretations of Christian symbols and doctrines in which speculative fancy is quite unhindered by any regard for historical fact or the results of critical research. This is quite legitimate, he considers, when once you hold that all these dogmas are an expression of the unconscious, that they originated in visions, dreams, or trances, that they "occur just as often in pagan religions, reappearing spontaneously as psychical phenomena."[3] It is not the most fanciful, though it is perhaps the most offensive of his illustrations, when he declares that the idea of the Trinity is taken from phallic symbolism and specifies in detail the anatomical basis for this doctrine.[4]

2. Leaving to one side such free mythologizing, we consider the more serious question, whether religious belief is mere wishful thinking and religion simply the attempt to escape from the hard realities, which man is unwilling to face, into a world of pleasant dreams. Two facts must be recognized here. First, feeling and desire are much the stronger part of man's life. That is true in the childhood alike of the individual and of the race. Rational reflection

[1]Footnote, p. 37. His justification is that the material is untrustworthy in any case and, further, that he is a psychoanalyst and not an ethnologist. The conclusions of critical historians, however, receive almost as little attention here as does the work of the historians of religion when psychoanalysts speculate as to how religion originated.

[2]*Psychology of the Unconscious,* pp. 258, 259.

[3]*Psychology and Religion,* pp. 56, 57.

[4]*Psychology of the Unconscious,* pp. 227, 228.

comes late and is even yet but little developed. A world war sweeps entire nations off their feet, press and Church and university included; and men's conclusions are determined not by fact and reflection but by interest, prejudice, fear, and passion. The fascist states show us whole peoples surrendering free rational inquiry for unquestioning submission to the "Leader." These emotions inevitably are strongest where the highest values are involved, as in morality and religion, but equally where other individual and social interests are concerned, as in politics and economics. Religious thinking has certainly been in danger here.

But the presence of interest need not militate against reason. "The cosmic religious experience," says Albert Einstein, "is the strongest and the noblest driving force behind scientific research." And this cosmic religion is for him "an insight into the mystery of life," the knowledge, the feeling that there is an "impenetrable" that really exists, "manifesting itself as the highest wisdom and the most radiant beauty."[5] Sometimes modern science is more practical in aim; its first impetus came from Bacon with his idea of *scientia* as *potentia,* and the control of nature for man's ends as the real objective of knowledge. But even where its motivation has been an apparently impersonal search for "truth," there has been operative a very definite human need, namely, that of a unitary, orderly, and intelligible world demanded by man's reason. A human being unmoved by desire would be not only monstrous but useless even in the search for truth. William James was right: "If you want an absolute duffer in an investigation, you must, after all, take the man who has no interest whatever in its results: he is the warranted incapable, the positive fool."[6]

But the deeper question involved here is in the underlying assumption of a basic dualism between the order and forces

[5]From *Has Science Discovered God?* E. H. Cotton, ed., pp. 97, 101, 102.

[6]*The Will to Believe,* p. 21.

of nature on one side and the desires and needs of man on the other. Of course, there is no perfect harmony here: the conflicts of life and the task of adjustment are evidence. But the other side must not be overlooked: Man and nature constitute a unity. It is as a unitary whole that both have evolved in constant and mutual interaction. The necessary condition of man's evolution has been as much the fitness of the environment for man as the adjustment of man to the environment.[7] Human needs and longings as such determine nothing, but it is fair to say that on the whole they point to truth rather than illusion, and that the presence of a basic and persistent need of man expressed in terms of universal and ineradicable desire is in so far forth a presumption in favor of some objective correspondence in reality. Modern science, viewing things genetically, sees the whole man, mind and feelings included, as part of a developing whole, of which "nature" is the other member. "Hopes and fears," writes John Dewey, "desires and aversions, are as truly responses to things as are knowing and thinking. Our affections, when they are enlightened by understanding, are organs by which we enter into the meaning of the natural world as genuinely as by knowing, and with greater fulness and intimacy."[8] And William James' comment is in point: "Certain of our positivists keep chiming to us, that, amid the wreck of every other god and idol, one divinity still stands upright—that his name is Scientific Truth, and that he has but one commandment, but that one supreme, saying, *Thou shalt not be a theist,* for that would be to satisfy thy subjective propensities, and the satisfaction of those is intellectual damnation. These most conscientious gentlemen think they have jumped off their own feet—emancipated their mental operations from the control of their subjective propensities at large and *in toto.* But they are deluded. They have simply chosen from among the entire set of propensities at their command those

[7]See *The Fitness of the Environment,* by L. J. Henderson.
[8]*The Quest for Certainty,* p. 297.

that were certain to construct, out of the materials given, the leanest, lowest, aridest result—namely the bare molecular world—and they have sacrificed all the rest."[9] The Freudian discussions of religion hardly justify the conclusion that here at length we have thinkers who have "jumped off their own feet" and at last attained pure rational objectivity.

But if we cannot exclude interest and emotion from the process of thinking, we can see to it that desires are purified and interests and motives elevated; and in so doing, we not merely escape the danger of illusion but advance the knowledge of truth. Lawrence Hyde draws the right conclusions from this psychological study. "What, we must now ask, is the condition of attaining to a direct rather than an illusory vision of reality? To this question all enlightened psychologists, ancient and modern, have returned a perfectly decisive answer: emancipation from the dominion exercised on the mind by the infantile, egoistical, phantastic self. Purify nature and you will perceive things as they are. . . . A deeper integration of being cannot but result in a new order of vision."[10] The knowledge of the truth is not secured by the effort to suppress all but cold and dry reason; the whole man must be engaged if the truth is to be known, and the quality of that life, its richness in relation to its world, its moral purity, and the degree of its integration will condition this knowledge.

3. But to secure this is the function of religion, and the first requirement in this connection is to get rid of the error of lumping all religion together and assuming naïvely that religion is the one exception in human development and can never rise above its primitive levels. Our concern here is with high religion, theistic and ethical. In such religion there are other motivations than that represented by Freud's pleasure-pain principle, and other forces operative than the all-

[9]*The Will to Believe,* p. 131.

[10]*The Prospects of Humanism,* pp. 22, 30. Compare our earlier discussion of "The Way of Moral Insight and Loyalty," Chap. X.

explanatory libido of Jung which he defines simply as psychic energy. One is the concern for truth. In its greatest representatives, philosophy is concerned with life as well as truth; it is *Lebensanschauung* as well as *Weltanschauung.* And high religion seeks truth as well as life; the passion for reality is fundamental with it, and its basic faith is the conviction that the good and the real are one. That is what it means by God. To despair of truth is atheism, to be false to it is irreligion. The psalmist's word voices this note: "My soul crieth out for the living God." And here belongs the almost savage Hebrew contempt for idolatry, for gods that are vanity, mere emptiness, a human fabrication, the great passage in Isaiah 44:9–20 being one example among many. It is only the persistent preoccupation with the lower expressions of religion and the assumption that the pathological offers the clue to the nature of religion that cause men to shut their eyes to such facts. Ethical religion, when it appears, demands sincerity and intellectual integrity. Leuba himself has recognized this in pointing out the comparative absence of myth from the central elements of Hebrew-Christian faith, due to the moral earnestness of this religion.[11]

The second motivation also springs from the moral quality of high religion; it is the concern for what is right and just. The God who is real is good, and goodness is not simply a kindly disposition which man posits because he desires it; it is justice and mercy and righteousness. In an ethical religion the goodness which man trusts is one which he must follow. Obsessed with a hedonistic interpretation of life, men overlook the religion of high demand. Here is no mere wishful thinking that shapes a God after its desire. Here are men who come into the presence of the Holy with fear and awe, who know God as the one who has the right to command, indeed, as the one before whom evil man stands condemned. "The morally perfect Being who confronts conscience is experienced as morally hostile to the individual interest or de-

[11] *A Psychological Study of Religion,* p. 205.

sire."[12] Religion is no mere refuge of ease; it is a judgment, a challenge, a demand.

And these considerations give the answer to the charge that religion as wishful thinking is a soft and selfish escape from a world of stern reality too hard to endure, too difficult to face, into a world of dreams. There certainly has been much religion of this type, day dreaming, otherworldly, self-deluding, and futile. But ethical religion is not of that kind. In action its great proponents have faced laborious days and met hard tasks; they have been among the most intense realists and most unselfish servants of mankind. In thought they have been equally realistic, but with a higher realism which believes that the appearance of things is not the last word of truth. They have found God as the most real, have refused to flee him, and have dared to live their life in the light of that supreme reality.

The basic error in this criticism is not simply a hedonistic misinterpretation of religion, but a hedonistic misconception of man. Happiness is not the supreme value for man or his supreme object of search. Berdyaev is nearer the truth when he says that it is not happiness or pleasure that man strives for but concrete values or goods. "Man is a free spiritual and creative being, and he prefers the free creation of spiritual values to happiness."[13]

4. We have still to consider the objections to the validity of religious belief expressed under the terms "projection" and "rationalization," some answer to which has already been given. Certainly there is in human thinking auto-suggestion and projection. Every idea that we have of the world about us is a projection. The question is: Do these ideas "hit something" when projected? Do they have their source in a real experience, one that involves a give and take between man and his world? Do they represent an adequate interpretation of that experience? Are these interpretations approved when used in

[12]R. H. Strachan, *The Authority of Christian Experience,* p. 185.
[13]*The Destiny of Man,* pp. 95, 96, 132.

further experience? These questions must be answered by our theory of knowledge. Psychology as such has no competency here; it describes the inner process but cannot decide the objective reference, a fact persistently disregarded by these psychologists.

Rationalization, as commonly employed, is the use of the reason not in its own right but to support actions or ideas already determined by need or desire. Abundant illustration can be found in all human life. Action comes first with man in point of necessity and in relation to human development. Our needs and desires are imperative; reflection and explanation come later. The progress of man, however, depends upon his capacity to understand and explain. In other words, the development of the reason itself becomes a practical necessity. To gain food, to live safely and happily with his fellows, to satisfy his driving desire, man must think and think correctly. That is equally true in religion. The religious writings of the Old and New Testaments are full of illustrations of the appeal to understanding, criticism, and reflection. The prophets and Jesus summon men to look upon life, to criticize conduct, to consider consequences, to judge what is far by what is near at hand and known. "What think ye?" is one of Jesus' frequent phrases. "Come now and let us reason together" is a prophetic summons.[14]

What we find then is this. Action precedes reflection and constantly outruns it. The use of reason marks a later and higher plane. There is constant temptation to prostitute reason in defense of an action that has no rational grounds. A nation seizes territory and then lets its "statesmen" invent lofty terms about manifest destiny and the white man's burden to justify the *fait accompli.* Religious myths grow up to account for established rites and customs. Men tend to believe what they would like and then find a philosophy for it. But if there is rationalization in religion, there is also

[14]See Matt. 18:12; 21:28; 22:42; 26:66; Luke 12:51; 13:2; Isa. 1:18.

reflection and criticism. It is interesting that the Freudian psychology, with its tendency to select facts to support its hypotheses, with its bent to mythologizing, should jump from the presence of rationalizing in religion to the conclusion that all religious ideas are rationalizations. To assume that your processes of thought are strictly rational and your opponent's are rationalizations is, of course, to beg the question, and seems to be a clear example of rationalizing. The conclusions of theology, as of Freudian psychology, must be settled one by one on their own merits.

To summarize our discussion: The psychological objection rests on the assumption that a full account is given of religion and its beliefs when these are described as a subjective process. The answer is: All knowing is a subjective process on the one side; the real question is whether there is something objective that corresponds to this and that is known. The problem is the same for all knowledge, religious, social, scientific; and psychology as such cannot settle it, for the task of psychology as a science is simply to describe.

Chapter Sixteen

SCIENCE AND FAITH

PREVIOUS discussions have already dealt with the bearing of modern science upon the religious world-view, but some specific questions remain to be considered.

1. Is not the Christian doctrine of creation excluded by the teachings of science as to evolution?

(1) We must distinguish here as elsewhere between the central Christian conviction and the form in which traditional theology expressed this. The question at issue is not that of a universe six thousand years old, or of a six-day creative period, or of a world created *ab extra* by a series of fiats. It is whether back of this cosmos and the ages of its development there is a creative Spirit of Good Will that has shaped its course. (2) The theory of evolution, so far as it is legitimate science and not a theory of philosophy, simply seeks to determine the facts and describe the process. It does not, and cannot, show the source or sustaining ground or end of it all. It must assume such facts as the basic and unitary order of the cosmos, change (the "fortuitous" variation of Darwin), heredity (not explained when its mechanism is described, as by Mendel), the organismic tendency, and the emergence of higher levels; but it has no explanation of these facts. (3) The new science recognizes a real creativity in evolution. That does not as such involve the idea of a Creator but does recognize the appearance of what is new and different. Evolution is a creative process. (4) The con-

ception of God's method in creation is being profoundly modified. Whether this visible universe had a beginning in time and was created out of nothing can be left to debate. If there be a creator God, however, his work would seem to be that of an artist, working slowly, shaping his material toward certain ends, and conditioned alike by these ends and the character of his material. Yet the figure of the artist is inadequate. The artist stands outside his work; the Creator Spirit is immanent. The material of the artist is passive and his work is compulsive; God works by a principle of freedom. Even on the lower levels we see in his material spontaneity and a life urge; in man this "freedom" rises to rational and purposive cooperation. The finite becomes co-creative with the Eternal.

2. A second problem for faith is raised for many minds by the bigness of the universe and the littleness of the earth and man. "If we had not discovered another solitary scientific fact in the last century," says one critic, "the implications of the size and distance of Betelgeuse would be adequate to blow sky-high the foundation of the whole set of moral conceptions of Judaism and Christianity."[1] The objection is put less crudely by Santayana, who sets forth the "Christian Epic" of creation and redemption as held by traditional theology, the familiar story of creation, sin, fall, the chosen people, the coming to earth of the Son of God for man's redemption, the final issue of all things in judgment and heaven and hell.[2] Is not this, we are told, a patent absurdity, a pitiful human megalomania? Man, creature of a day, clinging to this tiny fragment of matter in the midst of unmeasured spaces counts himself and his Earth as the center of this vast Universe and the supreme object of regard for that Cosmic Force which moves in all things! In the words of Tennyson's *Vastness,*

[1]H. E. Barnes, *Living in the Twentieth Century,* p. 37.

[2]From Santayana's *Reason in Religion,* as quoted by J. H. Randall, Jr., *The Making of the Modern Mind,* pp. 18–20.

"Many a planet by many a sun may roll with the dust of a
vanished race.
What is it all but a trouble of ants in the gleam of a million
million suns?"

But have the proponents of this objection really stated the issue? The question is not, How small is man in comparison with the universe? but rather, What is the yardstick by which to measure greatness? That is the crucial issue between naturalistic and idealistic philosophies. The objection brings not argument but assumption, the assumption that the material alone is real. It is not an appeal to reason, but the surrender of reason and an effort to terrorize the imagination. If reason counts at all, if the world holds any discernible element of the rational, then the astronomer who can discern this rational order counts for more than the enormous bulk of a Betelgeuse which, after all, is nothing more than a mass of flaming gas.

Let us note now the position of a Christian theism in the light of this new sense of cosmic vastness.

(1) The final reality is not things but God, the God who is alike goodness and power. The reality of God is the real issue. (2) Religion exalts God, not man. Its universe is not man-centered but God-centered. To find the highest and confess its absolute right over us is religion. Its spirit is not self-assertion but humility, not self-sufficiency but dependence. (3) It is the Christian faith in God which gives high meaning to human life. It is not the vastness of the universe that man has to fear, but the indifference of the universe and the consequent meaninglessness of life. Tennyson, bidding farewell to Carlyle late at night under the stars, spoke of their glory. To which Carlyle could only answer, "Man, it is just terrible, terrible." If there is nothing but bigness there, then it is truly terrible. The psalmist has another answer—for this problem of bigness is not so new as some think: "When I consider the heavens, the work of thy hands, the moon and

the stars that thou hast made, what is man that thou art mindful of him, or the son of man that thou visitest him?"[3] If once we can believe that Goodness is there, then the fact of bigness or power only adds to our reverence and joy. It is God that is the issue. If there be such a God, if the ultimate Reality be rational and moral, then man becomes significant. For only such a being as man can perceive this God, can reverence him, can enter into fellowship with him, and in some slight measure express this divine Spirit. Man is the one creature we know who, as rational being, can discern the meaning of events, and who as free being can act creatively in the stream of events. And in this his distinctive nature appears, as Tennyson suggests in his *De Profundis:*

"We feel we are nothing—for all is Thou and in Thee;
We feel we are something—that also has come from Thee."

(4) In all this there is nothing egoistic or exclusive. The old geocentricism is no necessary part of the Christian faith any more than the old Jewish nationalism. Its God is concerned with all creatures and equally with all worlds in which life may have appeared. If there be other spheres where creatures exist who have reached the plane of reason and morality, it will be through the creative Spirit of this God whose work is not limited by our ignorance. But certainly such a God will not be concerned with the size of the orb on which such creatures dwell, or fall prey to the "buncombe of bigness."

Our greatest need is a more adequate conception of God. We are still too much limited by the picture of a Carpenter Creator and a Manlike Monarch, a picture that does not go with the new cosmos. But the critic, too, needs to envisage this larger conception of God before he passes judgment. Is it not both naïve and narrow to assume a God so limited that he can have neither knowledge nor concern for anything except galactic systems and inter-stellar spaces? Mod-

[3]Ps. 8:3-5.

ern science has been quite as much interested in the microcosmic as the macrocosmic. It has found atom and cell as marvellous and significant as the stars in their island universes. (Curiously enough, as has been pointed out by Eddington, man seems to be in size the mean between the atom and the star.) The universe which science reveals is one in which order and beauty are equally present in great and small. If there be a God, why should not his goodness reach as far as his reason and beauty and power? If these last are present in the atom, why should not the love of God be present with man? Is it because the critics are still too anthropomorphic in their conception of God?

3. The third objection is in some ways the most subtle and powerful today in its anti-religious influence: If there be a God, what difference does he make? Where is there room for him in the actual ongoing processes of the world? Is not the appeal to God and the dependence upon God as outworn as the use of magic? The only forces that we know are the forces of this visible world of ours, of man and nature. If we are to be saved—physically, mentally, socially, economically—it must be by our effort, using and controlling the forces that we know through our science. There is no power that can come in from outside to change this course of events, and it is superstition to call upon it. The reply of religion to this objection can be briefly made. It involves, first, an understanding of the position of modern theism, second, an appreciation of what that Nature is which modern knowledge shows us.

(1) The first error is to set nature and supernatural over against each other. Religion does not require the old dualism. God is not one thing among many others in the universe; he is not a rival of nature. The world is not outside God, it is within God. These forces are his, for he is the power that moves in all things. These "laws" which we seek to learn by our science and to utilize in practice are his thoughts. This order is his reason working immanently in the uni-

verse. Science is our understanding of his way of working. There are not two worlds; there is one world. There are not two kinds of causes, natural and supernatural. All the cosmic processes are supernatural in the sense that all have their ground in God and are shaped by him to his ends; but the same processes are to be studied and traced out "naturally," that is, in their physical, psychical, and historical causes or relations. Human action within the natural order offers a simple analogy: first, processes which are to be studied and described scientifically in their causal relations; second, behavior seen as that of a rational and purposive being working within this order to secure his ends.

(2) The crucial question is: What is the nature of that final Reality which underlies all, which moves in all, in which all things, in Paul's suggestive phrase, hang together?[4] For religion the ultimate reality is the spiritual, not the material. The physical universe is real. Whether in its essential nature it be "thought" or "thing" we do not here need to decide; that is a philosophic question, not a religious one. But it is not ultimate, not self-sufficient; its source and its being are in the spiritual, in God.

(3) The world of our modern knowledge, including both natural and social sciences, does not, indeed, demonstrate God, but it does point beyond itself and leave open the way to faith in God. The physical universe, as we have seen, is not a sum of *disjecta membra,* or a mere collection of separate forces acting each by itself; it is more like a living organism, than a dead assemblage. There is a unity, a single pervasive order, with a creative and purposive energy at work in it. And if we are truly empirical, we must include the world of values, beauty and truth and goodness, and so seek an ultimate which is an adequate source for these.

(4) To say that the world has its being in God is not to identify God with the world or make him one with nature, whether we write this with a capital or not. So soon as you recognize in God the qualities of the rational and purposive

[4]Col. 1:17, translating thus συνέστηκεν.

and good, you have reached the idea of transcendence. So the spirit of man, reasoning, recognizing goods and goals, and working towards them, transcends the body in and through which it works. The God who transcends this universe is not by that fact outside of it; the God who is immanent in the cosmos is not by that fact identical with it.

(5) It would take a separate treatise to consider the question how God works in the world. The answer can, however, be indicated, and it should be empirically based. The order of nature and its unity, the principle of coordination or integration which works through it, the creative energy which has achieved the ascending levels of emergent evolution, the purposiveness which nature shows, these show how God works in the world of nature. The historic-social process is the second sphere. Here we can conceive of God's work in a double way: as that organic moral order which works as judgment and destruction in relation to evil and as support to all human labor for the right and good; as immanent Spirit of love and truth and justice which is alike appealing vision and inspiring presence. The third sphere is the individual life. To be truly empirical we must include the witness of those who assert a religion of personal fellowship with the divine Spirit, who have found through this strength and joy and peace and light, and who declare that in some way their life is at once the heightened activity of the human and the deed and gift of the divine.

The concern of religion then is simply this: to assert the supreme reality of the spiritual, to show that man is akin to this, to make plain that vital and active fellowship with this is possible and that through this man achieves life. The new theism welcomes every "natural" explanation, whether in the physical or spiritual realm. If there is anything to be gained from Freud or Watson, from a knowledge of hormones or ductless glands, it wishes to know it and use it, for only so can it work effectively with God. But it holds too that there are higher levels of life with laws and forces of their own. With Michael Pupin in the last chapter of his *New*

Reformation, it sees a realm of spiritual dynamics in which Christ was the great discoverer, with love as the supreme coordinating force in a universe in which coordination is the guiding principle for the whole course of development.

4. The last objection to be considered appeals somewhat more to the scholarly than to the popular mind. It rests upon the second law of thermodynamics. Of these two great laws, the first deals with the conservation of energy and the correlation of forces. It declares that the sum of energy in the universe is constant; energy is neither lost nor added to, though it is convertible from one form into another. The second law declares that in this conversion of energy, there is a certain one-way, or irreversible, movement. No energy is ever lost, but some of it is always escaping in the form of diffused heat that is no longer available for work. We must consider the quality as well as the quantity of energy. The energy in coal can be used to make heat, motion, electricity, all of which can be creatively employed. But some of it escapes as heat that is diffused and never will be available again. This is the increase of entropy. The kinetic energy is constantly decreasing, the potential increasing. There can then be only one issue, we are told: all the energy which has worked in the creative processes of the world will finally become diffused as uniform heat, or warmth. All life and movement will cease. This *Wärmetod,* or heat-death, will, of course, bring to an end not only the physical processes but all life, all personal beings and spiritual values which have appeared in the episode which we call human history. It is impossible, therefore, to conceive our universe as having a spiritual origin or spiritual end. This conception is the exact reverse of the idea of a creative process of development which we have been considering and which is presented not only by biology and psychology but by chemico-physical science. Its universe is one of steady degradation or dissolution.[5]

[5]*Cf.* L. T. Hobhouse, *Development and Purpose,* p. 355.

Professor R. A. Millikan has been the most vigorous opponent of this theory among physicists. He makes a threefold suggestion. This is an attempt, he declares, at a purely mechanistic account of the universe, and modern physics "has thrown the purely mechanistic view of the universe root and branch out of its house." More specifically he thinks that with the process of degradation of energy, there is a building-up process going on constantly somewhere in the universe. "If atom formation out of hydrogen is taking place all through space as it seems to be doing, it may be that the hydrogen is somehow being replenished there, too, from the only known form of energy that we know to be all the time leaking out from the stars to the interstellar space—namely: radiant energy." Finally, he insists that we know too little to dogmatize. "Gain of entropy always means loss of information and nothing more."[6]

The plain man, without special scientific knowledge, can see the inadequacy of this "law" as a total explanation of the cosmic process. Two alternatives seem clearly to face us here. (1) If this space-time universe has always existed as a self-sufficient and self-explaining whole, according to this law it should have run down before this time. For the essential point of this theory is that the universe must run down within a given time. If it has always existed, then that time would have elapsed ere this. Why then has it not already run down? (2) The other alternative is to assume that the universe came into being in time, that is, that it is not self-sufficient or self-explanatory, but that some creative Power brought it into being at some time in the past. This is the position reached by Jeans, who, with Eddington, has been especially insistent upon this idea of the impending "death" of our universe.[7] Jeans puts the age of the stars at as much as five

[6]Address at 1930 meeting of The American Association for the Advancement of Science.

[7]James Jeans, *The Universe Around Us,* Ch. VI; A. S. Eddington, *The Nature of the Physical World,* Ch. IV.

to ten million million years. The atoms existed in the nebulæ perhaps an equal time previous to this, and the present matter of the universe not more than 200 million million years in all. The conclusion is "creation of matter at some time not infinitely remote."

So we have scientists assuming a doctrine of creation in time. The question is whether this particular theory of creation is adequate to the facts and satisfactory to the mind. Dean Inge seems right in saying: "The working hypothesis of the astronomers seems to be a naïve deistic doctrine that some billions of years ago God wound up the material universe, and has left it to run down of itself ever since."[8] If creativity must be assumed, why not a continuous creative action? This whole effort to give a comprehensive explanation of the cosmic process and its conclusion in terms of a law of physics calls for the comment of L. T. Hobhouse: "It is clearly a one-sided account, as might be expected of a purely mechanical view, and rightly interpreted it is an admission of the inadequacy of mechanics to explain Reality."[9] Once more we see that this difficulty for religious faith has back of it a begging of the whole question.[10]

The consideration of these various questions has shown

[8]*God and the Astronomers,* p. 34. The volume contains an extended discussion of the problem. For a biologist's view, contrasting building-up and running-down aspects, see H. S. Jennings, *The Universe and Life,* pp. 16–19.

[9]*Development and Purpose,* pp. 355, 356. *Cf.* Pringle-Pattison, *The Idea of God,* p. 300.

[10]This unconscious naturalism into which so many scientists fall while conceiving themselves to be strictly "scientific" and without any philosophical assumptions is well indicated by Arthur S. Eddington in his work, *The Philosophy of Physical Science.* "Because a man works in a laboratory it does not follow that he is not an incorrigible metaphysician. . . . The physicist is by origin a philosopher who has specialized in a particular direction. . . . Generally he [the physicist] prided himself on being a plain matter-of-fact person—which was his way of describing a man who accepted the naïve realism of a Newtonian epistemology." Pp. 33, 52.

that they concern equally those who start with science and those who start with religion. The thoughtful man, beginning with nature, but not omitting man, is driven to ask what accounts for order and unity, for purposeful change, for the creativity which issues in higher levels of being and which is productive of values. The religious man, starting with this ideal or spiritual element, taking in the total picture of nature and process, must inquire just how his God is related to this world and how he works in it. Theology has long recognized that its traditional formulations are inadequate. The inadequacy of the old naturalism is even more evident. What is needed now in religious thought is to turn away from the merely defensive side of this question. It is not enough to argue the reality of the spiritual and its primacy; we must move on to a new doctrine of nature and of the relation to it of divine creativity. Such a doctrine must take into account the darker side of nature: conflict, suffering, not only movement in development but hindrance, delay, blind alleys. But it must also make clearer the need of such a world of nature as the necessary sphere of spiritual activity and development, and the way in which the Creative Spirit has worked. These considerations belong to the discussion of the problem of evil.

Chapter Seventeen

HISTORY AND FAITH

I. THE ISSUE

OURS has been called an age of science; it may with equal right be called the age of historical study. What we have, in fact, is the same point of view underlying the two great fields of human research, nature and man. The modern man thinks of a unitary, dynamic, and developing world, whether he is considering nature or history. Historical study is the effort to see all things as parts of one process of development, to understand all ideas and institutions and events by describing how that which is came from that which went before. It is therefore no longer one field of study among others but a method applied to every field.

It is easy to see why this viewpoint clashed with traditional religious thought. That thought embodied a philosophy of history which we may call naïve supernaturalism. It was dualistic in character; it saw two streams of history, one sacred, the other profane. Profane history dealt with ordinary human happenings; sacred history recorded the direct deeds of God. These formed a world apart, and here everything took place according to a special order, not, of course, unrelated to the historical and the human, but yet independent of these. The sacred writings were directly given by God, the turning-points in Israel's history hinged on God's deeds, the Redeemer came direct from heaven, the Church with its orders and sacraments was the act and prescription of God, its heads (at least for Rome) were divinely moved to infallible act and teaching, the creeds embodied the pure truth given by revelation and formulated under divine direction.

This externalistic supernaturalism has suffered at the hands not only of historical study but of Christian theology itself. Christian thinkers see that it is impossible to isolate a group of writings like the Christian Scriptures, or a group of events called sacred history, or a set of ideas whether found in Scripture or creeds, to lift all this out of the stream of history and make it the result of supernatural action. Something akin to this, it is true, is being attempted again today in the effort to avoid historical relativism and to assert the uniqueness and sole authority of the Christian revelation. So for Karl Barth there is real revelation only in the Christian religion, elsewhere only the human search. In more moderate form Hendrik Kraemer holds to the same general position in his work, *The Christian Message in a Non-Christian World.* He would not deny the presence of truth in other faiths. But this does not imply revelation; rather it is its virtual denial. For it suggests something discoverable by man, and thus always relative, while revelation is an objective deed of God, disclosing his will and his mind, and claiming unique and absolute validity. Revelation is thus an irruption of the divine into history; history itself is human, and all its products, including its religions, are to be judged by this revelation, though the latter is not to be identified with empirical Christianity, whether in terms of its life or its developed doctrines.[1]

But the problems that arise for faith from the modern historical viewpoint are not settled by the elimination of an externalistic supernaturalism. Christianity is both a religion of the historical and of the supernatural, or suprahistorical.

[1]See especially Ch. IV and pp. 142–147.

On the one hand it is bound up with history. Its God is one who enters into history and works through history; it believes in a revelation that has come through history and finds its abiding center in a historical personage, Jesus of Nazareth. On the other hand it holds that this history is more than history, more than the human and the relative. The living God shapes this history and "the mighty acts of God" are discerned in it. Jesus, though he appeared in time, a man among men in a given historical setting and succession, is yet seen as the deed and revelation of the Eternal, transcending time and having final meaning for all time. So far from being just one link in history, Jesus is seen as the clue to all history, including that which is yet to be.

To all this there are vigorous objections raised in the name of history. They may be summarized in four points: (1) Christianity claims a divine origin, but history shows us that all religions have had their origin in crude beginnings and are the result of long development. This is the objection from evolution. (2) Christianity claims absolute truth, but it is a historical religion and in history everything is imperfect, changing, and relative. This is the objection from the relativity of the historical. (3) Christianity identifies itself and its claims with a particular individual, Jesus of Nazareth, but the truth should be sought in eternal principles and truths and not in some single historical expression. This is the objection from the limitation of the historical. (4) Christianity ties up religious faith with past events, but we can never be absolutely sure of anything in the past, and that applies to our knowledge of the life and teachings of Jesus. This is the objection from historical uncertainty.

Before considering these objections we must inquire more clearly as to the Christian viewpoint. There are, of course, varying formulations of the Christian view of God and the world, or of the relation of time and the Eternal. The common denominator is the belief in a transcendent God, in the supreme reality of a world of spiritual meanings and values and forces. This common conviction has taken four main forms. (1) Where Hellenistic philosophy has influenced theology, men have conceived this spiritual order as a world apart, perfect and unchanging, while the world of time and change has been regarded as evil or at least as unmeaning. (2) Where a dualistic supernaturalism obtained, the action of the divine has been piecemeal and externalistic.[2] (3) Apocalypticism is a special form of dualistic supernaturalism. It sees the coming divine order as something *toto genere* different from the present world of time. This age is for it evil and hopeless, belonging to God's plan, indeed, but without apparent meaning. The new age comes by a deed of God which does not so much fulfill history as put an end to it. In contrast with these, however, we must think of Christianity as being (4) in the prophetic succession. Here the living God, always transcending history, yet acts through history. There is a dualism recognized but it is moral rather than metaphysical. Man as creature is dependent upon the transcendent God, but he may set himself over against God in self-will and disobedience. The transcendent God, however, does unite himself with human life in his redemption and does enter into history. And, so entering, the Eternal gives meaning to time; human life gains significance and history ceases to be mere endless change and becomes the outworking of a divine plan and a sphere of divine creativity. For Christianity the supreme deed of God is an event in history, his self-revealing and redeeming act in Jesus Christ; and its great goal is the kingdom of God, whose consummation, indeed, is beyond human history, but which is already present as the work of a transcendent God operative in history. Historical and suprahistorical both come to their rights here; the Eternal and time, God and man, the enduring and change are joined. Christianity sees in time and change a world of real meaning. It seeks from history the story of this age-

[2]*Cf.* the conception of a "holy history" described as "divine interference with history," p. xx, *God in History,* by Otto Piper.

long movement, but it gives to history a meaning which it would not otherwise have. The Eternal is the scene and setting of time, and time cannot be understood apart from the Eternal.[3]

If now we look more closely at the objections that have been raised in the name of history we shall see that they come in part from a misapprehension of the Christian position, whether by critic or defender, in the main, however, from a naturalistic philosophy underlying this "historism." It is the task of history to describe the ongoing change in the human scene. The assumption of naturalism is that there is nothing but bare events joined in ceaseless change. Against this, two considerations may be advanced. First, the historian himself constantly transcends this scheme, for his concern is not just with events, but with meaningful events, meaningful for the men of their time, meaningful for us because in their value and influence they live on. Second, so far as the values that appear in history commend themselves to us as real, we are moved by history itself to ask whether there may not be revealed in these values a purpose which gives meaning to history. Such inquiry does not fall in the field of historical science, but it cannot be excluded in the name of that science.

II. THE OBJECTIONS CONSIDERED

Let us turn now to specific objections from the historical standpoint.

1. Can we claim a supernatural source and a divine reality for Christianity when we know the crude beginnings of all religion and can trace in history the development of Christian beliefs and practice? To this a threefold reply must be made.

[3]*The Kingdom of God in History,* Vol. III of the Oxford Conference Books, gives a valuable discussion of the general subject by six authors of varying viewpoints.

(1) The value and truth of any achievement is not determined by its beginnings. That is the error of geneticism, the fallacy of historicism, "which consists in evaluating ethical ideals in terms of their historical origins, or even in depriving them of value altogether merely because they have origins," says W. P. Montague,[1] who points out how Huxley the naturalist and James the pragmatist protested against this naturalistic and pragmatistic irrelevance. There are two possible ways, says C. D. Broad, of studying any important item: Consider the most important and highly developed instance of the phenomenon in question or treat the problem genetically. That is, you can begin your study at either end. "Neither line of approach can be dispensed with, but the former is the more fundamental of the two."[2]

(2) God works "historically," whether you call his work education, revelation, or redemption. Religious insights, moral ideals, spiritual character, Christian institutions are not dropped down from heaven complete. Initial perfection is not the test of the divine as Christian apologists and their critics have both been wont to assume. Ours is a God, immanent in presence, instant in toil, who works in and through the process of history and the hearts and minds of men. Such a method necessarily involves lowly beginnings and slow progress.

(3) But there *is* progress and it attests the presence of God in the religious history of mankind. Primitive religion everywhere is marked by a sense of the Higher; it has taken long ages for man to learn what this Higher is, but he has been learning. The Eternal has always been with him, knocking at the door of mind and heart, of conscience and will, just as the order of nature has waited for the discoveries of science. We do not condemn physics because once—and not so long ago—it held to a universe whose varied forms were all constituted of small, hard, impenetrable bits of matter.

[1]*The Ways of Knowing*, p. 171.
[2]*The Mind and Its Place in Nature*, p. 11. *Cf.* pp. 12–14.

Physics still talks of the atom but its conception is wholly changed. So there has been growth in man's understanding of God. Primitive religion is marked by fear in the presence of the unknown, by doubt as to what might be expected, by all manner of sacrifices and rites of magic and dependence upon priests in order that the strange forces might be placated or controlled. *Mana,* spirits good and evil, gods of this and that are here in confusion. Out of it emerged the vision which the Hebrew-Christian faith has held. There is the great prophetic insight: the God of power is good; he is one, the God of all being, of all peoples; he is the living God, not a distant Being, an abstract principle, or a static order, but a God creative in nature and history. Jesus brought this to its simplest and profoundest expression, revealing this God as the God of redemptive good will. The early Church knew him as indwelling Spirit, the source of man's true life. Involved in all this was the idea of a God of fellowship, a personal God. From power to goodness, from the many to the one, from impersonal to personal, from the remote to the near, such has been the movement. With this went a transformation of religion that made it ethical, inner, social, human. Science and religion are both marked by such advance from crude beginnings to high achievement. It is curious that the same critics should judge religion by its crude beginnings and science by its high attainments, or imagine that we have disposed of God because man's first conceptions were so faulty. Bernard Shaw's comment is in point. The Chinese, he remarks, saw a solar eclipse as the work of a demon devouring the sun, whom they proceeded to frighten off by beating drums and pans. Their delusions, however, did not alter the reality of the eclipse itself. "Many people, seeing how many childish fables and ridiculous ceremonies have been attached to the conception of divinity, have rushed to the conclusion that no such thing as divinity exists. When they grow out of believing that God is an old gentleman with a white beard, they think that they have got rid of everything that the old gentleman represented to their infant minds. On the contrary, they have come a little closer to the truth about it."[3]

2. It is said, Christianity claims absolute truth, but history shows only the relative and imperfect; what we have is not a sure knowledge of God but changing human opinion. The answer to this is a right statement of the Christian position. The old absolutes and inerrancies must be given up. They represent traditional theology, not Christian faith. "Orthodoxy is intellectual Pharisaism." Perfection is not in our knowledge, but in God. But this God has revealed himself. True, "now we see in a mirror darkly," and yet we do see. The living God has touched our human life; we know him as truly as we know the world of nature, of which also we have absolute knowledge at not one point. Jesus is the challenge to men to trust in God as infinite good will and to live by that spirit; faith is the acceptance of that challenge. Ignorance remains; the technique of the religious life waits on experiment, and the thought forms change with the generations. But the light remains for our guidance and the light is from above.

3. Why narrow religion, it is asked, and halt its progress by tying it up with one individual of the past, Jesus? Here we must refer to our discussion of the finality of the Christian religion. Two reminders are needed. (1) Call it human insight or divine revelation—they are the same thing seen from below and above—Jesus represents man's supreme vision of God and of life's way. The truth of that vision has not changed with the passing years; it remains the base line of religion. But the base line serves to orient advance, not to mark its end. Jesus has been for man not a limitation, not the end of the way, but inspiration and guidance as he has pressed on. (2) If there be a God like that of the Christian faith, personal, good, a living God and not an abstract idea

[3]*The Intelligent Woman's Guide to Socialism and Capitalism,* p. 366.

or order or essence, then we should expect to know him best not in abstract principles or impersonal ideals, but in a living deed of history and in personal life. Only so can the Highest be expressed. And this expression in a person has a vividness, an appeal, a power such as abstractions can never possess.[4]

4. The final objection concerns historical uncertainty: It is a mistake to base any religious faith on a figure from the past since nothing that is past can ever be certain. Has not the very existence of Jesus been questioned? At the best our gospels are products of the second generation after his death. They were written in Greek, not in the Aramaic which Jesus spoke. They grew up out of the life and work of the Church, and reflect its background, its problems, and its faith. And we have no sources for Jesus outside the New Testament.

(1) The first matter to be considered here is historical. The question of the historicity of Jesus may be considered settled. Men like Conybeare, Thorburn, and Case have given it the necessary discussion. We may freely accept the date of the gospels as given above and recognize, as they themselves clearly indicate, that they were not written as scientific history but to set forth the faith of the Church. Undoubtedly they reflect the controversies of their day and legendary elements have crept in. It has long been recognized that the writers were not concerned about the order of events; a biography of Jesus in the modern sense is not possible. Nor can we say of the reported teachings of Jesus that we are absolutely sure of this one or the other, or that they were

[4]See the discussion by Bergson, *The Double Source of Morality and Religion.* The objection is the old one classically expressed by David Friedrich Strauss in the often incorrectly quoted passage from his *Leben Jesu.* "This is not at all the way in which the Idea realizes itself: to express itself completely in that one example but always incompletely in the rest." The background of his remark is the Hegelian philosophy. See *Leben Jesu,* third edition, 1829, Vol. II, pp. 766, 767.

Christ, speaking to men, winning inner conviction, summoning them to the decision of faith and life. For that we have what is needed: (*a*) Not certainty in detail, but, clear and definite, the personality of Jesus himself, his spirit in which we see God, his message of God and life, and his life itself not as a biography but as a deed, a deed of pure love and faith and devotion consummated in his death. (*b*) We have the witness of the early Church, its faith and life and message, as given in epistles and Acts and gospels. Here is the crucial point, not that these men were infallible chroniclers, but that they gave to their day, and to us, something more valuable than *ipsissima verba,* the spirit and word of God as seen in the spirit and life of Christ.[8] (*c*) The crucial matter, however, lies still further on. All this is history, is of the past, and religion is of the living present. It is not what God once did, it is what he does now. And that is the test which is met by the gospels and the New Testament as a whole: through them the living God still reveals himself, still speaks to men, still brings them into fellowship with himself. This is no mere past history. Despite the intervening centuries, our experience is still that of the first disciples and of those to whom they brought this by word of mouth: these words bring us face to face with the God of grace and judgment and with the decision of life.[9]

But if history offers problems to faith, faith is indispensable to history. History is not the mere succession of events; it is meaningful happening, and without a religious interpretation you do not have history. "Everywhere except in the religion of the prophets or in revealed religion, history becomes fundamentally meaningless. . . . A goal for history and for the progress of the world is found only in the

[8]See the valuable chapter on "Jesus in History," by F. C. Porter, in *The Mind of Christ in Paul.*

[9]On this whole matter, see the excellent treatment by Konrad Velte, *"Wort, Geschichte, und Mythus,"* in *Zeitschrift für Theologie und Kirche,* nos. 4 and 5, 1931. Velte opposes the extreme anti-historicism of the Barthians.

prophetism of the Old and New Testaments from which the creations of Islam and Zoroaster have inherited the conception of purpose in the world."[10] The task of faith in relation to history is not simply to assert this spiritual purpose and to meet objections as indicated above; it must show how time and the Eternal belong together, and how the Eternal enters into time. If time without the Eternal is meaningless, there is equal danger in the effort to posit the Eternal as something apart from time. Then we come to the static conception of God. He appears as the spiritual essence, pure being, for whom time and change have no real interest or meaning. Or he is the *actus purus* of Aristotle, who remains immobile since all possibilities have already been realized in his perfection. Such a God is morally deficient, remote from the Christian conception. There is no place here for a compassion that suffers, for a God that seeks to incarnate himself, for a creative Good Will that enters into the stream of time.[11] Rightly apprehending this relation of the Eternal and time, Christian faith will still find in history dark and difficult problems. They will not be problems to be met in mere defensive fashion, however, but rather by the shaping of a Christian philosophy of history which will show why the historic scene and movement are needed for the creative activity of a God of love, and how conflict and suffering and vicarious sacrifice necessarily go with this since it is an ethical and social process.

[10]N. Söderblom, *The Nature of Revelation,* p. 202, note.

[11]Suggestive comments are found in N. Berdyaev, *The Destiny of Man.* See especially pp. 37, 38.

Chapter Eighteen

FAITH AND THE FACT OF EVIL

THE FACT of evil has always been the greatest single obstacle to faith. At the heart of all high religion is the conviction that in some real and ultimate way goodness and power are one. That is what faith in God means: the power that is back of all things is good; goodness has ultimate power. But on every hand the facts of life seem to contradict that faith. The indictment may be summed up in four points. (1) Nature is cruel. "Nearly all the things which men are hanged or imprisoned for doing to one another," says John Stuart Mill, "are nature's every day performances. Nature kills, burns, starves, freezes, poisons."[1] (2) Nature is non-moral. It makes no distinction between the evil and the good. If it sends its rain on the just and the unjust, the obverse is also tragically true, that storm and flood and plague descend alike on the good and the evil. And this impersonality, this seeming total indifference to moral distinction and desert, is to many more terrible than nature's cruelty. (3) The world seems positively immoral. The innocent suffer for the deeds of the evil. A handful of men, selfish, ambitious, foolish, blind, bring on a world war; and all round the world the common folk who want only to live and love and labor in peace pay for these misdeeds with starvation, disease, and death, and the curse lasts on through genera-

[1]*Three Essays on Religion,* p. 28.

tions still unborn. (4) Such forces for good as there are in the universe seem everywhere to meet resistance. Advance comes only with conflict. Progress is terribly slow, whether we think of the long ages of biological evolution or of the possible million years of human life on this globe. A dead inertia seems to belong to the nature of things, or even a positive opposition to the creative process; and human history, like biological evolution, shows endless blind alleys where the struggle of generations apparently came to naught.

I. HISTORIC ANSWERS

The answers to the problem of evil run the whole gamut of possible creeds. At the one end we have the terrible and unrelieved pessimism of James Thomson in *The City of Dreadful Night.* He is describing a sermon by night in an unlighted cathedral. One of the congregation has exclaimed over the wretchedness of his own life: these few years are his sole chance, this chance frustrated from birth, his life but poison mixed with gall. All the preacher can say is, that

> "It ends soon, and nevermore can be;
> And we know nothing of it ere our birth,
> And shall know nothing when consigned to earth."

But as for the Maker of all this,

> "The vilest thing must be less vile than Thou
> From whom it had its being, God and Lord!
> Creator of all woe and sin! abhorred,
> Malignant, and implacable!"

At the other end is the optimism for which this is the best of all possible worlds, or that type of idealism for which all evil is illusion. A few of the more typical positions may here be indicated.

1. Dualism is perhaps the simplest answer, as it is one of the oldest. Its classical form is Zoroastrianism, nobly ethical in its ideal of God and its demand on man, seeking to save

the goodness of God by setting over against him the evil Angra Mainyu as responsible for the ills of the world. Of pre-Christian faiths it stands closest to Judaism in moral emphasis and in seeing the meaning of history in an age-long conflict between the forces of good and evil. Later Judaism, in its apocalyptic writings, though not necessarily by borrowing, shares with it the elaborate doctrine of angels and demons, of opposing spiritual beings, lesser and higher, the "angels and principalities and powers" of whom Paul writes, as well as the emphasis on a final conflict in which evil shall be routed. But dualism affords no real answer. If it is absolute, and good and evil rank as equal forces, then faith in a supreme God is endangered and the triumph of good left uncertain. If the dualism is relative and the final power rests with the good God, then why is not the devil sooner routed, or why, if the hour rests solely with God, is the final apocalyptic conflict so long delayed?

2. The second type of answer may be called legalistic, or, better, nomistic. It rests on the principle of retribution. The universe is under law, and evil is simply the consequence of wrongdoing. The legalism of later Judaism applied this to individual life: prosperity followed upon piety and suffering was evidence of sin. Hence the question put to Jesus: "Who sinned, this man, or his parents, that he should be born blind?" So the doctrine of the fall of man was used by theology to explain why a world perfectly good became evil, with man's own corrupt nature as the most tragic result. But pain was in the world long before man, and a just God could hardly curse all mankind for the deed of one; and in the face of facts we cannot hold that suffering and evil coincide. Most rigorous and terrible is the expression of this viewpoint in India's ancient doctrine of Karma. Karma means literally *deed*. Suffering is explained as the consequence of a man's deeds, whether committed in this present life or in some previous existence. There is something noble and profoundly true in the idea of an inclusive order to which all

our life belongs. But the theory is applied individualistically and mechanically, the fact of social solidarity is disregarded, and there is no place for the idea of vicarious suffering that may be redemptive, nor for faith in a merciful and saving God who works through the sorrow and pain of the world and makes man to triumph over it.

3. There is the position of absolute idealism in its various forms. Sometimes it denies the reality of evil altogether. That is the answer of Christian Science, which is idealistic in intention at least: Only the good is real, only spirit, only God; evil is simply man's delusion. But the realities are too strong for this view. The idea of evil, cast out of the door, comes in through all the windows. The Christian Science healers are dealing with it constantly. Only the name is changed; evil becomes the errors of "mortal mind," and the devil reappears as "Malicious Animal Magnetism." Absolute idealism in philosophy may either deny the reality of evil or declare that, looked at from the standpoint of the Absolute and the whole, evil is only seemingly such, while in fact a necessary component of total and ultimate perfection. But the anguished sufferer does not feel that his question is answered by reference to the perfection of the Absolute to which his pain contributes. And the Christian faith which follows Jesus in his belief in the sacredness of a moral personality cannot let even God (God, indeed, least of all) use human beings as mere means to some supposedly higher end.

4. There is the answer of religious absolutism as illustrated by Calvin: All that happens, good and ill, is determined by the will of God. The fall of man was determined by divine decree equally with the consequences which flowed in punishment from this. "By the will of God all the sons of Adam fell into that state of wretchedness in which they are now involved. . . . God not only foresaw the fall of the first man, and in him the ruin of his posterity; but also at his own pleasure arranged it." This, of course, is not to answer the question but to rule it out, as is done when Cal-

vin declares that "everything which he wills must be held to be righteous by the mere fact of his willing it."[1]

5. There is the disciplinary view: Pain and sorrow are here to develop character and lead men to God. The truth in this view must be considered later. By itself it is too individualistic and too narrow. It does not take account of the suffering of brute creation, of the endless instances where suffering works the other way, of needless pain going beyond all possible service, and of the realm of moral evil.

II. THE DOCTRINE OF A FINITE GOD

We may consider in a special group those who in one way or another have set forth a limitation of the power of God as the answer to this problem. It is their reply to the old alternative: in the face of the fact of evil, God must be lacking in either goodness or power.

Here, as at so many points, Plato exercised his far-reaching influence. For him the motive of creation was the love of God: "He was good . . . and he desired that all things should be as like himself as possible." But the world of the seen, the finite world, cannot be the direct expression of the unseen world, the world of ideas. For the real world is one and pure and unchanging, and the visible world is one of change and endless division. In his creation God seemingly had to use the world of empty space, the world of not-being, of nothing, which from its nature is endlessly divisible. This material is plastic to the creative action, so that the mathematical "forms" can be imposed upon it. At the same time it is under its own law, the law of the mechanical, that of the power which Plato calls "Necessity." This basic idea of Plato's appears again and again in later thought: God is a creative artist working with a material which is at once receptive-plastic and resistant-intractible. The nature of this material and the necessity of using it is the explanation of imperfection and evil.

[1]*The Institutes,* Bk. III, Ch. XXIII, Secs. 7, 2.

Nicholas Berdyaev, modern exponent of the theology of the Orthodox Church, shows the influence of Plato and of the mystics, Eckhart and Boehme. His system has a strong emphasis on duality, which appears not only in man and the world but in God himself. This duality has a non-rational basis, an element of the mysterious, the inexplicable. In terms gained from the mystics, he declares that God himself is born out of the divine Nothing, the *Gottheit* or *Ungrund.* The duality in God is not that of good and evil, but rather a conflict between equally good values; yet here there enters in an uncreated, nonrational element which is basic or elemental in the universe. In the resultant conflict is found the source of evil in the world.[1] There is, it is true, another and more fruitful element in Berdyaev's philosophy of man and history, appearing in his volumes on *Freedom and the Spirit* and *The Meaning of History,* as well as in *The Destiny of Man,* from which his ideas bearing upon the problem of evil have here been taken; that is the significance of freedom and creativity in man. Man's true life lies in moral freedom, with its capacity to receive the grace of God and to live a creative life by the help of God. Thus Berdyaev transcends his dualism; he sees the meaning of life for God and man in this creative work. The dualism is here to be overcome in a higher unity. The distinctive element in Berdyaev's position, however, is not found in this prophetic position, but in his theory of a metaphysical duality. Evil is not here, he declares, because of the fall of man. Back of the world, back of man, there is the "nothing" out of which the world is created. That "nothing" is "primeval uncreated meonic freedom." God is in his world as gracious and creative Providence. Freedom is here, rich in noble possi-

[1]The idea of the "demonic" has been coming into vogue in recent efforts to shape a philosophy of history that will take account of the element of the evil and irrational as something more than merely incidental to human freedom. The treatment of this concept by Paul Tillich in his work *The Interpretation of History* may be compared with Berdyaev's idea of the meonic.

bilities, as well as in tragic elements. But so also is "fate or destiny, *i.e.,* nature, the solidified, hardened outcome of the dark meonic freedom." Thus we have a God who is limited and a world that is conditioned by a non-rational ultimate, not unconquerable, it is true, but the source of tragedy and suffering.

John Stuart Mill was first among the moderns to suggest the idea of a finite God. "If the maker of the world can [do] all that he will, he wills misery, and there is no escape from the conclusion. . . . Not even on the most distorted and contracted theory of good which was ever framed by religious or philosophical fanaticism, can the government of Nature be made to resemble the work of a being at once good and omnipotent. The only admissible theory of Creation is that the Principle of Good *cannot* at once and altogether subdue the powers of evil, either physical or moral; could not place mankind in a world free from the necessity of an incessant struggle with the maleficent powers, or make them always victorious in that struggle, but could and did make them capable of carrying on that fight with vigor and with progressively increasing success."[2]

Two interesting and more recent discussions develop this suggestion of Mill: *The Problem of God,* by E. S. Brightman, and *Belief Unbound,* by W. P. Montague. For both the idea of evolution is important and both find in this developing world a creative and directing Power. But for both it is equally clear that this Power is limited or hindered. For Montague God is not an omnipotent monarch, but "an ascending force, a nisus, a thrust toward concentration, organization, and life." But there is a world of finite existences, "that in God which is not God," in God and yet each with "its measure of a self-affirming spontaneity or primary causality, and also its inertia or passivity." God's will is pure and good, but it is finite; it is one force among many in this world which he finds within himself, and which he is

[2]*Three Essays on Religion,* pp. 37–39.

trying to perfect.[3] As mind God is infinite, extending through the whole universe. As will he is finite, "a self struggling to inform and assimilate the recalcitrant members of his own organism or the recalcitrant thoughts of his own intellect."

For the personal idealism which Professor Brightman represents, the problem of evil is especially acute. Holding that the only existent reality is personal (finite persons and the Infinite), he can account for moral evil by the freedom given to men, but not for evil in the physical universe. For Doctor Brightman the world of nature has no such "measure of spontaneity or primary causality" as Montague gives it; it exists only as the functioning of the divine mind. Holding this, the evil that is found in nature, the cruelty and suffering, as well as the "drag," the hindrance to the process of development, affords apparently insuperable difficulty. For God is here directly and solely responsible, since all this exists only in God and as the direct expression of his thought and will. Brightman takes here what seems like the only available answer on the basis of his general premises: the will of God is pure and good, but there is something within God that hinders the expression of his will. If the achievement lags, if there are imperfection and suffering and long delay, it can only be because there is some obstacle in God himself. So he holds that God finds within himself, as a part of his nature, a "Given," an element that is irrational, passive, and resistant. This Given, like the Space of Plato, is that upon which God's will and reason act to produce the world and achieve value in it, and, similarly, it is both plastic and resistant to the good purpose of God.

There are questions that need to be raised with each of these theories. Berdyaev brings notable insights as to the tragic element in God himself which is inseparable from the love that calls for sacrificial self-surrender, and as to

[3] *Belief Unbound*, pp. 74, 83, 84, 91.

the place and importance of freedom and creativity in the world of the finite, especially in man. But one may well ask whether the recourse to an irrational *Ungrund* is not a dubious and unnecessary speculation. Montague protests against the "two-God theory" (apparently of H. G. Wells in his *God the Invisible King*), "the one an Invisible King, the other a sort of Captain Courageous"; but his own theism is a kind of halfway affair. On the side of consciousness his God is cosmic, aware of the total universe of being. On the side of power his God is one force among many. In other words, he has simply united the Invisible King and the Captain Courageous in one God. Both he and Brightman escape a cosmic dualism by introducing a dualism into the nature of God. Brightman courageously faces the difficulty which is involved in his philosophical position, but his solution leads one to question his premises. Why draw the sharp line between the personal and subpersonal, which are both a part of the developing world that science portrays, and deny any real independence and causality to the latter? Why not rather say: divine creativity involves, not merely at the human level, but in a measure at every level, a certain spontaneity, a certain free activity, a chance to achieve? Evil, then, is not the result of the nature of God but is incidental to the work of creation whose pure source is his love.

III. WHERE THE PROBLEM LIES

The whole problem of evil needs a new consideration involving, first, an analysis of underlying ideas whose meaning has been taken for granted, and, second, a better use of our present knowledge, that is, of the great Christian insights on the one hand and of modern knowledge on the other. The underlying ideas that demand our study are the good as it relates to man and the ideas of goodness and power as they refer to God. It is not only the popular writers but the philosophers whose treatment has been superficial; and too often the high insights of the Christian faith have been lacking in the discussions of the theologians.

1. What do we mean by the good for man? Back of most discussion is the hedonistic assumption: hardship and toil and pain are the great evils of life, pleasure and ease are its great good. Thus for John Stuart Mill[1] the benevolence of God means that the one aim of creation is "the happiness of his creatures." Against this we must set the Christian conception: Life is the only good, life in which man's highest possibilities are being achieved. That means vision and desire, truth as liberating insight and never-ending search, love that brings both joy and pain, ideals that are infinitely above us and that yet are our only true life. It means God, the God who casts down and lifts up, who is our judgment and our hope, our endless quest and our only peace. But one thing it is not, this good that is life: it is not something outside us. It is not any possible creation of engineer and architect, though this were God himself. The English composer of a sprightly fantasy tells of a pilgrim who visits hell and finds it a most comfortable place, well organized and strictly controlled, apparently rather like one of Mr. Wells' recurrent pictures of a scientifically planned utopia. But the hero leaves it with a lament: "What have I done to be sent to a realm where everything is provided for a man and only his heart and his hope and his spirit are taken from him?"[2]

Far sharper and more realistic is the satire of the hedonistic ideal that Aldous Huxley gives in his *Brave New World.* Science and engineering and social control, developed to the highest degree and applied in strict autocratic manner, have wrought a "brave new world" in which there is no anxiety, no insecurity, no hunger, no pain. Food and pleasure and work are for all, and in the Pavlovian labora-

[1]*Three Essays on Religion,* p. 192.
[2]Marmaduke Dixey, *Hell's Bells.*

tories psychological "conditioning" sees to it that all shall like the work which they have to do, including those intended for menial tasks. Scientific processes of human propagation make it possible to abolish the home, with all the grief and pain that come with childbirth and family responsibilities and relations, while contraceptive devices make sexual indulgence safe for all. Into this world Huxley introduces "The Savage." He comes from a land, walled off and preserved as a horrid example, where home and love, toil and pain, dreams and devotion still are found; and he knows the Bible and Shakespeare, long since banished from the new world which could not understand them and whose satisfied life might be disturbed by them. The Savage at last rebels. "I don't want comfort. I want God, I want poetry, I want real danger, I want freedom, I want goodness, I want sin." "In fact," said Mustapha Mond (the "Controller"), "you're claiming the right to be unhappy." "All right, then," said the Savage defiantly, "I'm claiming the right to be unhappy."[3] Which is not unlike Gilbert Chesterton's word: "I insist on the right to be damned."

2. What, we must ask next, is our conception of the goodness of God? It is certainly not that sentimental indulgence which often passes for this with men, especially in the idea of parental love. The goodness of God is, indeed, as tender as that of a mother, as patient as a father's love, pitiful as belonging to one who knows all our need and enters into all our pain, and wide as the heavens above and the race of men below. But this love is ethical, redemptive, creative. His goodness is good will, that is, it is a high and fixed purpose aiming at the supreme good of man. It is redemptive and therefore set against all evil. It is creative: it is goodness at work, active, unswerving, sparing no toil or pain in itself or in its object, seeking to give its own life to this creature man, not intent on granting pleasure and sparing sorrow, but rather on the creation in men, and

[3]*Op. cit.*, p. 283.

the sharing with men, of its own life, the life of truth and wisdom, of holiness and love.

3. The concept of the power of God needs even closer scrutiny. At no place has shallowness of thought been more in evidence. "Omnipotent, I fear," says James Ward, "is one of those question-begging epithets that everybody uses and nobody defines."[4] Consider, for example, the offhand manner in which C. E. M. Joad settles the question: "Pain and evil are either real or unreal. If they are real then God, who, being omnipotent, was bound by no limitations and constrained by no necessities, wilfully created them. But the being who wilfully creates pain and evil cannot be benevolent." If evil is due to man, he argues further, remember man is a creature of God. If man was not evil to begin with but wilfully generated evil, then how can man coming from God have a will of his own which is not also a part of God's will?[5] There are three elements in such a conception of divine power. Power is thought of in the abstract, as power in general; it is conceived as absolute, irresistible; it is treated as external force. The criticism of these ideas will help us to a true conception.

(1) It is a mistake to talk of power in the abstract: power is always of a specific kind. To speak of power in and by itself is simply to deal in words. Power is the ability of any being to act or function according to its peculiar nature and to accomplish its ends. The strength of a Hercules is physical. His five-foot wife may possess a moral power which can wrap him around her finger. An "absolute" dictator with all his armies cannot compel confidence and affection. The idea of power in the abstract is like that idea of being in the abstract, or "pure being," which, taken over by theology, led to the idea of a God wholly opposite to man and utterly remote, to whom, since every determination was supposed to mean negation, not even moral character could be ascribed because that would limit his pure "being." Such

[4]*The Realm of Ends,* p. 354. [5]*Mind and Matter,* p. 119.

a God is no God, is nothing. All being is determinate being, being of a definite kind, and that is true of God. So the power of God is determinate, since it is his being in action and thus is conditioned by his nature.

(2) The idea of irresistible power is equally unmeaning and untenable. It is a part of that abstract absolutism which has afflicted theology. There is an absoluteness which belongs to the Christian concept of God as one from whom all things come, upon whom all things depend, and who is perfect in goodness. But the traditional absolutism, with its denial of every kind of condition or limitation, is of another kind. Power, whether human or divine, is conditioned by the nature of the being that acts, by the ends that are set, and by that with which it works. It is, therefore, never absolute or irresistible. When God seeks a moral end, the idea of irresistible power is ruled out by that very fact; instead, God "stands at the door and knocks." When God wishes to create, he limits himself by that very fact; for creation means giving something of his own life to lesser beings, and life in any creature means a certain power of its own. Similarly he is conditioned by his own being. He is reason, and so he acts according to that reason and order which form his very being. He is wisdom, and so he must by his very nature choose high ends and use appropriate means. He is love and so he must suffer in sympathy and must toil and sacrifice. At none of these points can it be a matter of bare will acting with irresistible force. But that does not mean a God of inferior power. The greatest spiritually creative force in human history is linked to the figure of a man who lived the humblest of lives, who wrought in a limited sphere, who had no influence with the great ones of earth, who died unresisting upon a cross. That cross is the revelation, not only of God's love, but of his power—its might, its limits, its nature, its method. Theologians have gone to the wrong place for their analogies. Not in nature, with its suggestion of forces irresistible—and blind,

not with the kings of earth, autocratic but impotent to work moral good, but in the gospel of the Son of Man we are to see what is the power of God and how it works.

(3) Underlying these errors is the third, the conception of divine power as externalistic and compulsive. This is to think of power on the lowest plane, as physical force. Only physical force can be conceived as irresistible. Power on the higher levels from its very nature is not irresistible: truth waits upon the receiving mind, love is not compulsive. The power that develops life and shapes character must work indirectly. The conception of a divine compulsion working from without is as mechanistic in its way as the old materialism. It must be given up for a concept in which the transcendent God is seen to work immanently; and that means not irresistibly.

It is interesting once more to refer to Mill at this point. Why, he argues, should man be able to do for himself what God could not do? Why imagine that God could endow a Bosjesman or an Andaman Islander with the power of raising himself into a Newton or a Fénelon, and so accomplishing "by a succession of efforts what God himself had no other means of creating"? To Mill it seems an odd notion of the limitation of divine power that he could not give man these blessings outright instead of at such frightful cost. Mill wrote two generations ago. The years have made plainer that from their very nature the gifts of life, and the highest gifts most of all, can come only through human effort. The fact that "it is God that worketh in us" does not exclude the other fact that we must "work out our own salvation with fear and trembling." History is making terribly plain that the liberty of which Mill once wrote can remain our possession only as it lives in the minds and hearts of the people and is constantly won anew. And of what other high gift must not this be said? If we see its full scope and meaning, we may rightly quote here the word of H. Wildon Carr: "The evolution principle has not merely transformed the problem of evil; it has deprived it of its ground."[6] For what is the story of evolution but this same tale of a being that is possible only through becoming, of life that can come only through ceaseless toil and pain?

IV. A WORLD THAT IS GOOD AND WHAT IT REQUIRES

And now the outline of our problem begins to grow clear. We leave aside as non-Christian the hedonistic conception of the good; and the idea of God's power as an irresistible force that can accomplish any end by direct action we perceive to be a childish transfer from the physical world to the moral realm where it is simply irrational. Our problem now becomes, not so much that of evil, as that of the good. If the good can never be handed over as a finished product to a passive recipient, if it can only be an achievement, then a good world will be one which is adapted for such attainment. Then our great question is: What kind of a world is fitted for this end? That question is not an easy one to answer. How many, in hot revolt at the world's pain, have been ready to say with Omar Khayyam:

"Ah Love! could you and I with Him conspire
To grasp this sorry scheme of things entire,
Would we not shatter it to bits—and then
Re-mold it nearer to the Heart's Desire!"

But the more the matter is probed, the farther we move from such easy assumption of wisdom, and from the naïve conception of what is good and of what is possible to mere power that lies back of these words.

As we turn now to consider the world that is demanded if the highest good is to be achieved, we shall find not only that it is like the world which God has given to man, but that the evils which weigh most heavily upon us are incident to those elements which are essential to such a world.

[6]*Changing Backgrounds in Religion and Ethics,* p. 197.

1. In a world where good is to be achieved, there must be freedom. That is most obvious in the case of man. There can be no life of reason and affection, nor of moral and religious attainment, except as there are free spirits that can see and reflect and choose. Indeed, all life involves something of this kind; as against the merely mechanical, wherever there is life there is a certain spontaneity, a degree of indeterminateness, a movement from within, a capacity for awareness and adjustment. J. Y. Simpson, in his *Man and the Attainment of Immortality,* has traced the development of this "freedom" from the lowest levels to the rational and moral self-determination of man. As Baron von Hügel has pointed out, the very idea of creation involves the thought "that God has somehow alienated a certain amount of his own power, and given it a relative independence of its own." Only this makes a human selfhood and real religion possible, for as he goes on to say: "God is no more God for us, if we cease to be relatively distinct from him." And we cannot "show our apprehension of the secret of his law of spiritual life for us all, or cooperate in building it up, better than in ever remembering, ever vividly realizing, ever practising, ever suffering the true and real independence which God has chosen to give Creation, by the very fact of creating it, and still more by incarnating himself in its head and center, man,"[1] Call it evolution or creation—both terms are indicated—life comes as achievement and involves such freedom.

What we need to do here is to see what is involved in this and to accept it. It is this necessity which makes life a long, slow, and costly struggle, whether we think of the biological or the spiritual, the individual or the social. This freedom, of course, is not the only factor. It moves within an order, divinely set, which is at once its limitation and its support; and we believe there is a divine direction or a divine "pull" of the immanent Creator Spirit, not merely with man but on every level. But whether we speak of God or of an order

[1]*Selected Letters,* ed. by Bernard Holland, p. 93.

of nature, there is always something more than mechanical determination. Step by step we have experimentation, lessons slowly learned, tentative advances insecurely held, inevitable mistakes, age-long movements that end in blind alleys, and on the human level the whole story of ignorance, folly, and sin, with consequent failure and suffering. Especially clear does this appear in the history of social advance. The only way of advance is from below upward, from within outward, the way of freedom, never that of dictatorship, even if a benevolent dictatorship could be supposed. God himself can help us only as in faith we see him and in obedience receive his Spirit, only as his love and truth come to be our own inmost life. The way seems tragically slow and expensive, but it is the only way.

It is this necessity, not only of moral freedom, but of a certain spontaneity and freedom of all life, that has been so constantly overlooked, to left and right, in this discussion. So we have Thomas Huxley's words, strange as coming from so alert a mind: "If some great Power would agree to make me think always what is true and do what is right on condition of being turned into a sort of clock, I should instantly close with the bargain. The only freedom I care about is the freedom to do right; the freedom to do wrong I am ready to part with."[2] But no "sort of clock" can do what is right or think what is true, or indeed think at all. Nor can any man learn without the possibility of going wrong, any more than a child can learn to walk without the possibility of falling. Archbishop D'Arcy rightly protests against the same error as found with those on the right: "We can imagine a Creator," he writes, "designing to produce a universe in which every element must contribute to the making of a perfect order, so framing all the parts that none can go wrong. This is the kind of a world conceived by the theologians as that originally planned by the Almighty, yet disorganized by the sin of

[2] *Collected Essays,* I, 192.

man. But those who think in this way forget that the only way to secure such a result would be to make the world a perfect mechanism from the start." And a mechanical perfection can never become a moral universe.[3]

And here the dark shadow of sin appears. The necessity of freedom brings the possibility and practical inevitability of sin, and sin seems the one point of unrelieved darkness. We have still a long way to go so far as human knowledge is concerned, but even so, it may be asserted that we know enough today to assure us of the conquest of practically every major ill that threatens human life. We could conquer poverty, for there are resources enough for all peoples. We could furnish decent living conditions for all if we used only the means that went into one item, the preparation for war and the prosecution of war. We know enough, if we could all work together, to wipe out all the great plagues. The difficulty does not lie here. It is the indifference, the selfishness, the greed, the lust for power and love of pleasure—in a word, it is the sin of man that is the great source of our ills and that prevents our working together for their abolition. And that is even more obviously true when we come to the deepest source of human unhappiness, the suffering of the spirit. Yet a good world must be one of freedom.

2. A good world will be one of toil and struggle and resistance. One of the hardest facts for faith to face is the resistance that everywhere meets man's creative effort as he seeks to achieve the good, whether he tries to master nature, to shape his own character, or to secure social advance. The materials with which we work yield stubbornly to our efforts. Why is the ceaseless struggle demanded? Why should not the way to good be the easy way?

Traditional thought, as we have seen, has tried to meet this problem by some form of dualism: the devil and his angels form a kingdom of evil over against the kingdom of God; or, there is some element in the universe—matter,

[3]*The Christian Outlook in the Modern World,* p. 166.

space, the *Ungrund,* the Nothing, the demonic, or some "Given" which God finds in himself—sometimes conceived at once as resistant and as the necessary material for the divine work of creation.

There is an element of truth in these ideas, but it can be expressed in a simpler and less speculative form for which the creative work of man affords analogy. The good is always a creative achievement. But for all creative work there must be a material, or medium, and such a medium will necessarily be at once plastic and resistant, that which lends itself to the purpose of creativity and yet resists its efforts. That is certainly true of all man's creative work. The forces of nature as seen in wind and water, in electricity and fire, in expanding steam and the pull of gravitation, are always resistant and often destructive, and yet, rightly understood and used, though always carrying latent danger, they are the media through which all man's technical advance has come. The artist illustrates this most clearly, whether he be a sculptor working with marble, or an architect and builder with cement and steel and brick and stone.

The paradox of this resistance and support is merely on the surface; only that which offers resistance can yield the needed support. The atmosphere which resists the airplane supports it in its flight. The friction that impedes the railway train enables the locomotive wheels to grip the rails instead of whirling helplessly around. Man's efforts are conditioned here in the same way as God's; creative work is not done in a vacuum. If man is to create, he too must work with a world of independent being, that is, with a world of determinate being and character, with things and forces that have a nature of their own and act according to that nature. A characterless world, purely passive and wholly non-resistant, would offer no opportunity and be of no value. Indeed, there could not be such a world, for existence is being of a particular kind, it is energy in action after a particular manner. Opportunity and resistance are thus the converse of each other. And usually each varies directly with the other. Marble has more "character" than soft clay and offers more resistance; clay will do for the model, the masterpiece of the sculptor calls for marble. Human nature is the hardest of all materials with which to work; it has the greatest capacity for resistance, as God and man both know. But with it you can create character that is like to that of God and a kingdom of God in which love and justice shall dwell, and you cannot do that with a flock of docile sheep. We may conclude with Principal L. P. Jacks that "We are evidently made, in both body and mind, for life in a resisting medium."[4]

All this helps to explain why evils and hardships which are the greatest problem for man have been at the same time the occasion of his highest achievements. The supreme attainments of the human spirit have not been found in climes where nature was most gracious and life most easy, nor yet in those where man's strength was exhausted in the mere struggle for existence, but in those lands which afford at once opportunity and resistance to his efforts. "The enemies of life," wrote Fridtjof Nansen once, "are not care, not privation, not distress—they are its stanchest aids."[5] Miguel de Unamuno means the same thing by the words with which he closes his paradoxical work, *The Tragic Sense of Life:* "May God deny you peace and give you glory!" So the conclusion of Sir Henry Jones suggests itself: "If the spiritual process of learning to recognize and realize the best has the supreme value which we attribute to it, then the world that makes the process possible is the best world. It is a better world than the so-called 'perfect world' of ordinary opinion."[6]

3. A world fitted for the achievement of life must be one of order, and an order that is universal and dependable.

[4]*Elemental Religion,* p. 9.

[5]*The Saga of Fridtjof Nansen,* p. 221.

[6]*A Faith that Inquires,* pp. 354, 355.

The inexorable order of nature has been for many a chief count against the goodness of God. Nature seems to show not a personal God but an impersonal system, not a just and kind Father who shields his children from evil and helps them to the good, but a system of blind forces that knows neither good nor evil. "Beauty and hideousness, love and cruelty, life and death keep house together in indissoluble partnership; and there gradually steals over us, instead of the old warm notion of a man-loving Deity, that of an awful power that neither loves nor hates, but rolls all things together meaningless to a common doom."[7] Over and over again we are challenged by the questions of men in anguish: Why should this good man be taken while the evil are left? Why should this innocent child suffer from dread disease?

Part of this comes from certain persistent errors: the old retributive idea that suffering follows upon sin, the idea of a God who stands outside his world and constantly checks this and moves the other in its machinery, the conception of providence as interference in individual life. But a chief cause of trouble is the failure to see the spiritual significance of just that unvarying order whose seeming impersonality so disturbs us.

Let us make clear what we mean here by order. It means first of all that there is one world ground and that this is rational in nature and dependable in character. It means that all things have their own specific nature and behave accordingly, and that they will always and everywhere behave the same way. Water, for example, will always follow a given course: become vaporous with heat; as vapor will expand and rise; will condense as it becomes colder, as when struck by a cold-air current; will then be heavier, fall to earth, and seek its lowest level; becoming still colder and solidifying, will expand as ice. Upon that order depend fertile fields, pleasant streams, equable climate, power for man's

[7]William James, *The Will to Believe,* p. 41.

use, beauty of rainbow and clouds, and indeed the very existence of life. At the same time its inevitability may mean tornado and flood and destruction in which the good suffer perforce with the evil.

But such a universal order, which makes our world cosmos instead of chaos, is not only necessary for physical existence; it it the indispensable condition of the achievement of all higher life. (1) Only in such a world could reason develop in man, for man's reason develops in response to the reason, or order, that is in the universe. (2) Only in such a world is science possible, for science is simply the discovery of this order and its setting forth in terms of what we call natural laws. (3) Man's mastery of nature, resting back on science, is equally dependent on such order, and with it all material progress, all advance in culture. (4) Here too is the necessary setting for moral development. It is the school of nature's inexorable order that offers the stern but needed tuition. It compels industry and the overcoming of inertia and vagrant impulse. It develops self-control and character. It drives men to live together and work together in mutual confidence and support. Nothing is so demoralizing in home and school and state, even when the intent is good—as a rule that is arbitrary and erratic—where indulgence alternates with severity. And the tragic moral consequences of economic uncertainty are one of the gravest counts against our present economic system. The inflexible order of nature has been one of the great masters in the school of man.

It is the presence of such an order that, while it brings certain evils, at the same time makes possible their overcoming. The evils are inevitable just because order cannot be piecemeal; but the order itself is the means for their correction. The floods may destroy, but we can halt forest destruction, impound waters, and change the process from destruction to service. A shrinking earth, elevation here and depression by its side as seen when mountain range and unusual sea depth are found together, faults in stratification which leave an unstable condition of the earth's crust, all this is part of the process of orderly earth evolution though it brings earthquake peril to certain regions. But the knowledge of this same order of nature makes it possible to avoid such areas or to erect buildings which will be proof against such damage. Frank Lloyd Wright's great Imperial Hotel at Tokio stood unscathed when the earthquake levelled lesser structures. And so with the evils of injurious germs and parasitic forms, which have been incidental to a process of free evolution; a study of the order of nature not only shows a way of meeting such danger but of advance in human well-being. The typhoid scourge reveals itself as a filth disease and compels new standards of cleanliness. Tuberculosis has taught us to value sunshine, pure air, wholesome and adequate food, and right housing, and so helped to lift the level of human living. Every disease is a challenge, not simply to destroy a foe, but to rise in the scale of life.

The principle finds a still wider application in human relations. After all, it is in the moral realm, especially that of social relations, that the supreme evils of life are found. Our problem, as we have seen, lies not so much in nature as in human nature, in man's inhumanity to man, in selfishness, indifference, hate, greed, lust, cruelty, or simple inertia and acquiescence in the face of evil, in needless hunger and unjustifiable wealth, in oppression and exploitation and war. But there is a way of overcoming this, and it waits upon us. The divine order is not simply that which is—the impersonal order of nature; it is that which is yet to be, the order of the spirit, waiting to be seen by man, and by the help of God to be expressed in human life and relations. Slowly we are discerning that order does not mean death but life, whether it be in the physical or the spiritual world. Suffering and pain and destruction are warning signs, telling us that we are leaving the road, pointing us back to the way of life. Without them we should be helpless. Within the order which they help to reveal are all the redemptive forces that we need, and they summon us to relate ourselves to them and so to be saved.

Finally, only such a world of order comports with the Christian conception of God. If he be a God of reason, then his world must be grounded in order as the expression of that reason; if he be the one God, then that order must be unitary and universal; and if he be a God of moral character, then this must be a dependable world. Men are to find God in a dependable nature and not to fear: "While the earth remaineth, seedtime and harvest, and cold and heat, and summer and winter, and day and night shall not cease."[8]

4. A good world must be one of social relations and social solidarity. We must face certain facts here at the start. As we have just seen, no evils of life are so terrible as those which come through human relations, and the most tragic aspect of all this is the suffering of the innocent for the guilty. Multitudes hunger because leaders are too stupid or too selfish to find a new and better order. The youth of the nation perish in war, not the warmakers. Men cannot escape from these relations, and each brings its ineluctable evils. And it is just the more personal and intimate ties, those of home and friendship, of human sympathy and high loyalty, that bring the more poignant pain and sorrow in their train.

Here once more is the need of seeing things whole, of thinking things together as against the piecemeal approach to the problem of evil. The principle underlying this has already been considered in our discussion of organicism. To live is to belong to a whole; there is no existence on any plane apart from this. But if we seek the highest, not mere existence but life, not just *esse* but *bene esse,* then we must welcome the ties that bind us to wholes that are ever larger and of higher meaning. Faith and work, friendship and

[8]Gen. 8:22.

family, bonds of community and nation and world fellowship, these are ways to larger life. Clearly they are also the ways of toil and suffering and sorrow. In a measure we can avoid the latter but only as we give up life itself. So the great souls of our race have been those who have given themselves unselfishly, unstintedly, even joyously to this common life of humanity, and then have found in it life for themselves. They have understood with Browning that

> "Life with all its yields of joy and woe,
> And hope and fear . . . .
> Is just our chance o' the prize of learning love."
> (*A Death in the Desert.*)

Here in these bonds of love and friendship, of loyalty and service, with all the toil and suffering of body and spirit that they bring, mankind has found the way to higher insight, to inner peace and strength and wealth, and to God himself; in finding our brother, we find ourselves and God. It is this that the Persian poet, Firdausi, sang a thousand years ago:

> "No one could tell me what my soul might be.
> I searched for God, and God eluded me.
> I sought my brother out, and found all three—
> My soul, my God, and all humanity."

5. A world that is fitted for the achievement of life will be one of suffering and pain. One may say flatly: a world without pain would be one in which life would be impossible, and out of suffering has come the noblest fruitage of human life.

It must be stated, first of all, that the defense of pain as ordinarily presented is inconclusive. Men note the biological value of pain but do not consider that pain is often excessive in amount, and that, as with cancer, for example, it may not function when it would be most useful (in cancer's earlier stages) and lasts on when it no longer serves any end. Men speak of the school of suffering but fail to note that its fruit is often bitterness and rebellion. In part the error lies, alike in the indictment of pain and in its defense, with the piecemeal treatment. Here, as always, we must look at things whole. The question cannot be settled by pointing out that here and there suffering is useless or ineffective, or, *per contra,* productive of high good. We must look at life whole and inquire as to its place. But it is an even greater error that we do not realize that pain is not primary, that it is incidental to something basic which demands first consideration, namely, sensitivity. It is with sensitivity, then, that we must begin our study.

To be sensitive is to feel, or to become aware, of our world, to "sense" it. Its primary reference is to the physical organism and its "senses," but mind and spirit are equally included with body. This sensitiveness is the basic condition of life. In contrast with the whole realm of the inorganic, life is a matter of continuous adjustment dependent upon sensitive awareness of environment. He who does not feel cannot live. The keenness of this sensitivity and its increase in range and variety condition the ascent of life, alike in biological evolution, in individual development, and in social progress. The mark of man is the degree and range of this sensitive awareness, with its attendant possibility of pain. It is this which makes him citizen of many worlds, physical, rational, social, ethical, æsthetic, reaching to God himself. In his striking drama, *R. U. R.,* Karel Čapek has brought out the significance of this sensitivity for human living, while penning an indictment of a socal order that tends to make machines of men. Rossum, the inventor, has found a formula for manufacturing "robots." Human in form, in intelligence, and in skill, they lack but one thing, sensitivity. There is no pain of body when the hand is crushed in the machinery. Nor do their spirits feel; there is no pride, no sense of shame at being treated as machines, no feelings of friendship or love. The stark tragedy of the close is relieved by the fact that these creatures have at last begun to feel and to revolt at their lot, while a last revealing scene shows the dawn of love. They have ceased to be machines and have become human because they have learned to feel and suffer.

The basic fact in all this is not pain, but sensitivity. The great mistake has been to begin with the fact of pain and to think of this as something existing by itself. But pain is simply incidental to sensitivity. Heightened stimulus is one cause; increased sensibility is another, whether appearing in specially endowed individuals or coming, in general, with the ascent of life. In any case, to abolish pain would mean to make us insensate and so to destroy life. To reduce the capacity for pain would be to dull sensitivity and to force life back to lower levels. No life without sensitivity, no sensitivity without possibility of pain, the increase of sensitivity as life mounts higher, man as the most sensitive of creatures, both physically and spiritually, and the greatest spirits as those with greatest capacity for suffering and pain—that is the picture we must face. And that can be accepted only by those who, individually and as a race, "for the joy that is set before them, endure the cross, despising shame."

But aside from the fact that pain is an inevitable incident to sensitivity, there are special items concerning it to be noted. (1) Sometimes the heightened stimulus is a warning. Pain is nature's red flag. To ask that pain be abolished, or to content oneself with deadening it through drugs instead of reading its warning, is like imagining that we have rid ourselves of danger on the road by tearing down the warning signal. No physician would want to practise medicine in a world without pain, or could do so; pain is not the real enemy that he aims at, it is his aid in discovering the true foe. And the reverse is true: the feeling of satisfaction, of well-being, is one of life's guides. It is not the only guide, and it must not be limited to the physical; but life that is on the right way, that is lived in sane and true and wholesome fashion, in so far forth brings satisfaction and pleasure, and, on the higher levels, what we call joy. And joy, as the New Testament makes plain, belongs essentially to the life of religion: "that my joy may be in you, and that your joy may be made full," is the word of the Christ of the fourth gospel.[9] (2) There is no fixed line to mark the change in stimulus where pleasure ceases and pain begins. Even on the physical level, pleasure and pain are often mingled in the same sensation: on higher planes it is far more true. In William Blake's words:

> "Joy and woe are woven fine,
> A clothing for the soul divine."

(3) Pain and sorrow are not simply the inevitable accompaniments of life and joy, they may themselves become the road to their attainment. There come with sorrow and suffering a broader sympathy with all life, a deeper understanding of its meaning, a truer realization of its higher values. Not the comfortable and well fed, undisturbed in their enjoyment, but the Jeremiahs suffering for their people, the Pauls in deaths oft and labors more abundant, the Dantes in exile perhaps gaining more with Beatrice lost than if Beatrice had been gained, and Christ himself on the road to his cross—these have found God and life and have left their world the richer. That is not true of all who suffer. Pain does not work mechanically and necessarily to produce good; but it may become the way to truth and life.

(4) And here we must consider what is perhaps the supreme Christian contribution to the problem of evil: the idea of vicarious and redemptive suffering. It is this thought that marks the highest reach of religious insight in the Old Testament as expressed in the moving words concerning the suffering Servant in Isaiah 52:13 to 53:12. For this seer, the sufferings of Israel can no longer be wholly ex-

[9] John 15:11.

plained in terms of punishment for sin, for the good suffer with the evil. Whether the reference be to an individual figure, a righteous remnant, or the nation as a whole, the conception is clear: men are bound together indeed, in common suffering, but such suffering may be for the sins of others, and, rightly borne, it may be for the saving of men. Here is the union of three significant ideas: human solidarity, vicarious suffering, and the possible redemptive value of such suffering. It is probable that Jesus, pondering the tragic end that awaited him, turned to this passage.[10] Certainly the early Church found here its best clue to the meaning of his death.

Archbishop Söderblom has developed this thought. He tells the story of Bengt Nylund, who suffered from hip disease and spent most of his life in the hospital. First of all, he won out in his own life: bedridden, he found his vocation as a writer of books of adventure for boys. Meditating on his pain, he found meaning in that suffering: "Sin, guilt, and suffering affect all mankind; therefore it cannot be exclusively the fault of the individual, or of those nearest to him, that he suffers. No! he bears a burden which belongs to humanity. All mankind is one living organism, whose parts—that is, individuals—must bear in solidarity the burdens laid upon them. One has one vocation in life, and one another; we sick have ours in suffering. When we bear our burden with submission and with gladness, then we, even we, are doing our part, even we can take something of the guilt which rests on ourselves and on all mankind, and even in us God's glory is manifested." Then Nylund quotes from a fellow-sufferer: "If we take up our cross and unite it with that of Christ, and suffer in small measure what he suffered in great, we may in some slight degree help to hasten the final triumph of good over evil."[11]

6. We have considered the sort of world needed for the achievement of good. We need, however, to guard against

[10]Mk. 10:45. [11]*The Mystery of the Cross,* pp. 1, 21.

the idea that this means simply a passive or neutral order that is merely permissive of achievement. That would fall far below the religious faith which believes in an immanent Spirit of Good working constantly and creatively in the world. And it is far below the observed fact. Equally mistaken is the conception of two forces, good and evil, arrayed against each other. The order of the Universe is not impersonal and negative; it is positive and creative. The evil of the universe is not a fundamental principle, or power, ranged against the good. It is, indeed, real, but it is the temporary defeat of order, the frustration of the cosmic purpose. "There is no evil principle," writes L. T. Hobhouse, "in the sense in which there is a good principle. All evil is traceable to the failure of purpose to coordinate things which so far as uncoordinated act in mutual indifference. Evil is not inherent in the tendencies of elements as such."[12] Similarly Philip S. Richards: "Everywhere good is the positive, harmonious element, evil the negative and discordant. Good is the principle of integration and life; evil of disintegration and death. Of these two things which are radically and eternally opposed, one must be relatively fundamental and primary.[13] James Ward has stated the basic principle: "We are wont to say that a struggle between good and evil is constantly going on, and then our question takes the form:—which side, so far as we can judge, bids fair to win? But in fact the question in this form is not truly put. There is no such dualism of good and evil; they are not two coordinate powers; in a word, there is no principle of evil. There is a moral order, but evil is disorder."[14]

The conception then of a kingdom of evil, even in the modernized and modified form of Walter Rauschenbusch,[15]

[12]*Contemporary British Philosophy,* p. 186.

[13]*Belief in Man,* pp. 97, 98.

[14]*The Realm of Ends,* pp. 375, 376.

[15]*A Theology for the Social Gospel,* Ch. IX, "The Kingdom of Evil."

is not descriptive of the situation. Evil, in the social forms which Rauschenbusch was considering, is mighty and persistent. Inertia and ignorance help maintain it. It appeals to powerful human impulses. It is organized, as we know only too well. But evil is not solidaristic; the union of its forces is always temporary and external. The very selfishness which unites these forces for common ends bears the seeds that must inevitably grow to division and self-destruction. Not only are the forces of good set against evil, but evil works against itself; "sin, when it is fullgrown, bringeth forth death."[16] Aldous Huxley quotes Professor Whitehead's phrase, "The fact of the instability of evil is the moral order of the world." And then he adds: "Evil is that which makes for separateness, and that which makes for separateness is self-destructive. . . . The evolutionary history of life clearly illustrates the instability of evil."[17] Not the power of evil in the world, but the weakness of the good in man, forms our problem.

V. THE CONCLUSION

Evil remains the great problem for religion, alike on the side of faith in relation to its belief in God, as on the practical side in its goal of the good life for man and the rule of God on earth. The Christian religion is not committed to any theory as to the origin of evil or the reason for its presence in the world. It stands definitely for the faith in a God of goodness and power, a goodness seen in his purpose for man and the world, a power adequate to the ends that he has set. And it offers to men a way for the overcoming of evil through insight and faith and a life in right relations with God and man. This is its gospel, the word of God that it brings to men.

It is inevitable and right that men seek all possible light on this darkest of problems. The denial of the reality of evil is no solution. To refer to omnipotent and inscrutable

[16] Jas. 1:15. [17] *Ends and Means,* p. 349.

will is to deny the faith in the goodness of God. To appeal to a meonic or demonic at the heart of things, mysterious and inexplicable, is a speculative expedient without direct meaning for a faith that wishes to remain ethical and that seeks to understand. The suggestion of a finite God moves toward dualism in lesser or greater degree, or toward a pluralism which gets rid of the whole problem of evil by giving up the idea of a God who is anything more than one among the varied trends and forces which the cosmos reveals to us.

Such light as we have gained in our discussion has come in the main from a truer conception of what we mean by the good and a deeper realization of the conditions of its achievement. Here the elements of the dynamic, developmental, social, and ethical all enter in. The highest reach of Christianity in relation to this problem is seen in its symbol of the cross, the revelation of what sin is and of what the cost of life and good is to God and man. Significantly, at this its highest point Christianity does not desert the prophetic for the speculative.

But even if we find light here, and some new light, on an ancient problem, we must recognize that here as everywhere we come at last to an ultimate that is no longer explicable. Then there is left to us the attitude of humility and trust and devotion to the highest which we see with Jesus when he faced his darkest hour, when he saw no light in the world about him and turned to God in obedience and faith as he cried, "Nevertheless, thy will be done." Here in the end is the distinctive Christian contribution, not speculative theory nor yet blind submission, but moral faith in its double aspect: faith as trust in the God of love who has spoken to us, faith as devotion to the way which this God indicates to us. "This do, and thou shalt live." "This is the victory that overcometh the world, even our faith."

THE BROSS FOUNDATION

With the publication of this fifteenth volume of the Bross Library, the Bross Foundation of Lake Forest University (the charter name of Lake Forest College) celebrates its fiftieth anniversary. When William Bross established the Foundation he designated that at fifty-year intervals a grand prize should be awarded for a single book selected by a competition, in addition to the lectures to be sponsored and the decennial competitions to be held. He desired that the contest be open to "the scientific men, the Christian philosophers, and historians of all nations." The Fiftieth Anniversary Bross Competition, to be completed in 1940, was therefore announced in 1936 throughout the world. The first anniversary volume now published as a result of this competition, *Christianity: An Inquiry into Its Nature and Truth,* by Harris Franklin Rall, Ph.D., D.D., LL.D., Professor of Christian Doctrine, Garrett Biblical Institute, Evanston, Illinois, was selected from a large number of entries from many countries.

Thus have been achieved the aims of William Bross to "call out the best efforts of the highest talent and the ripest scholarship of the world to illustrate from science, or from any department of knowledge, and to demonstrate the divine origin and the authority of the Christian Scriptures; and further, to show how both science and revelation coincide and prove the existence, the providence, or any or all of the attributes of the only living and true God, 'infinite, eternal, and unchangeable in His being, wisdom, power, holiness, justice, goodness and truth.'" This is the language of the Trust Agreement, which Mr. Bross felt was too elaborate to express his intent. The Foundation had its origin in a desire to establish a memorial for his son [Nathaniel], who died in 1856 at the age of five. In 1879, after completion of the Trust Agreement beginning the Bross Fund he stated his objective more succinctly in his diary: "God grant that he Nathaniel may through this fund preach the gospel of our blessed Savior to the end of time." The foundation thus conceived was the fruit of his sincere devotion, a practical way of doing his Christian duty.

In the Trust Agreement entered into by Mr. Bross and the Board of Trustees of Lake Forest University in 1879, he pledged the sum of forty thousand dollars to be paid in installments, the income of which was to accumulate in perpetuity for successive periods of ten years, the accumulation of one decade to be spent in the following decade. Provision was also made for the accruement of a special fund to be used for anniversary awards. The principal sum of forty thousand dollars was consummated at the time of Mr. Bross's death in 1890.

In 1900, at the end of the first decade of accumulations from the Bross Fund, the trustees began to carry out the provisions of the Trust Agreement. It was determined that the series of books published by the Foundation should be called the Bross Library. Mr. Bross had specified that Volume I of the series should be *Evidences of Christianity,* by Mark Hopkins, who was his revered teacher at Williams College and to whom he went for advice in planning the Foundation. Accordingly, the copyright of this book was secured and it was published in a presentation edition as Volume I. Succeeding volumes of the series were procured by the two methods prescribed in the Trust Agreement: (1) by conducting competitions and (2) by publishing lectures delivered under the auspices of the Foundation.

Up to the present, three decennial competitions have been held, the award in each being six thousand dollars. In the first competition, completed in 1905, the prize was awarded to the Reverend James Orr, D.D., Professor of Apologetics and Systematic Theology in the United Free Church College, Glasgow, Scotland, for his treatise on *The Problem of the Old Testament.* This book was published in 1906 as Volume III of the Bross Library. The second decennial prize was awarded in 1915 to the Reverend Thomas James Thorburn, D.D., LL.D., Hastings, England, for his book entitled, *The Mythical Interpretation of the Gospels,* Volume VII of the Bross Library. The third competition was won by Douglas Clyde Macintosh, Ph.D., Dwight Professor of Theology, Yale University, New Haven, Connecticut, in 1925, with his book entitled, *The Reasonableness of Christianity,* which became Volume XIII of the series. The fifteen thousand dollar prize of the Fiftieth Anniversary Competition was awarded, as previously explained, in 1940 for the present volume to Doctor Harris Franklin Rall.

All of the competitions have been announced three or four years in advance in order that prospective entrants would have ample time to prepare books for submission. Also, the administrators of the Foundation have sought to advertise them as widely as possible. The requirement that the work be in English has doubtless been responsible for the fact that most of the entries have come from English-speaking nations; however, several translations of books originally written in a foreign language were submitted in the Fiftieth Anniversary Competition. Recognized religious leaders and scholars have served as judges in the competitions, and to insure an objective judgment the names of the writers have been withheld from them. These contests have without doubt helped to realize the aims of William Bross to reward more generously those who make significant contributions to man's religious and intellectual progress and to stimulate men to greater achievements.

Ten volumes of the Bross Library consist of lectures delivered at Lake Forest University. The first course sponsored by the Foundation on *Obligatory Morality,* delivered in May, 1903, by the Reverend Francis Landey Patton, D.D., LL.D., President of Princeton Theological Seminary, was not published. Volume II of the Bross Library, published in 1905, contains a course of lectures on *The Bible: Its Origin and Nature,* delivered in May, 1904, by the Reverend Marcus Dods, D.D., Professor of Exegetical Theology in New College, Edinburgh. The third course of lectures, *The Bible of Nature,* delivered in September and October, 1907, by J. Arthur Thomson, M.A., Regius Professor of Natural History in the University of Aberdeen, was published in 1908 as Volume IV. The fourth course, *The Religions of Modern Syria and Palestine,* delivered in November and December of 1908 by Frederick Jones Bliss, Ph.D,, of Beirut, Syria, comprises Volume V. In Volume VI was published the fifth series of lectures, *The Sources of Religious Insight,* delivered in November, 1911, by Professor Josiah Royce, Ph.D., of Harvard University. The next course of lectures, *The Will to Freedom,* given in May, 1915, by the Reverend John Neville Figgis, D.D., LL.D., of the House of

Resurrection, Mirfield, England, formed Volume VIII of the Bross Library. A course of lectures entitled, *Faith Justified by Progress,* delivered in 1916 by Henry Wilkes Wright, Professor of Philosophy in Lake Forest College, was published as Volume IX. *Bible and Spade,* a series of lectures delivered in 1921 by the Reverend John P. Peters, Ph.D., of Sewanee, Tennessee, makes up Volume X. Volume XI, *Christianity and Problems of Today,* consists of a group of lectures given by several men on the occasion of the inauguration of Herbert McComb Moore, D.D., as President of Lake Forest University. The lectures of M. Bross Thomas, D.D., Professor Emeritus of Biblical Literature at Lake Forest University, on *The Biblical Idea of God,* were delivered in 1923 and published as Volume XII. *England's First Library,* a series of lectures delivered in 1929 by the Reverend James G. K. McClure, President Emeritus of The Presbyterian Theological Seminary, Chicago, Illinois, was published as Volume XIV under the title, *The Supreme Book of Mankind.*

Besides providing for the production of books, William Bross was concerned with their distribution. Moved by the desire to make them available to a large number of people, he specified that the copyright of all books obtained by competition or presented as lectures should be transferred to the Foundation. He limited the royalties from their publication to a small amount so that they could be sold at a cheaper price than is customary for books of a similar nature. Also, in order that they might be read by people who could not afford to buy books, he requested that they be distributed by the Foundation to selected libraries where they would be free to all who asked for them.

William Bross hoped that the foundation which he designed as a memorial to his son would be an instrument for the spiritual enrichment of life. In the minds of those who know the Bross Library there can be no doubt that his hope has come to fruition in the fifty years since his death. In publishing the Fiftieth Anniversary Volume we may hope that the next fifty years of the Bross Foundation will be as fruitful as the first fifty years.

HERBERT MCCOMB MOORE,
President of Lake Forest University.

Lake Forest, Illinois.

J. Dewey, *Reconstruction in Philosophy; A Common Faith.*
D. C. Macintosh, *The Problem of Religious Knowledge.*
W. P. Montague, *The Ways of Knowing.*
A. S. Pringle-Pattison, *The Idea of God in the Light of Recent Philosophy.*
I. G. Whitchurch, "Interpreting the Religious Situation," in *Theology and Modern Life,* P. A. Schilpp (Ed.).

REVELATION AND AUTHORITY

J. Baillie and H. Martin (Eds.), *Revelation.*
K. Barth, *The Doctrine of the Word of God.*
E. Brunner, *Erlebnis, Erkenntnis und Glaube.*
C. H. Dodd, *The Authority of the Bible.*
J. H. Leckie, *Authority in Religion.*
Edwin Lewis, *A Philosophy of the Christian Revelation.*
W. R. Matthews, *The Idea of Revelation.*
J. Oman, *Vision and Authority.*
E. F. Scott, *The New Testament Idea of Revelation.*
B. H. Streeter, *The God Who Speaks.*

THE EXPERIENCE OF GOD

J. Baillie, *Our Knowledge of God.*
C. A. Bennett, *A Philosophical Study of Mysticism.*
Kenneth Edward, *Religious Experience.*
Rees Griffiths, *God in Idea and Experience.*
W. E. Hocking, *The Meaning of God.*
Fr. von Hügel, *Essays and Addresses,* Ser. I.
T. H. Hughes, *The Philosophical Basis of Mysticism.*
A. C. Knudson, *The Validity of Religious Experience.*
D. C. Macintosh (Ed.), *Religious Realism.*
R. Otto, *The Idea of the Holy.*
D. L. Scudder, *Tennant's Philosophical Theology.*
D. E. Trueblood, *The Knowledge of God.*
Evelyn Underhill, *An Introduction to Mysticism.*
H. N. Wieman, *Religious Experience and Scientific Method; The Wrestle of Religion with Truth.*

BELIEF IN GOD: REASON, FAITH, AND CERTAINTY

D. M. Baillie, *Faith in God and the Christian Consummation.*
J. Baillie, *The Interpretation of Religion.*
C. A. Bennett, *The Dilemma of Religious Knowledge.*
P. A. Bertocci, *The Empirical Argument for God in Late British Thought.*
J. Dewey, *The Quest for Certainty.*
Wm. James, *The Will to Believe.*
F. J. McConnell, *Religious Certainty.*
R. B. Perry, *In the Spirit of William James.*
N. K. Smith, *Is Divine Existence Credible?*
W. R. Sorley, *Moral Values and the Idea of God.*
A. E. Taylor, *The Faith of a Moralist.*
F. R. Tennant, *Philosophical Theology.*

SOME PROBLEMS OF FAITH

(Chapters XIV, XV, XVII, XVIII. For Chapter XVI, *see* list above under SCIENCE AND RELIGION)

ETHICS AND FAITH

H. E. Barnes, *The Twilight of Christianity.*
F. R. Barry, *Christianity and the New World.*
H. Bergson, *The Two Sources of Morality and Religion.*
W. G. de Burgh, *From Morality to Religion.*
R. Niebuhr, *An Interpretation of Christian Ethics.*
J. H. Randall, Jr., *Religion and the Modern Age.*
A. E. Taylor, *The Faith of a Moralist.*
E. F. Tittle, *Jesus After Nineteen Centuries.*

PSYCHOLOGY AND FAITH

E. S. Ames, *Psychology of Religious Experience.*
L. Feuerbach, *The Essence of Christianity.*
S. Freud, *The Future of an Illusion.*
L. W. Grensted, *Psychology and God.*

C. G. Jung, *Psychology and Religion; Psychology of the Unconscious.*
J. H. Leuba, *A Psychological Study of Religion.*
D. C. Macintosh, *The Problem of Religious Knowledge.*
N. MacLeish, *The Nature of Religious Knowledge.*
W. R. Matthews, *The Psychological Approach to Religion.*
W. B. Selbie, *The Psychology of Religion.*
A. C. Tansley, *The New Psychology.*
C. H. Valentine, *Modern Psychology and the Validity of Religious Experience.*
C. C. J. Webb, *Religion and Theism.*
D. Yellowlees, *Psychology's Defense of the Faith.*

HISTORY AND FAITH

S. J. Case, *The Historicity of Jesus.*
F. C. Conybeare, *The Historical Christ.*
C. H. Dodd, *History and the Gospel.*
C. H. Dodd and others, *The Kingdom of God and History* (Oxford Conference Book).
John Macmurray, *The Clue to History.*
N. Söderblom, *The Nature of Revelation.*
A. E. Taylor, *The Faith of a Moralist.*
T. J. Thorburn, *The Mythical Interpretation of the Gospels.*
P. Tillich, *The Interpretation of History.*

FAITH AND THE FACT OF EVIL

N. Berdyaev, *Freedom and the Spirit; The Meaning of History; The Destiny of Man.*
E. S. Brightman, *The Problem of God.*
H. H. Farmer, *The World and God.*
Georgia Harkness, "The Abyss and the Given," *Christendom,* Vol. III, No. 4.
W. P. Montague, *Belief Unbound.*
H. W. Robinson, *Suffering, Human and Divine.*
R. Tsanoff, *The Nature of Evil.*
L. D. Weatherhead, *Why Do Men Suffer?*

INDEX OF NAMES

INDEX OF SUBJECTS